THE 100 BEST Movies You've NEVER Seen

Copyright © ECW PRESS, 2003

Published by ECW PRESS
2120 Queen Street East, Suite 200, Toronto, Ontario, Canada M4E 1E2

NATIONAL LIBRARY OF CANADA CATALOGUING IN PUBLICATION

Crouse, Richard, 1963-
The 100 best movies you've never seen / Richard Crouse.

ISBN 1-55022-590-1

1. Motion pictures. I. Title. II. Title: One hundred best movies you've never seen.

PN1993.5.A1C86 2003   791.43   C2003-902185-8

Editor: Jennifer Hale
Cover and Text Design: Tania Craan
Cover Photographs: Richard Beland
Production & Typesetting: Mary Bowness
Printing: Transcontinental

This book is set in Akzidenz Grotesk and Minion

The publication of *The 100 Best Movies You've Never Seen* has been generously supported by the Canada Council, the Ontario Arts Council, and the Government of Canada through the Book Publishing Industry Development Program. **Canada**

DISTRIBUTION
CANADA: Jaguar Book Group, 100 Armstrong Avenue, Georgetown, ON, L7G 5S4

PRINTED AND BOUND IN CANADA

ECW PRESS
ecwpress.com

THE 100 BEST
Movies You've
NEVER Seen

RICHARD CROUSE

ECW PRESS

Table of Contents

Introduction

"YOU'VE GOT *HATE* MAIL"

It is almost impossible to gauge how people are going to react to things you say. An innocent little remark can trigger a whole cascade of events. Such was the case a few years ago when I introduced a segment on *Reel to Real*'s favorite martial arts movies with, "I have to admit, martial arts films are a guilty pleasure of mine."

I recall the shoot day. It was a steamy hot August afternoon. We were shooting outside and I was cooking inside my suit. We banged off the intro in one take, and I didn't think about it again. Well, not until I received the most aggressively angry letter I have ever gotten — possibly one of the most hateful, profanity-laced pieces of mail to ever make its way into my, or anybody else's, inbox. Everyone in the public eye has gotten them. Usually the subject line reads something like "What were you thinking?" or occasionally the blunt "You are wrong."

This one was different. I knew I was in trouble when I read the subject line: RICHARD IS A SNOB. Clearly, subtlety was not this writer's strong point. What her letter lacked in sophistication, it made up in vitriol. Here's the breakdown: After spending a paragraph or so calling me some not-so-nice names and questioning my ability to review movies, she got to the point. She was offended by my use of the term "guilty pleasure." "What? Can't he just say he enjoys martial arts films? Why do they have to be a 'guilty pleasure'? I really don't think he would say something like 'I have to admit, those Fellini films are a guilty pleasure of mine.'"

The unladylike dispatch went on to describe me as pretentious and several other things that aren't fit to print here, before insisting that I respond. I did reply, although I'm not sure she received the kind of answer she was looking for. Her letter was clearly designed to offend and upset; instead, I have to admit I found it rather funny. I was frankly tickled that something I had said on television could elicit such venomous feedback. As Frank Zappa said, "It doesn't matter what kind of reaction you get, as long as you get a reaction." In my response I thanked her for the letter and explained that I enjoy a wide variety of movies, not just Fellini. I like Fellini; I think *8½* is a great film, almost as good as another favorite of mine, *The Poseidon Adventure*. You see, I explained, I have to see between 300 and 325 movies a year for my job, and when I sit down to view something that I am not professionally obligated to watch I consider that a treat — a guilty pleasure. I listed a few of the movies that I always turn to in my off hours — *The Bad and the Beautiful, Cane Toads: An Unnatural History*, and *Here Comes Mr. Jordan* — explaining why I liked each of them. I decided not to attack her in any way, but to kill her with kindness.

I'm not sure what effect my e-mail had on her, as I never heard from her again. I do, however, owe her a debt of gratitude. Her nasty letter got me thinking about all the movies that I love — my guilty pleasures — which led directly to the writing of this book. There were only two criteria for the movies included in this book — they had to be underrated and they had to be personal favorites of mine. These aren't really obscure movies — most are available on DVD or video, although you might need a police dog to find some of them — they are just films you might have missed the first time around. If she hadn't written that letter, I wouldn't have written this book. So it is to her, the pissed-off viewer, that I dedicate this book.

I also would like to extend a personal thanks to:

Dara Rowland; Jen Hale; Jack David; Tania Craan; Richard Beland; Andrea Bodnar; Vincent Monteleone; Stephen Peter Smith; Zacharius Kunuk; Norman Cohn; Ryan Gosling; Barry Blaustein; Forrest J. Ackerman; Nick Broomfield; Bruce Campbell; Don Coscarelli; Bill Wyman; Peter Lynch; Rob Sitch; Oliver Hirschbiegel; Jim Jarmusch; Emily Perkins; Katharine Isabelle; John Turturro; Christopher Heard; Jenn Kennedy; Denis Villeneuve; Hampton Fancher; Mira Nair; Cole

Hauser; Vin Diesel; Tom Tykwer; Franka Potente; Andrew Niccol; Lloyd Kaufman; William Phillips; David Hewlett; Ron Mann; Raymond DeFelitta; Sofia Coppola; Gary Burns; Frances, Carol, Wini, and everyone else at Southern Accent; Charles Wechsler; Bryan Peters; Kai Black; David Carroll; Brent Bambury; Kathleen Scheibling; Julia Caslin; Susan Smythe; Laura Quinn; Virginia Kelly; Nancy Yu; Bonnie Smith; Karen Neilson; Sherman Pau; Mark Pauderis; Shelly Chagnon; Julie Vaillancourt; Peter Lynch; Bill Phillips; Katrina Soukup; Jason at Rhino Home Video; Tim Goldberg; Paul Kemp; The Chiodo Brothers; Shelly at Starway International; John Bain; Max Films; Ron Mann; Andrew Currie; Kevin Hall; Rod Guidino and *Rue Morgue* magazine; Mike Scott; and Michael Fleisher at Anchor Bay Entertainment.

"May I pass along my congratulations for your great interdimensional breakthrough. I am sure, in the miserable annals of the Earth, you will be duly enshrined."
– LORD JOHN WHORFIN (JOHN LITHGOW)

THE ADVENTURES OF BUCKAROO BANZAI ACROSS THE 8TH DIMENSION (1984)

You wanna talk multi-tasking? Buckaroo Banzai (Peter Weller) must be the busiest renaissance man in the galaxy, listing not only rock star and comic book hero on his resumé, but also race car driver, samurai, and of course, world famous neurosurgeon.

In the opening moments of this, the first in a proposed series of *Banzai* movies, Buckaroo is giving his latest invention, something called an Oscillation Overthruster, a test run. As he drives his newfangled Jet Car through a solid rock face he enters the 8th dimension. Once there he encounters the wicked Red Lectiods from Planet 10, who were banished to the 8th dimension and now see a way out through Buckaroo's technology. While Buckaroo is wowing the ladies and performing with his band, the Hong Kong Cavaliers, the Lectiods (all named John, strangely enough) plan to steal the Overthruster to escape their earthly prison and do battle with their sworn enemies, the Black Lectiods. The Black Lectiods respond by threatening to unleash a nuclear war, which would not only devastate the Red Lectiods, but earth as well. Life as we know it could go up in a huge mushroom cloud unless Buckaroo Banzai and the Hong Kong Cavaliers step in to save the day.

It's a wild ride, and one that motors along at such a clip that it demands your attention, or you'll get hopelessly lost in the confusing story. The muddled plot may be the reason that the proposed sequels never materialized, or maybe it is as Weller says, "It just didn't get the press or publicity it needed. The picture got lost in the shuffle." At any rate, audiences in 1984 stayed away. Since then it has gained a cult following, no doubt driven by fans of the *Robocop* movies, a character Weller originated.

Buckaroo Weller is stoic, delivering lines like "Remember, no matter where you go, there you are," with a mock seriousness that borders on camp. It's a nice balance to John Lithgow as the insidious Dr. Emilio Lizardo/Lord John Whorfin, a performance so over-the-top that it borders on insanity. The movie is great fun to watch. A strong supporting cast includes Ellen Barkin as the maudlin Penny Priddy, Jeff Goldblum as Banzai's medical colleague with the unlikely name of New Jersey, and Christopher Lloyd as John Bigboote.

Poor box office receipts killed any chance of 20th Century Fox turning *Buckaroo Banzai* into a franchise, but rumors persist that a sequel might be made someday, or possibly even a television series. "Your guess is as good as mine," says Weller. "The director is hiding out in Boston somewhere, the guy that owned the rights shot himself in a hotel room in Century City, and the rest of us have gone on to happy lives. We've all been approached a hundred times, and I'd certainly do it if it all came together — I don't understand the movie myself, but people love it . . . we'll see."

Annigoni: PORTRAIT OF AN ARTIST (1995)

When documentary filmmakers Richard Bond and Stephen Peter Smith were filming in the Cathedral of Santo Antonio in Padova, Italy, a curious thing happened. They were there to shoot Pietro Annigoni's final fresco from the walls of the great cathedral when a wizened old man approached them and asked what they were doing.

"We told him we are shooting the last fresco," said Smith. "He said, 'No! No! This is not the last fresco. Follow me and I'll show you.' And he led us through the back interior [of the cathedral]. Low and behold, he opens a door into this huge workspace that hadn't been used for a hundred years or more, and was just a storage space. Annigoni had created this incredible fresco that was 15 meters high. It was amazing. It had been covered immediately after finishing it."

The piece had simply been lost to time. Not even Annigoni's secretary or his estate was aware of its existence. "It was really extraordinary," says Smith. "Italy is sort of like that. A lot of their ancient art treasures aren't properly cataloged, so they lose literally hundreds of thousands each year."

The making of *Annigoni: Portrait of an Artist* was a four-year journey of discovery for Bond and Smith. Shot on location in Annigoni's home of Florence, Italy, the filmmakers immersed themselves in Annigoni's world, interviewing his students and family to gain insight into this largely forgotten painter.

"I went around Florence and checked out his work, and I thought it was incredible that nobody had ever made a film on this painter," says Smith. "We started exposing the first frames in 1991 in the fall and went on from there. It just became a larger and larger film as we got deeper into his work and his ideas. Annigoni was such a prolific artist we really needed a feature length to tell his story."

The Annigoni presented in this film is a complex person. His students called him "The Maestro" because of his mastery with a paintbrush — he was, simply put, the Karsh of the canvas. He was a philosopher, with the skill to capture a person's soul on canvas, but also had a reputation as a heavy drinker and brawler. He was an intellectual with the soul of an artist, whose favorite pastime was knife throwing. Painter John Angel characterized him as a "cynical and pessimistic man," while his peer Giorgio de Chirico called him "one of the few artists worth respecting."

Director Smith says Annigoni was an enigma. "He was a very gentle and generous man, but he was a perfectionist and could be severe at times. Especially when it came to his work."

Annigoni's work provides the heart behind this 1995 film. Students of 20th century portraiture will be familiar with Annigoni's celebrated paintings of John F. Kennedy and Queen Elizabeth, and Bond and Smith take pains to ensure that the painter's other great works are well presented.

Photographing the enormous frescos presented the biggest challenge. To avoid distortion, cameras had to be positioned on the same plane as the frescos to properly film their two-dimensional surfaces. "We had to build scaffolding and shoot on extension ladders," says Smith. "We also had to run external generators because the churches aren't equipped to handle cinema lights." It was time consuming and difficult, but Smith found it rewarding in the end. "You don't want to make a film like this and take short cuts. We really wanted to do justice to his work, and also take pride in the kind of film we were capable of making."

That kind of pride is something that Annigoni himself might have appreciated. "Annigoni really believed in the technique of drawing as being one of the most important aspects of painting," says Smith. In the film Annigoni says, "If you can draw, you can paint." He was a perfectionist as a painter and teacher, and would only take on students of the highest caliber. According to the film, he once had a potential student work for three months on a single drawing before he would agree to teach him. "It was a pretty rigorous process to get accepted into the studio," says Smith.

> "At the dawn of the first millennium . . . evil lurks in the form of an unknown shaman . . . two families divided by power, jealousy, murder, and revenge . . . one man must fight for his life and community . . . battling natural and supernatural forces . . . can harmony finally be restored?"
> — Advertising tagline for *ATANARJUAT: THE FAST RUNNER*

ATANARJUAT: THE FAST RUNNER (2001)

Originally planned as a two-hour movie for Canadian television, *Atanarjuat: The Fast Runner* has found worldwide success, scooping up awards in Cannes and finding theatrical distribution at home, in the Netherlands, Germany, and the United States. Based on an Inuit legend passed down orally through the years, this 173-minute epic is a stunning achievement for director Zacharius Kunuk. He perfectly captures the rhythms of the North, allowing the story to unfold little by little against a backdrop of ice and snow. The result is compelling both as a story and an anthropologic study.

Set in the eastern Arctic wilds near Igloolik at the beginning of the first millennium, *Atanarjuat: The Fast Runner* begins with the murder of a camp leader. Sauri (Eugene Ipkarnak) takes command, and proceeds to humiliate his old enemy Tulimaq through maltreatment and derision. Tulimaq regains some of his lost prestige years later when his two sons, Amaqjuaq, The Strong One (Pakkak Innukshuk), and Atanarjuat, The Fast Runner (Natar Ungalaaq), become the main providers of food for the camp. Old rivalries arise as Sauri's bad-tempered son Oki (Peter Henry Arnatsiaq) becomes resentful of Amaqjuaq and Atanarjuat. When The Fast Runner wins away Oki's promised bride-to-be, the striking Atuat (Sylvia Ivalu), Oki schemes to murder the brothers.

"It is a story that was taught to us, a story passed from generation to generation," director Zacharias Kunuk told *Reel to Real* in March 2002. "It's like a lesson on how you want to lead your life when you grow up. These stories were taught to us, they were like bedtime stories for us when we used to sleep side by side. Mothers told the stories to put their kids to sleep and give lessons."

At first glance director Zacharias Kunuk's style recalls that of the 1922 landmark documentary *Nanook of the North*. Like the 80-year-old classic, *The Fast Runner* was shot entirely in Igloolik and the North Baffin area of Arctic Canada and is set against vast vistas of snow and ice, an unrelenting background of stark white and icy blue. The cold acts as an emotional trigger, as the audience can relate to it on a primal level. Kunuk wisely lets the severe climate speak for itself, quietly telling the viewer of the hardships of Inuit life.

Also like *Nanook*, Kunuk's slow-paced cinema verité method reveals the cultural values of the Inuit people, but that is where the similarities cease. Yes, *The Fast Runner* is historically accurate, carefully reconstructing ancient Inuit traditions and lifestyle, but, unlike its predecessor, is far from being just a clinical examination of time and place. Blending realism with legend, Kunuk tells a story that is both compelling and universal in its appeal.

"Once you hear the story you can't get it out of your mind," says Norman Cohn, the film's cinematographer, co-writer, and production manager, and a native New Yorker who moved to Igloolik in 1985. "The centerpiece of this story is a man, naked, running for his life across the Arctic ice as three guys are chasing him with spears trying to kill him.

Zach has talked many times about what it is like to be a kid and have that image in your head: you could see it, imagine it. There are lots of legends you can choose from, but once you've heard this one, you say, 'Wow, that would be a great movie.' We were evolving as a company and as a creative production team to larger and larger projects, and when we decided we were ready to try and make a feature film, this story seemed like a really good place to start. Paul Apak Angilirq, who was the screenwriter, said, 'Let's try and do this one.' And we really thought it was a good idea."

The otherworldly setting may seem foreign, but the moral of the story is anything but. Through the actions of Oki and his father Sauri we learn of the consequences of greed and the misuse of power. The theme has been covered hundreds of times in all art forms from the Bible to *Othello* to television's *Dallas*. Rarely on screen has it been so moving, so memorable. It is a timeless morality tale, but as Kunuk s-l-o-w-l-y unravels the story we are treated to a beautiful retelling that is more than worth the wait.

One main ingredient of the film's success is the ensemble cast. Wonderfully naturalistic performances breathe life into the roughly hewn characterizations. These are simple, primal people living a harsh and unforgiving life, without a trace of self-pity or regret. Natar Ungalaaq is particularly haunting in the lead role. His understated turn as Atanarjuat reveals an inner strength that is exposed by his actions and facial expressions rather than through dialogue. Through him we learn the virtues of perseverance and forgiveness. While the film has been praised, and won the 2001 Camera d'Or at Cannes, the Guardian Award for First Directors at the 2001 Edinburgh International Film Festival, and the Toronto City Award for Best Canadian Film at the 2001 Toronto International Film Festival, it is a shame that Ungalaaq's remarkable performance has been all but ignored.

Another standout is Peter Henry Arnatsiaq. In his first professional job as an actor, the former full-time hunter is very convincing as the wicked Oki.

Near the midpoint of this three-hour epic is an extraordinary scene. Fleeing the evil band of killers who has ambushed him and his brother, Atanarjuat runs naked across the frozen tundra. The scene is allowed to play in real time, and lasts an eternity. We see him jumping from ice floe to ice floe, his bare feet bloody and freezing, pounding agonizingly against the snow. His flight is a testament to the human spirit. Harrowing and painful to watch, the scene is shot simply and realistically and is an unforgettable display of mind over matter and the will to survive.

Spoken entirely in the Inuktitut language (with English subtitles), Kunuk's retelling of an ancient Inuit legend doesn't just inform, it entertains.

> "I don't want to win awards. I want a picture that ends with a kiss and puts black in the books."
> — HARRY PEBBEL (WALTER PIDGEON)

THE BAD AND THE BEAUTIFUL (1952)

The film industry has never been shy about turning the camera inward, exposing the ins and outs of "that business called show." Hollywood was satirizing itself as early as 1928 in King Vidor's *Show People*, the story of Peggy Pepper (Marion Davies), a talented comedian who unsuccessfully tries to make a go of it as a dramatic actress. Ripe with in-jokes and behind-the-scenes footage, this one pretty much set the tone for those to follow.

With the popularity of tabloid magazines like *Confidential* came a thirst for the seedy underbelly of Hollywood and a number of harder-hitting films. One such movie is *The Bad and the Beautiful,* a cliché-ridden melodrama that is at once over-the-top and incredibly insightful. Based on a story that originally appeared in a February 1951 issue of *Ladies' Home Journal*, the film opens with actress Georgina Lorrison (Lana Turner), writer James Lee Barlow (Dick Powell), and director Fred Amiel (Barry Sullivan) arriving at a film studio for a meeting with hot shot executive Harry Pebbel (Walter Pidgeon). Pebbel's mission is to convince the trio to make another film with blackballed producer Jonathan Shields (Kirk Douglas). "Don't worry," he says, "some of the best movies are made by people who hate each other's guts."

In a series of flashbacks, we learn about the trio's troubled relationships with the scheming producer. Amiel and Shields had cut their teeth together, making a string of successful B-pictures. They were tight until Shields stole Amiel's idea for a classy film called *The Faraway Mountain* and leapt into the big time without him. Next is Georgina's story of alcoholism and spurned love. She is the daughter of a faded screen star, who fruitlessly battled the bottle until Shields showed up, romanced her, helped her kick booze, and cast her in a movie. When the film was done, so was their relationship. Last is southern writer James Lee Barlow's tale of woe. Wooed to Hollywood, he made it big, but lost his wife Rosemary (Gloria Grahame) after Shields engineered an affair between her and the studio's resident Latin lover Gaucho (Gilbert Roland). Both were killed when Gaucho's plane crashed en route to Mexico.

There isn't a hint of cynicism in director Vincente Minnelli's handling of the material. While he paints Shields as a manipulative, cheating gadfly, he also implies that each of these characters owes him something, suggesting they must put aside their personal animosities and make a decision based purely on professional considerations. The question remains, Will they acknowledge their debt to Shields, or take their revenge, kicking him when he is down? "Look folks," says Peebel, "you've got to give the Devil his due. We all owe him something and you know it." *The Bad and the Beautiful* is a far cry from the negative, sad tenor of other contemporary Hollywood exposés like *Sunset Boulevard* and *A Star Is Born*.

Occasionally overwrought — check out the scene where Shields tells off Georgina after the premiere — the movie succeeds because of the larger-than-life characterizations of the main characters. Kirk Douglas is at his ruthless best (he lost the Best Actor Oscar that year to Gary Cooper in *High Noon*), and Lana Turner turns in the role of her life as Georgina. Her hysterical breakdown on a rainy road in the Hollywood Hills is the highlight of her spotty career.

Minnelli took great care casting the smaller roles as well. Look for Beaver's mom, Barbara Billingsley, in an uncredited cameo as a testy costume designer. Ned Glass's turn as a world-weary wardrobe man is a classic.

Another of the joys of *The Bad and the Beautiful* is trying to connect the dots between the fictional characters and their real-life counter-parts. Georgina likely is a thinly disguised Diana Barrymore, the beautiful but troubled daughter of acting legend John Barrymore. A composite of writers William Faulkner and F. Scott Fitzgerald seems to be the inspiration for Barlow's tale of woe, while there are great similarities between David O. Selnick and Shields. *The Bad and the Beautiful* is sophisticated, but still just trashy enough to be consistently entertaining, just like the tabloids that inspired the story.

"I'm the horned one. The Devil. Let me give you my card."
– GEORGE SPIGGOTT (PETER COOK) from *BEDAZZLED*

BEDAZZLED (1967)

In the 1960s and early '70s the duo of Peter Cook and Dudley Moore were Swingin' London's hippest comics. Their West End revues — *Piece of Eight* and *Beyond the Fringe* — heralded a new age of comedy that paved the way for *Monty Python's Flying Circus* and a new brand of satiric humor. No subject escaped their jaundiced eye — the Royal Family, social conditions, the BBC, even the Prime Minister. In 1967 they took on their most powerful subject ever, the Devil.

Bedazzled is a comic reworking of the *Faust* legend. Stanley Moon (Dudley Moore) is a lonely and timid short-order cook at a London Wimpy Burger restaurant. He's hopelessly in love with waitress Margaret (Eleanor Bron) who is oblivious to his affections. Spurned, he writes a suicide note — "Dear Ms. Spencer, This is to say cheerio. Yours Sincerely, Stanley Moon. P.S. I leave you my collection of moths" — and tries to hang himself. Like everything else in Stanley's life, his suicide attempt is a miserable failure.

He makes the acquaintance of the sarcastic George Spiggot (Peter Cook), a smooth-talking gentleman who claims he's really the Horned One, Beelzebub, The Prince of Darkness — The Devil. George offers to exchange Stanley's soul for Margaret's love and seven wishes. To act on his dreams, all he must do is utter the magic words, "Julie Andrews" (who is apparently in league with the Devil). Should Stanley wish to cancel any of his wishes all he need do is blow a "raspberry." Sounds like a win-win deal for a guy like Stanley, but Spiggot has a wicked sense of humor that prevents Stanley's wishes from turning out the way he wants them to. Stanley must be careful what he wishes for, because he just might get it. Enticed by the living personification of the Deadly Sins, embodied by Raquel Welch as Lilian Lust, Stanley begins his journey to win the heart of Margaret. Along the way his dreams are dashed over and over by the wily Devil, who always seems to be one step ahead of poor Stanley. Or so he thinks.

Bedazzled, based on sketches written by Cook for the stage, rides the line between satire and blasphemy, although to my mind lands squarely on the side of humor. Taking on the church and re-examining the interaction between Satan and humans may have ruffled some feathers, but they do serve the higher purpose of revealing the true nature of Stanley's greed and the role of the Devil as an entity who exists to reinforce people's belief in God. Don't let the examination of religion scare you off, *Bedazzled* is also very funny.

Peter Cook (best known in North America as the priest from *The Princess Bride*) has never gotten his due as a comic mastermind. His script for *Bedazzled* bristles with inventive lines and irreverent situations. His Devil, for instance, isn't malicious, but more of a wise guy. As the Dark Lord he scratches record albums, sets wasps loose on picnickers, and rips out the final pages of Agatha Christie mysteries. Hardly the work of a fiend, but fiendishly clever nonetheless. On screen the Carnaby Street-clad Cook plays up his impish character beautifully, giving him an amusing, self-important air.

Dudley Moore works well with Cook; their verbal jabs fly hard and fast, played with a comic timing that comes only with years of practice. Amusing though his Stanley may be for most of the film, Moore seems to run out of steam near the end, when his role takes on a slightly more serious tone. Moore was not yet a seasoned screen actor, and seems to be relying on stage-bound sketch comedy tricks rather than "acting." His onscreen performance technique would improve by the time North American audiences made him a star in *10* and *Arthur*.

Most notable among the supporting cast is the barely dressed Raquel Welch. As Lilian Lust (married to Sloth), she plays one of the Seven Deadly Sins. Not yet a major star, Welch adds an element of sex appeal to this comedy of (bad) manners.

Director Stanley Donen (*Singin' in the Rain*) handles the material with a nice light touch, and while *Bedazzled* may seem dated to today's audiences, the comic duo of Moore and Cook is well worth revisiting.

"What I loved so much about this movie is that it is about this kid who loved something so much it made him feel weak."
— **RYAN GOSLING on Danny, his character in *THE BELIEVER***

THE BELIEVER (2001)

■ ■ ■ ■ ■ ■ ■ ■

The Believer is a controversial film starring a former mousketeer (who once shared the stage with Britney Spears), as a Jew who becomes an anti-Semite. Ryan Gosling plays Danny Balint, loosely based on the real-life Daniel Burros, a Jewish teen from Queens so confused and filled with self-loathing he joined the American Nazi Party and the KKK. In 1965 he was arrested after causing a disturbance at a KKK rally in New York City, and then killed himself when the *New York Times* disclosed that he was Jewish.

The contentious subject of *The Believer* kept it off multiplex screens despite winning the Grand Jury Prize at the 2001 Sundance Film Festival and critical raves for its star Gosling. At the Toronto International Film Festival distributors were heard commenting that it is a great film, but they couldn't — or wouldn't — touch it with a 10-foot pole. Gosling's performance was compared to Ed Norton's turn as a neo-Nazi in *American History X*, but there was a difference — Norton's character seeks redemption, Gosling's doesn't. His Danny Balint constantly questions the roots of his faith, even as he faces death. This ambiguity led Rabbi Abraham Cooper of the Simon Wiesenthal Center to publicly condemn the film.

The overriding problem with the movie is also one of its great strengths. Screenwriter Henry Bean (*Internal Affairs, Enemy of the State*) has nailed the language of hate practiced by skinhead groups almost too well. *The Believers* could be seen as a how-to handbook for anti-Semites, an idiot's guide to neo-Nazism. The character of Danny is articulate and charismatic, and if seen through the wrong eyes, a poster boy for hate. By casting Gosling, an appealing, talented young actor, Bean may have inadvertently made hate sexy.

The wrong-headed anti-Semitism in *The Believer* skims the surface of Danny's character, whereas the difference between what he says and what he believes lies at the core. As a child we see an impassioned Danny arguing with his teachers about the story of Abraham, who was asked by God to kill his son Isaac as a test of faith. In the end Danny decides God is a power-drunk madman, and Isaac will be "traumatized, a putz the rest of his life." It's the first step in his tormented relationship with his faith. "Let him crush me like the conceited bully that he is. Go ahead," he dares.

As a teenager he attacks Jews on the street and subway, beating one person to a bloody pulp. His rage and hatred are born from the misguided belief that the Jews did not fight back during the Holocaust, and therefore are a weak race. Eventually his journey leads him into the welcoming arms of Lina Moebius (Theresa Russell) and Curtis Zampf (Billy Zane), leaders of a Fascist organization who see Danny as a natural leader to take their message to the mainstream.

Lina's daughter, Carla (Summer Phoenix), is drawn to Danny, attracted by his sexuality and his intellect. After Danny and a group of skinheads vandalize a synagogue and destroy the Torah, he steals and repairs the document. With Lina he explores both sides of his ideological fence, preaching hate by day while secretly studying the Torah by night. At the film's climax a final act of skinhead terrorism in a synagogue leaves Danny with a choice between life and death.

"The thing I thought was beautiful, an interesting idea, is the line in the movie when Danny says to Carla, 'Do you think people ever commit suicide out of happiness?'" says Gosling. "That was really important to me because I felt at the end of the movie — and this is the disturbing part — that Danny was happy. Probably never would be as happy as he was at that moment in his life because he was a Jewish Nazi. He was both. He had a girlfriend who was a Nazi, who was reading the Torah and learning Hebrew, who was making Yom Kippur dinner for him and going to shul [school], and he is daven [a prayer leader] at a Yom Kippur service on a bimah [altar where the Torah is read] in which he has placed a bomb. He's got them both. He was happy, and decided, Why can't I choose the day I die? Why can't I die out of happiness? It's a hard thing to come to terms with."

The Believer is a murky, unsettling film that offers no easy answers. "The reason I think it is a testament to the beauty of Judaism and the strength of his faith," says Gosling, "is that he could give you every reason not to believe it. And he does. He can tell you everything that is wrong with it, and he is so learned as to why you should hate it, but at the same time he loves it."

Danny is a complicated, profoundly troubled character, so in love with his faith that it makes him feel weak, and therefore must destroy it. "He's just one of those people who couldn't help what he thought," says Gosling. "He felt two ways about it." It's a confounding philosophy — the idea of showing love by embracing hate — and the product of an unstable mind. "He just wanted to feel strong, and as a confused kid he went in a confused direction."

The real find here is Ryan Gosling, an Ontario native who broke into show business following an audition for *The Mickey Mouse Club*. At age 12 he moved to Orlando, Florida, and performed with fellow mouseketeers Britney Spears and members of 'N Sync. His television work included lightweight syndicated fare like *Breaker High* and the lead in *Young Hercules*, and his lone film role before *The Believer* was as the thirteenth-billed Bosley in *Remember the Titans*. *The Believer* is a quantum leap forward for Gosling. In a powerhouse performance as the steely-eyed Danny he lends humanity to a paradoxical character. At no time does the performance hit a false note. It's a commanding performance that deservedly won the Best Actor award at the Independent Spirit Awards.

Chances are you haven't seen *The Believer* on the big screen. It played briefly in independent theaters, but found its main audience on specialty channels like Showcase.

"We had a hard time with it, but a beautiful time as well," says Gosling. "The film is about contradiction, and that is the response to the film. It's been a real rollercoaster. It went from Henry and I and a small crew stealing shots in New York with a very low budget, trying to make a movie that nobody really wanted us to make. Not thinking that anybody was ever going to see it, but just sort of wanting to tell the story. We never thought we'd get into Sundance, let alone win Sundance. That was such a high, and then everybody wanted the movie. And then everybody realized *what* they wanted, and got scared, then nobody wanted the movie. We couldn't find a home for the movie. Then we thought this movie is never going to be seen, and that was it, and then we found a couple of homes for it and alternative ways of getting it seen. That became more important than anything, making sure people saw the film."

The Believer is a very difficult film. Some will find the subject matter offensive, and while that is an understandable judgment — the anti-Semitic ravings of the skinheads are particularly difficult to watch — it is also an ambitious film that sometimes overreaches, but is anchored by a great performance by Gosling. We follow his progression from idiosyncratic self-hatred to liberation; all the while the camera never judges him, but merely observes him. Perhaps if director Bean had been less tolerant of Danny's Nazism the film might have had more appeal, à la *American History X*. It's a hot-potato topic, and certainly not for every taste.

BETTER OFF DEAD (1985)

The 1980s: the heyday of *Donkey Kong*, parachute pants, Cabbage Patch Dolls, New Coke, breakdancing, and of course, deliciously funny teen comedies. Hollywood still pumps 'em out by the cartload, but the Golden Age of adolescent humor dates back to the days when a new Brat Pack film was guaranteed to play to sold-out houses. Dozens were released, but only a few had the impact of *Pretty in Pink*, *The Breakfast Club*, and *Ferris Bueller's Day Off*, which became classics of the genre and cultural touchstones of the Reagan years.

One forgotten classic, *Better Off Dead*, is a gem of surrealistic teen comedy directed by Savage Steve Holland, best known for helming television shows like *V.I.P.* and *Eek! The Cat*. Nineteen-year-old John Cusack plays sad-sack Lane Myer, a 16-year-old with serious problems. His soulmate Beth (Amanda Wyss) has recently dumped him, with the brutally honest observation, "I really think it's in my best interest if I went out with someone more popular." He should be glad to get rid of her, but, frankly, she was the best thing in his life. His father (David Ogden Stiers) means well, but seems slightly disconnected from reality. Mom (Kim Darby) is a terrible cook, who subjects her family to the creepiest, crawliest entrees ever seen on film. Brother Badger (Scooter Stevens) is a creepy mad scientist who doesn't speak, and can't look anyone in the eye. On top of all that his best friend snorts Jell-O and a demonic paperboy (Demian Slade) endlessly harasses him for a two-dollar payment.

Despondent, and brimming with teenaged angst, Lane attempts a series of feeble suicide attempts. When a poorly timed leap off a bridge lands him in the back of a garbage truck, a witness comments, "Man, now that's a shame when folks be throwin' away a perfectly good white boy like that." Lane's salvation comes in the form of Monique (Diane Franklin), a cute foreign-exchange student determined to save his life and win his heart.

Much of *Better Off Dead* is typical teen underdog fare — Lane is in love with Ms Wrong, but ends up with the right girl by the time the credits roll — but there is an irreverence on display that sets it apart from the average kid flick. Holland seems to really understand the sense of isolation and displacement typical of the difficult teen years, but more importantly, also knows how to lampoon it. Everything about this movie has an off-kilter feel, as if reality has been tilted 45 degrees, creating a crazy world that is both unique and delightful.

At the core of this strange suburban tale is John Cusack, who puts in a performance ripe with the vulnerability of youth. Cusack's baby face reads all the awkwardness and self-doubt that occurs when you mix teen boys with raging hormones and high school girls. The blend of Cusack's charming performance with timeless gags, a killer soundtrack, and some really bad '80s fashions makes *Better Off Dead* a fun time capsule from the Me Decade.

"The Film Vince McMahon Didn't Want You To See!"
— Advertising slogan for *BEYOND THE MAT*

BEYOND THE MAT (1999)

Screenwriter Barry Blaustein had a terrible secret. A film and television veteran, Blaustein had written for *Saturday Night Live* and penned several successful Eddie Murphy movies, all the while keeping a unique personal preference under wraps. Then he was outed — Barry Blaustein

Richard's Favorite Lines from '80s Teen Comedies

1. "I wanna be just like you. I figure all I need is a lobotomy and some tights." – Bender (Judd Nelson), *Breakfast Club* (1985)

2. "Fuck me gently with a chainsaw." – Heather Chandler (Kim Walker), *Heathers* (1989)

3. "Gee, I'm real sorry your mom blew up, Ricky." – Lane Myer (John Cusack), *Better Off Dead* (1985)

4. "How would you like a nice greasy pork sandwich served in a dirty ashtray?" – Chet (Bill Paxton), *Weird Science* (1985)

5. "Hi, I'm Gary Cooper, but not the Gary Cooper that's dead." – Gary Cooper (Tim Robbins), *The Sure Thing* (1985)

6. "All I need are some tasty waves, a cool buzz, and I'm fine." – Jeff Spicoli (Sean Penn), *Fast Times at Ridgemont High* (1982)

7. "I mean, I've had men that have loved me before, but not for six months in a row." – Ginny (Blanche Baker), *Sixteen Candles* (1984)

8. "Are you telling me my mom has the hots for me?" – Marty McFly (Michael J. Fox), *Back to the Future* (1985)

9. "Money really means nothing to me. Do you think I'd treat my parents' house this way if it did? – Steff (James Spader), *Pretty in Pink* (1986)

10. "I'm so dead they're going to have to bury me twice." – Les Anderson (Corey Haim), *License to Drive* (1988)

was a professional wrestling fan. "It's like when some guys watch X-rated movies and someone comes into the house and they quickly try and hide the stuff," he says. "It was like that with me and wrestling."

You might not recognize his name, but if you are a comedy fan, you are undoubtedly familiar with Barry Blaustein's work. A prolific four-year stint as a writer for *Saturday Night Live* yielded some of Eddie Murphy's most memorable characters, including Tyrone "C-I-L-L my landlord" Green and Buckwheat. Having conquered the chaotic world of *SNL*, Blaustein (and collaborator David Sheffield) moved west in 1984 to write for the big screen. In Hollywood the working relationship with Murphy continued as Blaustein peppered the scripts of *Boomerang, The Nutty Professor*, and *The Nutty Professor II: The Klumps* with laughs. It was the success of that trio of movies, produced by Imagine Films, and a surprise birthday party that led Blaustein down the path to directing a documentary about his lifelong passion, wrestling.

"My wife threw a surprise birthday party for me about five years ago and invited everybody that I knew," Blaustein told *Reel to Real* in 1999. "I heard a familiar voice of a wrestler named Dusty Rhodes. He said, 'Come on out, This Is Your Life!' I walked out in the backyard, and there was everybody that I knew. My father had built a little podium that looked like a wrestling ring. I was totally humiliated because everybody found out that I liked wrestling." With his dirty little secret made public, he decided to document his love of the sport on film.

"It is hard to get funding for a documentary in the States," said Blaustein. "You can get a government grant if your film is about black lung disease among coal miners in West Virginia, but not for a movie about wrestling." Blaustein took advantage of his longtime association with Imagine and pitched the idea of a wrestling documentary, budgeted at a half-million dollars. "That is nothing for a documentary," says Blaustein. "It is the shrimp cocktail at the premiere of *Nutty Professor II*. A drop in the bucket. I think they did it as a favor to me. It was like, 'You know he's written a lot of movies for us, let's throw him a bone. It means a lot to him.' They had no expectations for the film whatsoever."

With Imagine on board, Blaustein was ready to rumble. Using his downtime on the weekends, he assembled a small crew and shot a variety of storylines over five years. "I just wanted to go out and do something for myself," he said. "It was revitalizing, like I was back in college again. When you are in college you feel like you can do anything, and you approach without fear. That is how I approached this film."

Over time Blaustein pieced together a film that works on an almost Shakespearean level. There is tragedy, rage, humor, violence, intrigue, hucksterism, and real human stories. It uncovers the carny aspects of wrestling, which is surprising as it was made with the complete co-operation of the World Wrestling Federation. Well, *almost* complete co-operation. "I say my knees are worse than any wrestler because of the begging," says Blaustein. "And my lips are pretty parched too; they're just getting their feeling back. It took about a year, or year and a half of chasing Vince [McMahon, owner of the WWF] to get him to agree to this. When I caught Vince, I caught him on a good day. Wrestling wasn't as popular, and I was able to convince him through passion and conviction that this would be good for wrestling.

"He gave me full access, but later tried to pull out of it. He wanted to invest in the movie, then tried to buy it outright. I said no, and this is a man who is not used to hearing the word no. He went out of his way to make sure people didn't know about it."

Before running afoul of McMahon, Blaustein captured some eye-opening images. He follows two wrestling wannabes, Michael Modest and Tony Jones, as they go for their big break, and then gives us a rare backstage look at McMahon's analysis of their performance and the wheeling and dealing side of the wrestling biz.

The theme of control runs throughout the film — from McMahon, who wields the biggest stick in the business, to the physical control the wrestlers must exercise in the ring to avoid grievous bodily injury. Sadly though, *Beyond the Mat* illustrates the lack of control most of these guys have in their personal lives and careers. One former king of the ring,

Jake "The Snake" Roberts comes across like a car wreck; you don't want to watch, but can't take your eyes off him. Blaustein unblinkingly shows his fall from the height of wrestling fame to a crack-smoking shell of a man who can't even stay off the pipe long enough to give an interview. It is heart-wrenching material, but further illustrates the toll that fame in the pro wrestling circuit can extract.

Veteran fighter Terry Funk fares better, yet inspires pity when the viewer realizes the physical anguish he suffers every time he steps into the squared circle. His left knee is damaged to the point where it barely functions, but he continues to wrestle, perhaps drawn by the fame, or maybe, feeling the weight of his golden shackles, he can't afford to quit.

Perhaps the biggest surprise is Mick "Mankind" Foley, who comes across as a nice man in an incredibly violent occupation. Scenes of him playing with his kids, the picture of normalcy, are juxtaposed with excerpts from his fights. Blaustein marries the two contradictory elements of Foley's life — family man and wrestler — in a potent segment that shows the dismayed reaction of his wife and kids at the Royal Rumble, a no-holds-barred match against The Rock.

I'm not a wrestling fan, but I was swayed by Blaustein's obvious passion for the subject. *Beyond the Mat* opened my eyes, forcing me to look past the manufactured personas that grimace and talk trash from ringside, and see the real people behind the muscles and sweat. There is real emotion here, outside the rage and showmanship usually associated with wrestling. For the first time we see these fighters not as cartoon characters, but as real people dealing with the effects of their job on their health and families. *Beyond the Mat* should be placed alongside *Pumping Iron* and *When We Were Kings* as movies that reveal the personal side of sports entertainment.

We all know wrestling is fake, but after seeing *Beyond the Mat*, it seems a little more real.

BEYOND THE VALLEY OF THE DOLLS (1970)

This is one of the most unlikely major studio efforts of the early '70s. Co-screenwriter (and future Pulitzer winner) Roger Ebert remembers the production of *Beyond the Valley of the Dolls* as "a movie that got made by accident when the lunatics took over the asylum."

In 1968, sexploitation pioneer Russ Meyer signed a three-picture deal with 20th Century Fox, based on the strength of the critical and commercial success of *Vixen*, an independent nudie set in a Canadian mountain resort. The first of these projects was a sequel to the trashy screen adaptation of Jacqueline Susann's novel *Valley of the Dolls*. Ebert and Meyers banged out the screenplay in just six weeks, not even taking the time to read the original book. The result is a trippy story about three young female musicians — Kelly (May '66 Playmate Dolly Reed), Casey (December '68 Playmate Cynthia Myers) and Pat (super-model Marcia McBroom) — who try to make it big in Hollywood.

After hooking up with Kelly's funky Aunt Susan (Phyliss Davis) and her friend, rock impresario Ronnie "Z-Man" Barzell (John Lazar), the girls become embroiled in the trappings of late '60s swinging lifestyle — sex, violence, and drugs. At a wild orgy at Z-Man's groovy Los Angeles pad, the band (and the audience) get acquainted with the sexual habits and individual excesses of the party-goers and "super-octane girls who are old at 20." The mysterious Z-Man provides a color commentary, uttering the famous line, "It's my happening baby, and it freaks me out," a quote later co-opted by Mike Myers in the first Austin Powers film. Despite the fact that the band's only other gig was at a senior prom, Z-Man offers the band a contract, gives them the name The Carrie Nations and they score several hits including *Talkin' Candy Man* and *Look on up at the Bottom*. This is, however, a morality tale, and even though the hits keep coming, things turn sour for the band, and each member experiences an ethical lesson amid the decadence and betrayals. A surprise twist at the end is confusing, largely because the filmmakers were making this up as they went along and apparently didn't bother to rework earlier scenes.

Ebert was a neophyte screenwriter at the time who lacked the experience to pen a coherent script, although film buffs will note that he is probably the only Pulitzer Prize winner to write a skin flick. "The story is such a labyrinthine juggling act," Ebert wrote in *Film Threat*, "that resolving it took a quadruple murder, a narrative summary, a triple wedding, and an epilogue." Looking back at the film today Ebert admits that the movie has a "curious tone."

Meyers ran the show on-set, and the personality of the rough and tumble former World War II newsreel cameraman intimidated the actors so much they couldn't work up the courage to ask whether or not they should play this material for laughs. "If the actors perform as if they know they have funny lines," said Meyer, "it won't work." As a result some ridiculous dialogue is given very strange line readings, lending a pseudo-serious feel to *Beyond the Valley of the Dolls* that helped turn it into a camp classic.

Viewed today, the movie seems like a time capsule back into what was considered cool in the late '60s, except that they didn't get it quite right. Meyers was too old to be involved in the Summer of Love, and Ebert seems to have only heard about free love from reading a *Time* magazine exposé. The wild scenes in the movie are a caricature of '60s speech and behavior, kind of like the beatniks on *The Beverly Hillbillies* or any other mainstream late-'60s fare that was trying to come to grips with the counter-culture. (Ebert and Meyer could have used a class or two at Jethro Bodine's "Cool School" before setting out to make this picture.) Z-Man is saddled with most of the outrageous dialogue. I can only imagine how difficult it was to deliver a line like, "You will drink the black sperm of my vengeance," without busting a gut. To compensate,

Meyer simply upped the ante by doing what he knew best, adding beautifully robust naked women into the clichéd mix.

Despite credibility problems, Meyer does hit the mark satirically. The unruly structure (intentional or not) lends a certain manic energy to the movie that echoes the pill poppin' culture he was trying to parody. Have you ever tried to follow a long, involved story told by a really high person? It makes about as much sense as this film does. The film is best watched as a series of wacky set pieces, strung together with scenes of sex and violence to make a whole. Watch for Pam Grier in her first on-screen role as a party-goer, and some delicious '60s psychedelia from one-hit wonders The Strawberry Alarm Clock, who perform their 1967 chart topper "Incense and Peppermints."

"The staggering tale of one man's relentless pursuit of imperfection."
— Advertising tagline for *BIG BAD LOVE*

BIG BAD LOVE (2001)

Big Bad Love is a surreal movie based on a short story collection by Mississippi writer Larry Brown. "A book and a film have as much to do with each other as a turkey does to a sandwich," says Arliss Howard in the press notes for the film. "Once the bread is involved, it is no longer turkey, it is a sandwich; and if you make turkey salad, it is something else again, and if you add mayo, humus, lettuce, salsa, if you broil it, slice it, well the idea is in there somewhere, and it gets more confusing if you see a wild turkey take flight, more so if you are walking with a three-year-old. What I mean to say is that Larry Brown understood this, having adapted his own work for the stage and screen."

That quote sums up the feel of the movie — tangential, and just a bit off-center. Arliss Howard directs and stars as Vietnam vet Leon Barlow, a drunken writer struggling to piece together the broken shards of his life, turning his personal experiences into deeply felt fiction. As the rejected manuscripts pile up around him, he must also deal with the demands of his ex-wife (Debra Winger), his children, and his war buddy and only friend (Paul LeMat). He's a self-centered man who struggles to balance his creative life — a need to write — with the wants and needs of those in his life. Even after catching up on his child support and alimony, and earning a weekend with his kids, he is left feeling empty and saddened with his ex-wife's lack of caring. His internal tussles, coupled with a mother (Angie Dickenson) who regards him as a disappointment and a personal tragedy, cause him to spiral downward.

Leon is a failure on almost every level — certainly personally and professionally — and Howard doesn't shy away from his protagonist's shortcomings. In one heartbreaking scene he has a drunken Barlow watch his wedding video — backwards. In the beginning we see him and Marilyn kissing and hugging, and as the film slowly reverses through the ceremony we see him waiting at the altar, and then wandering through the graveyard by the church. The way he sees it, even on "the happiest day of his life" he still wound up alone.

The movie is (Howard's real-life wife) Debra Winger's return to film after an absence of six years, and serves as a reminder of what a skilled screen actress she is. Her portrayal of Marilyn is as memorable when she is speaking as it is when she is still. In one scene she tells Barlow, "I went out to collect the laundry and I just couldn't make it. I'm too tired. I'm just lying here listening to the rain." The camera lingers on her face after the dialogue, and the look on her face is one of a woman at the end of her rope. In her silence we learn more about her character than we do in anything she says.

Big Bad Love is a meandering, surreal (check out the cow with the typewriter) look at the creative process, and how one man messed up his life. "Someone asked me what the movie is about," says Howard. "I said 'birth, death, love, work, friendship . . . pick 'em.' And trains." It's a well-crafted directorial debut from Howard who handles this quiet tale of an artist's redemption with a firm hand.

> "If this had been some ordinary drive-by shooting by some inexperienced gang-bangers we would've solved it a long time ago. You've got to think to yourself, 'Who could do this and get away with it?'"
> — Ex-LAPD Detective RUSSELL POOLE

BIGGIE AND TUPAC (2002)

Your enjoyment of *Biggie and Tupac* will be directly related to your enjoyment of director Nick Broomfield and his bumbling passive-aggressive approach to ambush journalism. He dominates the movie, integrating himself into the story in his search to uncover the culprits behind the slaying of the Notorious B.I.G. and Tupac Shakur, two of hip hop's brightest stars, gunned down within months of one another. No arrests have been made in the six years since the murders, and while Broomfield offers some possible suspects, he stops short of any definitive conclusion.

"It's a really complicated story," Broomfield told *Reel to Real* in 2002. "It took me nearly six months to put this thing together. There are so many different layers to it. On its simplest level it is the story of two guys who started off as best friends. Biggie loved Tupac. Then they got into a rivalry and what happened is that over the years the rivalry was used as a means of explaining their deaths. What I found in making the film, talking to the members of the LAPD who were handling the murder investigation, is that this is in fact not the case." Broomfield suggests several motives for the killings, but the point of the film is to chronicle his investigation — to present the facts and open a new dialogue about the culture of violence that is prevalent in hip hop — rather than pointing the finger at one guilty party.

I find Broomfield's approach highly entertaining, and while he veers off course occasionally — there is a long pointless sequence with an ex-girlfriend of two LAPD officers allegedly tied to Tupac's murder that hinges on the sex lives of the officers, not their criminal behavior — you have to admire his bravado in chasing down interviews in backrooms, prison yards, and anywhere the story takes him. "I think documentaries are about entertainment," says Broomfield. "They've got to be really entertaining, but I don't think that means they can't be *about* something at the same time. In a way one is almost like a contemporary historian or diary keeper. It's great to take subjects that tell the audience about something that we're all a part of. I think *Biggie and Tupac* is as much about the way society sees hip hop and sees those people — whether it is the police force or the FBI or whatever as anything else — but at the same time it is a funny and entertaining film. I think that makes it accessible to a much bigger audience."

In the film's final third there is an interview with Suge Knight, the head honcho at Death Row Records, a leading rap label. Knight was in prison at the time, and didn't want to do the interview, but through sheer persistence Broomfield got him on camera. You can sense the tension in the sequence. The camera is noticeably jittery, as though the camera operator was having an anxiety attack while shooting, and Broomfield is unusually subdued. Knight begins benignly enough with a "message for the kids" which slowly disintegrates into a hate-filled diatribe and death threat against rap artist Snoop Dogg. It is powerful footage, and worth the price of admission.

THE BRAVE ONE (1956)

■ ■ ■ ■ ■ ■ ■ ■ ■ ■

The Brave One puts a South American spin on the typical "boy and his dog" story. A lot of films have focused on young kids and their adventures with a favorite pet, but this may be a filmdom first — the pet in question is a bull. Based on a true story that took place in 1936 Spain, where a bull was pardoned and returned to its owner after a heroic performance in the bullring, the movie is set in Mexico. We meet young Leonardo (Michel Ray) who rescues a bull from certain death during a violent flood. A tight bond develops between the spirited boy and the animal, which he names Gitano. When the bull's ownership is disputed, Leo writes a letter to the former owner, who grants the young boy custody of the animal. Tragedy strikes when Leo's boss, the ranch owner, dies suddenly, and Gitano is auctioned off with the rest of the stock to fight in the Plaza de Mexico bullring.

Leo is determined to save his friend from death in the bullfighting arena and writes a letter to the President of Mexico asking for a pardon. Moved by the letter, the President grants the young boy's wish, but it is already too late: Gitano has been committed to face off with renowned matador Fermín Rivera (playing himself). Both warriors — man and beast — display bravery and brilliance in the ring, which leads to an exciting finale.

The Brave One has the best elements of a Disney film without the treacly sentiment. This is an uncomplicated but moving story, well told by blacklisted writer Dalton Trumbo (using the pen name Robert Rich) that will appeal to kids and adults alike.

BROTHERHOOD OF THE WOLF (2001)

Brotherhood of the Wolf is all over the place. It's a French Revolution/horror/martial arts epic with style to burn, and makes up for the gaping holes in its story with sheer energy and sensory assault.

Very loosely based on the legend of the Beast of Gevaudan, a mysterious creature that terrorized a rural area of France in 1764, *Brotherhood of the Wolf* begins its loopy journey in the closing moments of the French Revolution. To solve the mystery of the beast, who had attacked more than 60 women and children and was widely believed to be of colossal size, the king of France dispatched two investigators to the precipitous central area of France. Each member of the envoy brings special talents to uncover the mystery: Mani (Mark Dacascos), an Iroquois scout, not only has martial arts moves that would make Bruce Lee green with envy, but can also talk to trees! Expedition leader Fronsac (Samuel Le Bihan) comes to believe that the creature exists, though he surmises it is being manipulated by man.

At a dinner Fronsac meets Jean-Francois (Vincent Cassel) and his sister Marianne (Emile Dequenne). They are local gentry, and a blossoming relationship between the rough-and-tumble Fronsac and the demure Marianne causes a rift with those close to the king. Matters become even more complicated when Fronsac becomes involved with Sylvia (Monica Bellucci), a beautiful prostitute with some dangerous habits. When the king's lieutenant falsely claims to have killed the murderous Beast of Gevaudan, Fronsac arranges one last hunt using Mani's shaman techniques to track the murderous monster.

Director Christophe Gans packs every moment of *Brotherhood of the Wolf* with either bone-crunching action (imagine if John Woo had directed *Dangerous Liaisons*), crazy audio/visual effects, or busy scenes involving beautiful people. Though Gans knows how to amuse the eye, he isn't much of a storyteller; but *Brotherhood of the Wolf* is so entertaining that we'll forgive him just this once.

"Mr. President, we're going to have to kick some mummy butt."
— ELVIS PRESLEY (BRUCE CAMPBELL)

BUBBA HO-TEP (2002)

Since The King took his final earthly tumble from the throne at Graceland in 1977, there have been many Elvis sightings. He's been spotted ordering a Whopper at a Burger King in Kalamazoo, Michigan; riding in a Cadillac in his hometown of Memphis; and dozens of Web sites chronicle the king of rock and roll's rather hectic schedule in the afterlife.

Self-proclaimed champion "Mojo storyteller" Joe R. Lansdale added a new and unlikely chapter to the folklore surrounding Elvis's post-August 1977 activities in the form of a novella of speculative fiction called "Bubba Ho-Tep." It's a wild story about an aging Elvis and an Egyptian mummy that was nominated for a Bram Stoker Award in 1994.

Director Don Coscarelli discovered the story the following year. "I was in a genre bookstore down in Los Angeles. I was looking around for something fun to read," Coscarelli told *Reel to Real* in 2002. "I asked the guy behind the counter for something good, and he said, 'You should look at this Joe Lansdale, his books always have a high body count.' That sounds cool, I thought. He gave me one that I liked quite a bit, and I actually became a fan. I started reading all of Joe's stuff, and it turns out he lives down in East Texas, so I called him up. He invited me to come down there, and I visited with him. We were talking about some different kinds of projects. He had [written] a crazy film called *The Job* and also a great horror western called *Dead in the West* which would make a fun picture, but nothing ever came of it.

"A couple of years later I found this anthology of some of his short stories and I was looking through the dust jacket and it said, 'Elvis versus the Mummy.' I said, 'That's a cool idea,' and that's what really attracted me. Then I found that it was so much more layered and deeper and wonderful in its own way. I thought this is something that would make an interesting movie." Coscarelli set aside the *Phantasm* series of movies he had been churning out for a decade and adapted the "true" story of what happened to Elvis for the screen.

B-movie hero Bruce Campbell wears a ton of makeup to play the elderly Elvis, a resident in a Texas old age home. The story is that Elvis switched identities with an Elvis impersonator named Sebastian Haff, just after the 1968 comeback special. Unfortunately he missed his chance to switch back before Haff died, and ended up broke and in the rest home. There he befriended an old African-American man (Ossie Davis) who believes he is President John F. Kennedy. Together they battle an evil soul-sucking Egyptian entity that has been terrorizing the home.

"It was the weirdest script I had ever read," Campbell told *Reel to Real* in 2002. "It certainly jumped out. A lot of the crap you get is such miserable dreck, and I've been in a lot of miserable dreck so I can smell them when they're coming. Bubba was different. It had a different stink on it."

Campbell understands different. Finding cult fame as Ash in the *Evil Dead* movies, he has forged a career doing B-movies and in the process gathered a fiercely loyal fan base. Despite his reputation as a B-actor, Campbell is not to be underrated. He literally brings Elvis to life as a cranky, horny old man. "An Elvis impersonator came and I worked with him, but he quit after an hour," says Campbell. "He said, 'You're worthless. It's not going to work. I'm the one with the real talent.' I said, 'Yeah, who's playing Elvis and who's the fake Elvis? Who's playing him — me or you, pal?'" Despite the falling out with the Elvis expert, Campbell's portrayal of The King is reverential. Campbell cites the heavy makeup, fat suit, and the fact that he was hunched over a walker as the building blocks to creating the Elvis character. "The rest was just dicking around," he laughs. Veteran actor Ossie Davis is thoroughly believable as the deluded Jack, and is a perfect foil for Campbell's Elvis.

The premise is a startlingly original one for a film, and while over-the-top, has large dollops of humanity spread throughout. As the dynamic duo battle evil, they are making the most of their final years. These guys may be old, bad-tempered, and slightly crazy, but they can still make a difference. *Bubba Ho-Tep* is actually more entertaining and exciting than most Elvis movies, and should earn an enthusiastic "Thank you, thankyouverymuch," from open-minded fans of The King.

"When one species of cane beetle is in the cane fields, it just doesn't come in contact with the ground and we know that cane toads can't fly."
— DR. INGRAM

CANE TOADS: AN UNNATURAL HISTORY (1988)

Who would have thought a documentary about the cane toad infestation in Australia could be this much fun? Made in 1987 by documentarian Mark Lewis, the film is a cautionary tale about introducing non-native species to a fragile environment.

In 1935, 100 cane toads were brought in from Hawaii to Queensland, Australia, to battle the cane grub, a nasty little critter that was destroying the sugar-cane crop. Bad planning, as it turns out, because the cane toads didn't have a taste for the grubs and instead began procreating constantly. Just 50 years after they were introduced, these sex-crazed amphibians had spread from the initial nine farms to cover almost 250,000 square miles.

Equipped with two venom pouches behind their heads that shoot deadly poison, the toads have no natural predators; they can defend themselves against insects, birds, and mice all the way up to dogs, cats, and even humans who don't handle them properly. They are unstoppable. Queensland became overrun with these (I have to say it) horny toads that lay tens of thousands of eggs a year.

Lewis presents the facts, but washes them down with more humor than Marlin Perkins could ever muster on *Mutual of Omaha's Wild Kingdom*. Much of the comedy is derived from clever crosscutting between the citizens of Queensland, who have adopted the toad as a mascot, and the anti-toad faction, the scientists, who hate the little creatures. Lewis adds to this a series of real and staged shots that inspire dread and hilarity simultaneously. In one such scene a motorist witnesses the relentless sex drive of the male toad. Driving down a country road, the man stops when he sees a male toad mating with a female. Quite natural, except that she is roadkill, squashed pancake flat. The "What the hell???" look on the driver's face alone is worth the entire movie. In another scene a local displays his prowess in hunting the tiny toads . . . with his van. He swerves through a country road, flattening them under his wheels. Because the toads puff up when they sense danger, they make a loud popping sound when run over. Lewis can't boast that no animals were hurt during the making of his film, but this scene, and the ensuing loud bursts, do inspire some giggles.

The staged scenes are just as effective. Taking his cue from classic horror films, Lewis shoots several sequences from the point of view of the villain. The "toad cam" sequences are amusing as the wicked amphibians hippity hop toward their prey, in particular the one where they sneak up on a man in the shower singing a tune called "Queensland Toads." The single most disturbing scene involves a four-year-old girl playing with "Dairy Queen," her pet cane toad. She makes it dance and rubs its tummy, blissfully unaware of the lethal tendencies of her living toy. Lewis heightens the surreal goings-on by adding the lilting strains of a folk song about loving the cane toad "warts and all."

Cane Toads: An Unnatural History is an exploration into not only the biology of nature, but also human nature, as we learn that many of the locals have grown to love and admire these pesky creatures. Never preachy, but not without scientific merit, *Cane Toads* is the funniest nature documentary to date.

"We didn't set out to make a classic. We just wanted to make a movie that would make a little money . . ."
— Cinematographer MAURICE PRATHER

CARNIVAL OF SOULS (1962)

The success of *The Blair Witch Project* in 1999 took everyone by surprise. A no-budget, black-and-white horror film, it packed a punch with atmospherics and unexpected thrills. Almost 40 years earlier, another micro-budgeted movie, *Carnival of Souls*, breathed the same air, giving us a fear-inspiring story that relied on psychological terror rather than high-tech special effects.

Colorado-born producer/director Herk Harvey was born into a working-class family and christened with the unlikely name Harvey Harvey. Always fascinated with show business, he majored in theater at Kansas University, cutting his teeth acting and directing stage productions. In the late '50s he turned to film, working with the Centron Corporation of Lawrence, Kansas, a company specializing in educational and industrial films. Hired as an actor, he appeared in many short subjects before taking a job behind the camera as a director.

The idea for *Carnival of Souls* was born in 1961 during a road trip through Utah. Harvey had just finished shooting an industrial film in California, and while driving home to Kansas he passed Saltair, an abandoned amusement park located near the Great Salt Lake. "It was the weirdest place I'd ever seen," he later said. Once a popular resort, the grand structure was now in ruins, but it lit up Harvey's imagination, and he sensed it would be a good location to shoot a film. Harvey had aspired to directing features, especially now that another industrial filmmaker, Robert Altman, had recently made the jump to the big screen with *The Delinquents*, shot in Kansas City.

Harvey discussed the idea of shooting a feature with John Clifford, a friend from Centron. Clifford was an author with a western novel to his credit. They brainstormed, and in two months Clifford had a completed script.

Clifford's script begins with a drag race between a carload of young women and some testosterone-charged guys. The race ends badly and the women crash, plunging into a deep river. Hours later, as the police drag the river for bodies in vain, Mary Henry (Candace Hilligoss) appears, dazed but unhurt. She remembers nothing of the accident, and is viewed as a miracle woman, someone who defied death. She tries to lead a normal life, accepting a job as a church organist in Utah. As she pieces her life together, strange things start to happen. She loses touch with reality, able to see people who cannot see or hear her. A ghostly figure (played by Herk Harvey) plagues her, even though no one else will admit to seeing the phantom. What exactly is this hallucination?

The story is simple, if not completely original. Lucille Fletcher, wife of *Psycho* composer Bernard Hermann, had written a script called *The Hitchhiker*, which was performed on the radio by the Mercury Theatre and starred Orson Welles. There are vague similarities between *The Hitchhiker* and Clifford's script. In Fletcher's story a motorist who had previously been in a car accident driving across the country repeatedly encounters the same hitchhiker after a car accident.

The connections to *The Hitchhiker* are clear (both Mary Henry and

Fletcher's motorist see ghosts after surviving a trauma), although Clifford adds some elements that set it apart from Fletcher's radio play. This time the main character is a woman, who slips in and out of a supernatural state of non-being. Also, Clifford's Mary is a cold, distant character, a break from the stereotypical sympathetic horror movie heroine. The story may have familiar elements, but Clifford's handling of the material elevates a run-of-the-mill trifle into a nightmare of paranoid delusion. Its refusal to provide cut-and-dried answers leaves the viewer uneasy.

While Clifford was penning the screenplay, Harvey set out to raise the modest budget through private investors. He pieced together $17,000, a modest sum, even in the early '60s. With no money in the budget to pay actors, an amateur cast was assembled, and Harvey took a three-week leave of absence from Centron to shoot the film.

When it came to cutting corners on the set of *Carnival of Souls*, Harvey used some tricks he'd learned while shooting industrials. With no money for special effects, save for some wavy lines that appear between plains of existence, some ingenuity was required. In one scene a ghostly face appears on a car window. Today the effect could easily be accomplished with computer imagery, but in 1962 Harvey and cinematographer Maurice Prather came up with a much simpler solution. "We did it with a mirror," says Prather.

Budgetary concerns precluded the use of a process screen, a technique commonly used in film to give the illusion of movement in car scenes. These shots would typically be shot in a studio with any landscape seen through the windows of the car projected onto the process screen. In *Carnival of Souls* the car scenes were actually shot on location inside moving vehicles, using a battery powered handheld Arriflex camera. The shots are very clean, and have since become the industry standard. The use of the Arriflex, an extremely mobile camera traditionally used in news photography, gave them the opportunity to concoct elaborate camera moves without the use of expensive dollies or cranes. The inventive camera work of Maurice Prather is one of the things that sets *Carnival of Souls* above other low-budget horror films of the same vintage.

Another effective scene was shot for only a few dollars. Central to the story is the car crash at the beginning of the film. It is important that the viewer see the crash to understand its devastating nature. The cars were arranged through a contra deal, but having them smash through a bridge was a different and potentially more expensive matter. "What do you think it cost us for a city like Lecompton, Kansas, to let us wreck their bridge?" asked Prather, "Thirty-eight dollars. They said, 'Yeah, you can do that as long as you replace the rails you knock out.' It was nothing to replace the rails."

Carnival of Souls is a potent thriller, and like *The Blair Witch Project* rises above its humble beginnings to deliver some truly frightening moments. I particularly like the use of sound in a pair of scenes where Mary finds herself shut off from reality, unable to make herself known to those around her. Harvey heightens the tension of those passages by eliminating all sound except the clicking of Mary's heels. The eerie silence conveys Mary's alienation far more effectively than any musical score could.

The crisp black-and-white *Carnival of Souls* doesn't look or feel like a modern horror film and contains moments of wooden acting and stiff dialogue, but it has undoubtedly influenced a generation of filmmakers. Its steely-eyed look at the horror that can lie just under the surface certainly influenced David Lynch, while other horrormeisters like John Carpenter and George Romero have acknowledged its importance.

Herk Harvey never made another feature (he became a teacher at Kansas University), but he did live long enough to see his film become a cult classic. He died in 1996, eight years after it was theatrically rereleased to great critical fanfare.

"Paul loaded the camera. Andy pointed it and Gerard started the tape recorder – there were always endless amounts of waiting. Of course there were endless amounts of drugs too, which sort of made up for it."
— **MARY WORONOV, STAR OF *CHELSEA GIRLS***

CHELSEA GIRLS (1967)

■ ■ ■ ■ ■ ■ ■ ■ ■ ■

Any wine expert can tell you that certain bottles, when stored properly, improve with time. Think of *Chelsea Girls* as a nicely aged bottle of Meursault Sancerre 1967 — smoky, but displaying a tremendous presence; rich and boldly flavored. Viewed with a mix of curiosity and bewilderment at its initial screenings, *Chelsea Girls* has become Andy Warhol's best-known film and a true underground classic.

Pop artist Andy Warhol liked to hang out at the El Quixote restaurant, located downstairs from the fabled Chelsea Hotel at 222 West 23rd Street in New York. He would meet his entourage (most of whom were staying at the hotel) for a cheap dinner washed down with jugs of sangria and would discuss the events of the day. During one of these meals Warhol says he "got the idea to unify all the pieces of these people's lives by stringing them together as if they lived in different rooms of the same hotel."

Warhol had been tinkering with films since the early '60s. His pieces were primitive point-and-shoot exercises featuring ad-libbed dialogue and naturalistic performances. His films were studies of people doing mundane things — one film, *Eat*, showed Robert Indiana eating a mushroom for 33 minutes; another, *Haircut*, was a half-hour movie of one man ritualistically cutting another man's hair. His idea for *Chelsea Girls* was to be his most ambitious film to date.

Between June and September 1966 Warhol shot 15 one- and two-reel films at various locations around New York City, including the Chelsea Hotel and his Factory studio. The process was the same each time. Each scene was shot in one take until the 35-minute film load had run out. Warhol's thesis was simple: point the camera at exciting people, let it run, and something interesting was likely to happen. "This way I can catch people being themselves instead of setting up a scene and shooting it and letting people act out parts that were written," he said. "Because it's better to act naturally than act like somebody else." The short films had no plots or scripts, save for some rough outlines that were discarded early in the shooting process.

Warhol's direction of the scenes was minimal. Eric Emerson, credited as The Boy in the Kitchen, remembers Warhol simply instructed him to tell the story of his life, and "somewhere along the line to take off all my clothes." While Warhol didn't provide much guidance on the set, he did have other methods to draw incendiary performances from his actors. All the performers knew one another and were part of the scene that Warhol had created in his Factory art studio. The actors were using drugs, and all vying for Warhol's approval. He used this scenario to create tension among his "superstars" by spreading gossip and unkind remarks that the actors were allegedly making about one another. He encouraged them to express their feelings about one another in their scenes. This methodology was disagreeable and sometimes cruel, but it made for compelling viewing. Bob "Ondine" Olivio, who played The Pope of Greenwich Village in the film, called this manner of working unpleasant, but added with a bit of unintentional hyperbole, "he pulled out of these people, including myself, some of the best performances *ever* on screen."

Warhol did capture some unforgettable images. Transvestite Mario Montez cut his scene short after being reduced to tears by the insults of two boys sitting on a bed. The taunts and the tears are real, and the scene is harrowing.

In another scene real life and infighting take over. Before filming began, Susan "International Velvet" Bottomly told Warhol she was expecting a call from a modeling agency. He told her that would not be a problem, and to use the call in the scene. When the phone rings a fight ensues between Velvet and Mary "Mary Might" Woronov when Mary won't let Velvet answer it. "That's my call," says Velvet. "You don't have a call," Mary replies, "You have a fat ass." It may seem trite now in light of television's reality shows, but the realism drips off the screen, and the viewer is left wondering if what they are seeing is real or contrived. That feeling is enhanced when one of the actors, obviously growing frustrated with Warhol's process, looks into the camera and asks, "When is that fucking thing going to stop?"

Warhol pieced together *Chelsea Girls* after reviewing the reels at the end of September 1967. A close examination of the 15 half-hour scenes revealed an unintentional, rough story line. Warhol realized that he could piece all these loose bits of footage together into one film. The problem was he was unable to edit the footage because he had shot it all on newsreel cameras that recorded the sound directly onto the film. This technique prevented separation of sound and picture, so to keep the sound in sync he would have to run the 35-minute segments uncut. To prevent a prohibitive seven-hour running time, Warhol ingeniously used a split-screen presentation, with sound only on one side at a time, to cut the running time down to three-and-a-half hours. Warhol created a standard order for the reels, though by juggling the order of the scenes and remixing the sound it is possible to create a different movie each time it is screened. In 2000, director Mike Figgis used a similar approach in his film *Timecode*, which was shot on digital video and presented on a quadruple-split screen. Figgis would personally host screenings, remixing the sound based on the reactions of the audience.

Chelsea Girls isn't perfect, but at three-and-a-half hours it has enough compelling moments to make it worth watching. For example, Ondine's attack on the Roman Catholic Church, climaxing with the line, "Approach the crucifix, lift his loincloth, and go about your business!" is searing stuff, and is still shocking today, decades after it was first released. What I find most fascinating about the film is the way it blurs the line between reality and artifice. Warhol orchestrated a sordid look at the soft underbelly of his life in New York, and it is hard to tell what is real and what is performance art, although the drug use and infighting seem authentic.

Warhol was not a skilled filmmaker. He didn't concern himself with properly recording the sound. The camera zooms wildly, constantly refocusing and jiggling. This looks and sounds like an underground movie, but there is a punk rock DIY energy about the film that propels the action.

In 1967 *Chelsea Girls* was met with mixed critical reaction, and generated hundreds of column inches in the newspapers. Warhol was philosophical about fault-finding attacks from the establishment. "Until then the general attitude toward what we did was that it was *artistic* or *camp* or a *put-on* or just plain *boring*," he said. "But after *Chelsea Girls*, words like *degenerate* and *disturbing* and *homosexual* and *druggy* and *nude* and *real* started being applied to us regularly."

"She'd get out more . . . if it wasn't a felony."
— Advertising tagline for *CHERISH*

CHERISH (2002)

Cherish is one of those films that people like to call quirky. It is an odd little story about a fantasy-prone woman named Zoe who winds up under house arrest for a crime she didn't commit. Robin Tunney plays Zoe as a hapless 29-year-old computer animator hopelessly in lust with a co-worker named Andrew (Jason Priestly). Many drinks later at an after work party in a nightclub, Zoe finally gets Andrew's attention. Before accepting a ride home with him she checks her car, only to be hijacked by a mysterious man in a mask who forces her to drive drunk and steps on the accelerator as a cop stands in front of the car trying to flag them down. The police officer is killed, the strange man disappears, and Zoe is arrested for vehicular manslaughter.

To avoid hard jail time while waiting for trial, Zoe cuts a deal to live under house arrest, wearing an ankle bracelet that sets off an alarm if she strays from her loft. At the beginning of her sentence her living situation doesn't seem that bad — there are worse ways to do your time than in a huge Ikea-filled loft in San Francisco — but the limitations of movement soon become obvious, and you realize that any place can become a prison if you aren't allowed to leave.

Despite not being allowed to set foot outside her front door she forges relationships with several people — a pizza delivery man, her wheelchair-bound downstairs neighbor, and a gawky local deputy played by Tim Blake Nelson. Through her confinement and the friendship of outsiders Zoe sheds her emotional handicaps and blossoms into a confident, resourceful, self-reliant woman. She's innocent, and since no one believes her, she must find the proof that will set her free. At this point the movie breaks loose of its claustrophobic feel as Zoe takes control of her destiny and hunts down the obsessive man who ruined her life.

Robin Tunney rises above the occasionally messy script to actually give Zoe an interesting screen life. She's spirited, likeable, and delivers a heroine with a bit of edge. She's the offbeat girl you see at the coffee shop, the brainiac with a secret inner life. She makes interesting choices that her more mainstream contemporaries might have avoided. Jennifer Connelly might have played Zoe with steely determination, while Kirsten Dunst would have brought a veneer of sweetness to the role that would undermine the character's natural anxiety. Instead Tunney plays Zoe as a subtle oddball, a woman just slightly out-of-step with everyone else. It is this very quality that makes her transformation so much more interesting and believable. Few recent Hollywood movies have strong central female characters, so it is refreshing to see a film in which the female lead is in virtually every scene.

Tim Blake Nelson's lovesick deputy is an understated gem of a performance. At first he's all business, but he slowly warms to Zoe and finds his well-ordered life slowly turned upside down as he develops decidedly unprofessional feelings for her. His is a key character, on the one hand representing authority and incarceration, and on the other Zoe's ticket to freedom. It's a finely layered act without any of the showy aspects of his work in *O Brother, Where Art Thou?* or *Minority Report*.

Other well-known names pop up in small supporting roles. Alternative rocker Liz Phair fares well enough in the bland part of Brynn, one of Zoe's co-workers, but doesn't make much of an impression. Nora Dunn, best known for her five-year stint on *Saturday Night Live*, plays a no-nonsense attorney with gusto, but it is Jason Priestly as the object of Zoe's affections who steals the show. Age has rounded his handsome face somewhat, which makes him less a teen idol and more the good-looking guy who could actually work in the next cubicle to yours. It's a self-deprecating portrayal that slyly pokes fun at his former cheesecake status.

The pop music of the 1970s and '80s propels the movie, and is used to illustrate Zoe's inner life. The themes of stalking and unrequited love are underscored by radio hits by Hall & Oates and The Association. The songs may sound familiar, but in this context the lyrics to "Tainted Love" by Soft Cell or 10cc's "I'm Not in Love" resonate with creepy undertones.

Cherish isn't a perfect movie. The basic plot is implausible. Anyone who has watched *Law and Order* can tell you that people who are suspected of killing police officers are not treated to house arrest, and certainly no cop would treat Zoe the way that Blake's character does. If you can ignore the movie's key flaw, there is a great deal here to appreciate.

"It's a fucking good film, Robert, but if it ever shows in America
we'll never be allowed in the country again."
— MICK JAGGER to director ROBERT FRANK

COCKSUCKER BLUES (1972)

You probably haven't seen one of the best movies about rock and roll ever made, and Mick Jagger wants to make sure that you never do. *Cocksucker Blues*, the legendary documentary about the Rolling Stones, is so raunchy it even made the Fab Five blush. Although it was produced with the full co-operation of the band, they still took director Robert Frank to court to block its distribution.

The Rolling Stones first met the Swiss-born photographer Robert Frank at a mansion in Los Angeles during the sessions for *Exile on Main Street*. As Europeans they shared a common fascination with American culture. The Stones were walking encyclopedias of Southern blues, while Frank had traveled the States in the mid-'50s snapping a series of photographs that would be released as a book titled *The Americans*. By the time of their meeting in 1972 the Stones were the biggest rock band in the world, and *The Americans* was already regarded as one of the classic photography books of the century.

After their initial meeting Frank was hired to provide the cover art for *Exile on Main Street*. He gave them a photo he had taken in 1950 of a collage of circus freaks from the wall of a tattoo parlor on Route 66. The cover photo was met with such critical acclaim that the Stones decided to expand their working relationship with Frank, and hired him to shoot a no-holds-barred documentary of their 1972 American tour, to be produced by the legendary owner of Chess Records, Marshall Chess.

The Stones had not performed in the U.S. since the December 1969 debacle at the Altamont Racetrack, the final date on a tour that was filmed by Albert and David Maysles and released as a full-length feature film titled *Gimme Shelter*. Shot in the waning moments of the 1960s, *Gimme Shelter* not only documents the actual end of the decade, but its ideological end as well. During the Altamont concert the Hell's Angels, hired by the Stones to act as security, used pool cues and knives to beat an 18-year-old African-American audience member to death. As the Stones played "Under My Thumb" and Meredith Hunter lay dying on the ground, the image profoundly signaled the end of the era of peace and love. It was an historical moment, and the Rolling Stones had it on film.

Gimme Shelter is an above-average rockumentary, and the inclusion of the controversial Altamont footage assured that it would be successful. Three years later, it was time for a follow-up. Jagger decided to call the new movie *Cocksucker Blues* after a raunchy tune he had written about a gay hooker in London, and gave Frank an all-access pass to shoot wherever and whatever he wanted. That was a decision that would later come back to haunt the band.

Frank chose to shoot the film *cinema verité* style in crisp black and white, which lends a stark newsreel feel to the movie. His dispassionate eye neither judges nor comments, preferring to let viewers draw their own conclusions as he films Keith Richard's descent into heroin addiction, or a battered woman trying to hide her face from the camera. There are many outrageous sequences in the film: saxophonist Bobby Keyes and Keith Richard indulge in one of the great rites of passage for any rock star — throwing a television out of a hotel window; Keith advises Mick on the best way to snort cocaine; naked groupies masturbate for the camera — and one gets the feeling that they are genuine, despite the Stones' later claim that Frank staged some of the more decadent scenarios. As part of a legal settlement with the band Frank was forced to add a disclaimer at the beginning of the movie stating, "all scenes except the musical performances are fictitious."

To my mind the thing that makes this documentary special, setting it heads above the other anything-that-is-worth-doing-is-worth-over-doing music movies is not the sensational sex, drugs, and rock and roll footage, but the shots of the band in the downtime between concerts.

This, I suspect, is the side that the myth-hungry Rolling Stones didn't want you to see.

Frank unblinkingly shows us the tedium of life on the road, and allows the real lives of the band members to be revealed. Mick, the ultimate rock star, for example, is seen trying to deal with his high-maintenance wife Bianca, who is often seen crying and playing with a small music box. The band is shown killing time between gigs by ordering room service, engaging in inconsequential conversations, or simply by not speaking at all. This was hardly the high glam life that would be expected from the "World's Greatest Rock and Roll Band," although these are the scenes that humanize the group and put a pinprick in the bubble of fame that surrounded the Stones in their glory days. Director Jim Jarmusch called *Cocksucker Blues* "definitely one of the best movies about rock and roll I've ever seen. It makes you think that being a rock star is one of the last things you'd ever want to do."

There are also some great in-concert moments, although *Cocksucker Blues* is by no means a concert flick. In one memorable sequence Frank intercuts backstage antics of roadies snorting coke with the Stones on-stage performing "Midnight Rambler." The images pile up on one another, creating a hypnotic tableau that shows both the public and private faces of the band. In those frames Frank captures the true dichotomy of the group and life on the road. Other standout performances include an "Uptight"/"Satisfaction" medley (with Stevie Wonder), "Happy," and "Street Fighting Man."

The era when it would be possible to make a film like this showing a band at this level is over. Now publicists would run interference at every stop, and every media-savvy groupie would demand a release form and a fee. *Cocksucker Blues* may represent our last truly unfettered look into the lives of rock gods at the peak of their fame. The practice of celebrity journalism has been dealt a mortal blow by overzealous celebrity minders whose purpose in life is to sanitize their client's images and make sure that compromising situations like the ones in this movie never see the light of day.

Not everyone agrees with my assessment of *Cocksucker Blues* as the greatest (and most revealing) rock movie ever, least of all the Rolling Stones. "I thought it was a piece of shit actually," Bill Wyman, the Stones' original bass player, told *Reel to Real* in September 2001. "I thought it was so amateur and so poorly done, I just couldn't relate to it. [Robert Frank] was obviously just looking for anything sensational. That's why me and Charlie are hardly in it, because we weren't sensational. All the good bits, I thought, were cut out. It was just like a poor home movie, shot badly. I couldn't relate to it. I had no interest in it really."

The film has had very few public screenings. Frank's vision of rock-and-roll superstardom may have been too raw for the Stones, who sued to have the film shelved. Instead of suppressing the film completely, they reached a complicated settlement that allows Frank to show the film once a year, as long as he is in attendance. Bootleg copies — with a picture quality that "sucks as much as the groupies" as one critic has joked — have been widely distributed, and are available for rent in many cities.

"I just want to capture what's real and honest."
— PAUL (JEREMY DAVIS)

CQ (2002)
▬ ▬ ▬ ▬

Roman Coppola has worked on his father's films since he was a teenager, doing sound on *The Outsiders* and directing the second unit and special effects for *Bram Stoker's Dracula*. *CQ* is his feature film debut, although he is already well known for directing music videos.

The action takes place in Paris in 1968 and involves a character named Paul (Jeremy Davies), an idealistic American film student who ends up directing a sci-fi B-movie called *Dragonfly*. The movie within the movie has notes of Jane Fonda's *Barbarella*, featuring a sexy, butt-kicking heroine who embodies the late-'60s ideal of female empowerment. Paul is hired by a flamboyant Dino De Laurentiis-esque character (Giancarlo Giannini) to finish directing the movie after the original director (Gérard Depardieu) was fired for not providing a satisfying conclusion to the story. Paul feels pressure to wrap up the film, while fielding advances from his sultry American leading lady (Angela Lindvall), and fighting with his Parisian political activist girlfriend (Elodie Bouchez). *CQ* is an incredibly layered and stylistic film, maybe too much so. There are two films within the film, and Coppola cuts back and forth randomly, using Paul's black-and-white experimental film to provide the emotional core of the story, while the science-fiction film propels the action.

"During the writing process, I'd put music on and look through magazines and watch movies and get receptive to things that impressed me one way or the other," Coppola told *Hollywood Bitchslap*. "It was fun. You just collect all these ingredients and then start to weave them together and try to make some sense of things." It's a valiant try, and while it's not completely successful, I really liked *CQ*. Coppola has nailed the time and place perfectly — Paris in 1968 looks like the hippest spot on earth — and coaxed good performances from his actors. Another bonus is the groovy soundtrack by über-hipsters Mellow that actually adds to the movie, rather than just support it.

"The eye cams allows people to be me rather than see me."
— **STEVE MANN, the world's first cyborg**

CYBERMAN (2001)

- - - - - - - -

P.T. Barnum would have loved Steve Mann. The pitch would have gone something like this: "Step right up ladies and gentlemen! Have we got a FREAK for you! Half man and half machine, this *un*biological creature is one of the wonders of the world!" Barnum met his reward many years ago, so it has fallen to Canadian documentarian Peter Lynch to introduce us to the weird world of Mr. Mann, the planet's first cyborg.

Lynch has a knack for finding unusual subjects for his films. His last feature, *Project Grizzly*, focused on Troy Hurtubise, who built a suit so he could wrestle grizzly bears. Before that was *The Herd*, featuring Andy Bahr, who wanted to drive reindeer across the top of the world. As eccentric and compelling as those characters might be, the director struck pay dirt with Steve Mann, the subject of *Cyberman*. Mann, a University of Toronto professor, has spent the last 20 years outfitting his body with a variety of electronic gizmos that are linked to a computer. He is rarely seen without his wearable PC, even in the company of family and friends. Think of Mann as the bastard child of Bill Gates and Inspector Gadget. His electronic get-up gives new meaning to the term "personal computer."

Ideologically Mann is a cybergeek Michael Moore, an anti-establishment figure who is distrustful of big business and almost everyone else. One of the functions of his contraption is to keep an eye on the hidden surveillance cameras in stores. There are several scenes showing Mann accosting retail employees, questioning them about hidden cameras in their shops, while at the same time secretly recording their meetings. Therein lies the contradiction of Mann's work: he rails against hidden surveillance in franchise retail outlets while simultaneously violating the privacy of the store's employees. Mann doesn't acknowledge this conundrum, as if his academic ideas take precedence over the rights of the very people he claims to want to protect.

That said, Mann doesn't exactly try to blend in. His thick black glasses, equipped with eye cams, give him a mutant fly-like appearance, like a character from a Philip K. Dick novel. We see him wandering the streets of Toronto and New York, shooting a video diary of his life that he uploads to a variety of Web sites. While he attracts attention, he seems awkward and confrontational when dealing with non-techno hipsters. He maintains that his work will actually forge a stronger bond between people, but by its very nature it isolates him from real human contact. By acting as the director of an elaborate cyber-reality show he puts a layer of equipment between him and the rest of the world, preventing any real interaction with others. Not even Mann's wife, who has worn a similar personal technology for 15 years, is immune to his constant electronic observation. Mann claims that by monitoring her at meal times she was able to improve her table manners. It seems a rather elaborate way to teach etiquette.

There is a creepy element to Mann and his constant detached observation. He doesn't look at things, he inspects them. His mother reveals that Mann and his brother kept the family under secret surveillance for three years. College friends mention a hair fetish. This behavior isn't explored in the film, but doesn't exactly endear Mann to the viewer.

Mann is not a likeable character, exuding an "I'm-much-smarter-than-you'll-ever-be" vibe that could become obnoxious when presented by a less capable filmmaker, but Lynch handles the material with subtlety. Mann isn't treated like a sideshow attraction, a Lobster Boy or Bearded Lady. Lynch allows Mann to spout his unusual ideas while including several scenes that humanize him, including footage of the adult Mann taking his first swim. True to form, he learns the ins-and-outs of swimming from books and movies, rather than from the more direct experience of simply jumping in the water and moving his body.

We meet his mother, a woman resigned to the difficulties inherent in raising the world's first cyborg. As he sits next to her in full cybernetic regalia, she looks at him, and in a world-weary voice says, "This is Steve." The implied feeling is one of a long-suffering parent who can't quite get a handle on her own flesh and blood, but also of unconditional love.

In another sequence Mann recalls a story of a childhood friend who was forbidden to play with him. The boy's mother was concerned about the six-year-old Mann's "influence" on her son. Shot in close-up, it is the first time we see past the darkened glasses and into the soul of the subject. Mann appears vulnerable, his guise of superiority dropped as he momentarily steps out from behind the wall of technology.

Lynch wisely resists portraying Mann as a one-dimensional techno-nerd. Without these illuminating scenes he would seem to be a damaged person only able to deal with real life by creating his own reality. Lynch's unblinking camera manages to smooth Mann's rough passive-aggressive edges, which may be the film's greatest achievement. Mann is difficult to like, but through Lynch's camera viewers are engaged, even fascinated by a character they only get to meet through the screen. Observing the observer. Engaged but removed. I imagine that is the kind of cool detachment that Mann would admire.

"Three wishes I'll grant you, big wishes and small, but if you wish a fourth wish, You Lose Them All!"
— LEPRECHAUN KING (JIMMY O'DEA)

DARBY O'GILL AND THE LITTLE PEOPLE (1959)

Based on the Darby O'Gill short stories of Herminie Templeton Kavanagh, this movie is arguably Disney's best-ever live-action film. Uncle Walt tried to bring the story of Darby O'Gill and his tall tales to the screen for almost 20 years, but had to wait until 1959 to be able to create the sophisticated special effects necessary for the film's visual success. Technicians needed to create an effect that blended full-sized actors with tiny leprechauns. Using mattes was an option, as was optical patching, although both methods would have left the film with a grainy appearance that would have taken away from the story. The answer to his F/X problem was found in the art of optical illusion — forced perspective. Large-sized actors are placed in the foreground, while smaller ones are moved to the back. When lit properly, one achieves the desired illusion of leprechauns and full-sized people interacting in the same scene. It is this technology that lends *Darby O'Gill and the Little People* so much of its wonder.

The story is simple: devious old O'Gill (Albert Sharpe) learns that he is about to be replaced by the younger (and much better looking) Michael McBride (Sean Connery in one of his first film roles) as caretaker of Lord Fitzpatrick's estate. He stumbles down a well, only to discover the kingdom of the leprechauns. Thinking quickly, O'Gill captures Brian Connors (Jimmy O'Dea), the leprechaun king, and holds him captive until he agrees to grant three wishes that will secure a future for himself and his daughter Katie.

The screenplay, although serviceable, has a loose feel to it, mainly because it had been cobbled together from a number of stories. It isn't the script however, that makes this movie so enjoyable, it's the wonderful special effects and rambunctious performances of Sharpe and O'Dea, who turn in boisterous portrayals of O'Gill and the leprechaun king.

At the beginning of the film Disney added a title credit sequence thanking "King Brian of Knocknasheega and his leprechauns, whose gracious cooperation made this picture possible." He wanted kids to believe that this world really existed, and once they'd gotten an eyeful of the sprite kingdom with hundreds of leprechauns cavorting and racing around on horseback in front of a colossal O'Gill, I'm sure they were convinced. *Darby O'Gill and the Little People* is a solid action-adventure film, topped off with some great fantasy sequences.

"Forgive me Father, for I am 14."
— advertising tagline for *THE DANGEROUS LIVES OF ALTAR BOYS*

THE DANGEROUS LIVES OF ALTAR BOYS (2002)

The title, *The Dangerous Lives of Altar Boys*, sounds ripped from the headlines, but is actually taken from a 1994 novel by the late Chris Fuhrman, who died of cancer before the book was released. The story of four boys in Catholic school was based on his experiences as a child growing up in Savannah, Georgia. The Catholic Church will be relieved to discover that there isn't a single pedophile priest in sight.

Set in the early 1970s, the film revolves around a group of teenage boys who are obsessed with comic books. Their ringleader Tim (Kieran Culkin) is a prankster who schemes to get revenge on Sister Assumpta (Jody Foster), the joyless, strict nun with a prosthetic leg. Learning most of what they know of the world from the superhero adventures written by Stan Lee and Steve Ditko, they believe there are only two types of people — heroes and villains. Sister Assumpta falls into the latter category, and becomes the subject of a "blasphemous" comic book drawn by the boys featuring the evil motorcycle-driving Nunzilla. The guys imagine themselves as the heroes who do battle with Nunzilla's sisterly minions.

In their real lives they are careening towards maturity with varying degrees of success. Francis (Emile Hirsch) falls in love for the first time with Margie (Jena Malone), a girl with a sad and surprising secret. As his relationship with Margie intensifies his friendship with Tim becomes strained, and life becomes complicated for the first time.

Once the comic book is discovered the boys are expelled from school, with the grave assurance from Sister Assumpta that not only are they not welcome at the school anymore, they likely won't be welcome in Heaven either. Tim concocts a plan to kidnap a cougar from the zoo to give her a fright, but like many of his schemes, the plan has unforeseen consequences for everyone involved.

The Dangerous Lives of Altar Boys is a darkly comic, touching coming-of-age story that could easily have turned into by-the-book teenage drivel, but is rescued by the performances of its teenage leads. Kieran Culkin, who made his acting debut at age eight in his brother Macaulay's film *Home Alone*, shows real range and subtlety here. His line readings are good, no doubt helped along by the strong dialogue of first-time screenwriter Jeff Stockwell, but it is his body language that really impresses. He's reckless, but with a world-weariness the others don't have. In one scene we see Tim watching television, ignoring a knock-down-drag-out scream fest between his parents. His posture says it all. He's been in this situation too many times to show concern, but deep down the fighting and mayhem are slowly crushing him.

Emile Hirsch makes his big screen debut as the artistic Francis. Years of guest spots on *ER* and *NYPD Blue* seems to have taught him a thing or two about acting. His Francis Doyle is a normal kid caught in the throes of self-discovery. His childhood is slipping away, only to be replaced with a reality that he can't quite understand. He's not sure how to make this transition into adulthood, and his reactions to his evolving world keep his performance compelling.

As Margie, Jena Malone exhibits a torment that lies just beneath the surface, waiting to bubble over at any time. It's the kind of deeply layered performance that she hinted at in 2001's *Life As A House*.

The film's biggest stars play small but pivotal roles. As a priest and a nun Vincent D'Onofrio and Jody Foster play the theological good cop/bad cop routine with the boys. D'Onofrio's chain-smoking Father Casey is a firm but benign influence, while Foster's Sister Assumpta spits hellfire in every sentence. Foster plays the sister as a strict disciplinarian who truly believes she is doing the best to save her students from damnation. Her peg leg is just a physical manifestation of her rigid personality. It's new territory for Foster, who pulls it off with aplomb.

The rich inner lives of the boys are represented by the spectacular animation of *Spawn* creator Todd McFarlane. McFarlane's animated interstitials are Francis's inner thoughts shown in the form of the Nunzilla comic book come to life. It's a clever and entertaining way to weave extra character information into the story without resorting to needless verbal exposition. The scenes are dazzling and entertaining.

The movie isn't faultless — the pacing is a little slow in places, the climax is played for shock value — but whatever this film's devils may be, its angels more than compensate.

"You loved the others too. How long did that last?"
– CLAPET THE BUTCHER reprimands his daughter

DELICATESSEN (1991)

▬ ▬ ▬ ▬ ▬ ▬ ▬ ▬

The French are world renowned for their cuisine, so leave it to iconoclastic directors Marc Caro and Jean-Pierre Jeunet to set their first movie in post-apocalyptic France where there is very little food and no meat. Well, almost no meat. *Delicatessen* is a high voltage variation on *Sweeney Todd*, set in a time when people will eat just about anything . . . or any*one*.

The time is the near future. Louison (Dominique Pinon), a down-on-his-luck clown, answers an ad in the *Hard Times* newspaper and earns a janitorial job in a crumbling apartment building. His boss, Clapet (Jean-Claude Dreyfus), also runs a deli. Louison is grateful for the work, and tries to ingratiate himself to the tenants of the building, who for the most part seem to like him. But they'll like him even more in a few days when they are eating him with mint jelly or a béarnaise sauce.

You see, a catastrophic meltdown of some sort has left thick toxic yellow smog hanging over the city, and killed almost all the animals in the world. With lots of mouths to feed people had to seek out alternative forms of animal protein. This is where Louison comes in. The residents of this particular building have come up with an interesting way to procure meat: they hire it. Louison is the latest in a string of superintendents whom the tenants plan to butcher and eat. Clown stew, anyone?

A romance with the butcher's myopic daughter keeps him off his neighbor's dinner tables for a time, but as their hunger grows, his chances of survival get slimmer. To ensure Louison's safety the butcher's daughter betrays the cannibals to the Troglos, the subterranean vegetarian revolutionaries who actually live underneath the building.

Delicatessen's apartment building is populated with many memorably grotesque comic characters. First there is Louison, the ex-circus performer whose best friend and partner, a chimpanzee called Dr. Livingstone, was recently attacked and eaten by a ravenous circus audience. Then there is his paramour, the nearly blind butcher's daughter Julie (Marie-Laure Dougnac), who is so clumsy she buys two of everything so she will have a replacement when she inevitably breaks one. There are two men who spend their days making toy cylinders that moo like a cow when turned upside down. A man in the basement has turned his apartment into a snail farm, while a woman upstairs hears voices telling her to kill herself. She tries, building elaborate Rube-Goldbergesque suicide devices that always fail. The man next door patches his condoms with a bicycle repair kit, and most of the alienated tenants only communicate with one another through an old pipe that runs through the walls.

In their feature film debut co-directors Marc Caro and Jean-Pierre Jeunet show a great deal of control, keeping this disparate group of characters intriguing and captivating, while grounding a story that seems ready to take tangential flight. Their sense of comic pacing is dead on, particularly in a scene that starts off with the butcher and his mistress in bed, the motion of their lovemaking causing the mattress springs to squeak rhythmically. Soon, as the camera cuts from one apartment to another we are treated to a symphony of household sounds playing in concert with the squeaky springs. The toymaker's drill keeps time, as do the grandmother's knitting needles. The piece builds with the addition of a bicycle pump, a cello, and a metronome. Louison paints the hallway ceiling to the beat, using his suspenders as a bungee cord so he can reach the awkward parts. It is a beautifully realized sequence, expertly edited and paced, that ends with a frenzy of action.

Stylistically *Delicatessen* owes more to music videos and animator Tex Avery's feverishly wild Bugs Bunny cartoons than to other post-apocalypse movies like Richard Lester's fantasy *The Bed Sitting Room* (1969) or the Luc Besson end-of-the-world epic *Le Dernier Combat* (1983). Shades of Terry Gilliam and David Lynch shine through the motivation and execution of this film, but Caro and Jeunet are such mavericks that every camera move, every scene in this film feels fresh and alive. Cinematographer Darius Khondji, who created the look of David Fincher's menacing *Se7en*, helps put their dark vision on celluloid.

The script, by famous comic book author Gilles Adrien, constantly keeps the viewer off guard. The basic story is bizarre but fairly simple, but it is his eccentric vision of the dystopian future that confounds and amazes. He has created a dark and moody world worthy of any serious science-fiction movie, but at the same time filled it with belly laughs. While being propelled through this crazy world it is impossible to guess what will happen next.

As good as the direction and script are, it is the lead actors who really sell this film. The wonderful Dominique Pinon — a prolific French actor who is probably best known in North America as the bald hit man in 1981's *Diva* — uses his rubbery face to great comic effect, but can also pluck at your heartstrings with just a slight move of his eyes. Playing opposite him as Julie is Marie-Laure Dougnac who projects sweetness and likeability, particularly in the afternoon tea scene. Julie is so myopic she can barely see, but she doesn't want Louison to see her wearing her ugly glasses. She rehearses everything for their lunch so she can literally do it with her eyes shut, but when he sits in the wrong seat, her plan backfires, and their date becomes a comedy of errors. She is the lone beacon of sanity and innocence amidst the film's madness.

After the success of *Delicatessen*, Caro and Jeunet teamed up once more for the bizarre but entertaining *The City of Lost Children* (1995) about a scientist in a surrealist society who kidnaps children to pilfer their dreams, hoping to slow down his aging process. That was Caro's last film, although Jeunet has had international success with 1997's *Alien: Resurrection* and the enchanting *Amelie* in 2001.

"Do Not See This Film Alone . . . or if You Have A Weak Heart!"
— Advertising tagline for *DEMENTIA 13*

DEMENTIA 13 (1963)

Roger Corman brags that he made hundreds of movies in Hollywood and never lost a dime. He made his first film in 1953 as a producer and screenwriter before taking over the directorial reins in 1955. His work is the stuff of legend. Most films were shot quickly, with the kind of money that wouldn't even cover the catering budget on a mainstream movie. Fast and dirty, he shot practically all of his films in under a week, and set a record in 1960 by shooting *The Little Shop of Horrors* in just two days and one night. Productions were run with military-like precision, and Corman's trademarks included efficiency, resourcefulness, and the ability to surround himself with hungry young filmmakers.

Over the years he discovered many of Hollywood's top talents: Martin Scorsese, Robert Towne, Jonathan Demme, John Sayles, James Cameron, Peter Bogdanovich, and Joe Dante are just a few of the directors who caught their first break working for Corman. "If there's a heaven, and if Roger Corman has any expectation of getting there," said *Airplane* producer Jon Davidson, "what will open the gates for him is that he gave hundreds and hundreds of people a start." Another of his protégés went on to direct some of the classic films of the 1970s.

Francis Ford Coppola began his career with Corman editing, writing, and looping English dialogue on a Russian science-fiction film so it would make sense to American audiences. At $90 a week Coppola was a bargain, and soon found himself behind the camera, shooting second-unit footage. "It was a fabulous opportunity for someone like me," said Coppola. "It was better than money."

Corman recognized Coppola's talent, and soon had him working on larger projects. He became the dialogue supervisor on *Haunted Palace*, running lines with Vincent Price, before being given the chance to make his first feature film.

Corman had been offered a script about a young American who becomes involved with a bullfighter and his wife in Spain. The bullfighting scenes would have been too complicated to shoot, so he adapted the story into a car-racing tale. "Race car driving, bullfighting," said Corman, "same thing." To cut costs he decided to shoot at the Grand Prix in Monte Carlo, rather than stage the race scenes themselves. Corman recruited Coppola to work as first assistant, grip, and soundman on the European shoot for *Young Racers*. Coppola knew that when Corman went to exotic locations he always shot a cheap second feature for release in drive-ins. While on location he asked Corman if he could borrow the camera, some staff, and equipment to make a psychological thriller. Corman wanted to see something on paper, so after a day's shooting on *Young Racer*, Coppola went back to his hotel and wrote "a Hitchcock-type ax murder sequence."

Corman made some changes to the scene and gave the go-ahead, providing the rest of the script would be as interesting as that scene, and gave the neophyte director a budget of $20,000. Coppola had shot a couple of quickie nudie films before, but had never helmed a feature film. This was his foot in the door. Production on *Dementia 13*, as the script was now called, was to commence in Dublin at the end of the *Young Racers* shoot.

The film opens with an atmospheric sequence of a young married couple taking a rowboat ride. John informs his wife Louise (Luana Anders) that he doesn't love her and she will never receive any of his family's money. Upon delivering this unhappy news he drops dead of a heart attack. That could have been the end of the story, but hey, this is a horror film, so Louise forges a letter from John to convince his family that he has been suddenly called to America on business. She then goes to his ancestral home, Castle Haloran, to win over his family and find a way to line her pockets.

The creepiness factor gets kicked up a notch during Louise's visit with the family. Her efforts to brown-nose her way into a fortune go unnoticed by John's oddball mother (Ethne Dunn) and his two lame-brained brothers (William Campbell and Bart Parton), who seem more concerned with the fate of another family member, the dear departed Kathleen (Barbara Dowling). Secrets shroud her death, but it seems that years earlier she had accidentally drowned in the estate's pond. We soon discover there's a serial killer at work.

Family and guests start disappearing under mysterious circumstances, the killer's homicidal rage apparently triggered by his or her obsession with Kathleen. As the body count increases, so do the red herrings. The family's secrets are slowly exposed as the family doctor, Dr. Justin Caleb (Patrick Magee), starts assembling the facts about Kathleen's death.

Dementia 13 isn't Coppola's great, lost masterpiece. It is, however, a great example of the Corman school of filmmaking. Coppola learned to keep the story and visuals vigorous, a lesson that would later inform his best work — *The Godfather*, *The Conversation*, and *Apocalypse Now*.

Technically, Coppola makes the best of what must have been limited resources. The tension of the film is enhanced with the startling use of music. Ronald Stein provided a classic horror score, which is particularly effective in a bedroom scene where Louise is rummaging through Kathleen's clothes. Effective lighting further compounds the feeling of dread.

Coppola's work with the actors shows that his best days as a director are still to come. Patrick Magee (who would later appear as the wheelchair bound writer in *A Clockwork Orange*) is convincing as the doctor, building an acerbic and untrustworthy character that is fun to watch. Others don't fare as well, especially William Campbell as brother Richard. Campbell seems unable to control himself, threatening at times to literally chew the furniture. The rest of the cast is serviceable, but with only three days to shoot, the actors didn't exactly have a lot of time to explore their characters' motivations.

Dementia 13 is sometimes cited as the first slasher film, and while it does contain elements of the genre (the first-ever decapitation by ax on screen; a mysterious masked murderer in the woods) it has more meat on its bones. Coppola plays it by ear, inserting ghastly violence to spice up an already eerie Agatha Christie-like riddle.

Dementia 13 was a milestone for Coppola on several levels. It was his first legitimate feature film, it made money, and he met his wife Eleanor Neil on the set.

"What is a ghost? A tragedy condemned to repeat itself time and again? An instant of pain, perhaps. Something dead which still seems to be alive. An emotion suspended in time. Like a blurred photograph. Like an insect trapped in amber."
– CASARES (FEDERICO LUPPI)

THE DEVIL'S BACKBONE (2002)
▬ ▬ ▬ ▬ ▬ ▬ ▬ ▬ ▬ ▬ ▬

The ghost in Mexican director Guillermo del Toro's beautiful tale of the supernatural owes more to films like *The Haunting* than to the malicious spirits that inhabited *Poltergeist*. Santi, the sad spirit of *The Devil's*

Backbone needs to tell his story to the living so he can find peace and exact his revenge.

The film is set in 1939, near the end of the blood-spattered Spanish Civil War, when General Franco's right-wing Nationalists are about to crush the left-wing Republican forces. The story is built around the curiosity of Carlos (Fernando Tielve), a 12-year-old boy delivered to a remote orphanage after his Republican war hero father is killed. Carlos is uneasy in his new surroundings, despite the concern shown to him by the head mistress Varmen (Marisa Paredes) and the kindly Professor Casares (Federico Luppi). The youngster resolves a conflict with the orphanage bully, but finds a more determined foe in Jacinto (Eduardo Noriega), the aggressive groundskeeper. Jacinto strikes out violently when any of the students dares go near a deep well, located in the orphanage's storage room.

Human enemies are one thing, but Carlos is also troubled by the ghost of Santi (Junio Valverde), a former student, who visits him at night with the ominous message, "Many of you will die." The ghost's prophecy seems likely to come to fruition, as Franco's troops get closer by the moment. Step by step Carlos untangles the story of Santi, discovering the details of his brutal death and the mystery of the well.

"I think the ghost serves as a horrifying but ultimately pitiful reminder," del Toro told *Film Freak Central*. "That's why the ghost in the movie breaks the cardinal rule in horror films: less is more. I tried to show the ghost as much as I could in the film so that by the end you're not fearing the dead so much as the treachery of the living. It starts as a ghost story, but it's meant to be a war story with a ghost in it. If you read the seminal gothic romances there are huge elements of melodrama with a supernatural strand running through them — but they're much more than just the accumulation of, say, 25 supernatural occurrences or something. Look at a beautiful Gothic romance like *Wuthering Heights* — it opens and closes like a strange ghost story, but ghosts are not the main thrust of the story."

Guillermo takes his time with the story, letting the feeling of anxiety and dread build slowly, layering the atmosphere with thick slices of mystery and the supernatural. That, coupled with one of the best-realized screen ghosts of recent memory, makes this movie both unsettling and worthwhile.

"That's bullshit. You just bullshitted NASA!"
— ROSS "MITCH" MITCHELL (KEVIN HARRINGTON)

THE DISH (2000)

On July 19, 1969, the world witnessed one of the greatest technological triumphs of all time: man setting foot on the moon. Director Rob Sitch and his partners, a creative team of writers, producers, and directors who call themselves Working Dog, were inspired to write *The Dish* after realizing the sheer magnitude of the events of that day. Six hundred million people watched Neil Armstrong set foot on the moon, and for one night the world was united in front of their TV sets. The Melbourne-based production company found a little-known Australian connection to the story and wrote a semi-fictional account of the role a small town played in the Apollo 11 moon landing.

"*The Dish* is the story of people basically thrown into the deep end," says Rob Sitch. "These three scientists who spend their lives doing fairly routine, humdrum work out of an astronomical installation in the middle of New South Wales suddenly have the opportunity of greatness thrust upon them, a chance to be responsible for broadcasting pictures of the greatest television event of the 20th century."

The action takes place in Parkes, a rural town whose only distinction is that it houses the largest radio telescope in the southern hemisphere. NASA has commandeered the telescope as a back-up to their prime receiver in Goldstone, California. When an unexpected flight schedule change renders the Californian telescope useless, NASA relies on the Parkes satellite dish to track the whereabouts of Apollo 11, and to broadcast images of the trip and moonwalk. The 1000-ton radio telescope is roughly the size of a football field and is located in a sheep paddock.

The small staff is prepared for the momentous broadcast and are very aware of their unique place in history, but tensions run high as a NASA representative (Patrick Warburton) butts heads with the Aussie scientists. Cliff Buxton (Sam Neill), the "dishmaster," is knowledgeable and helpful, but joyless since the death of his wife a year earlier. Mitch (Kevin Harrington) is a hothead and Glenn (Tom Long) comically yearns for the sandwich girl. This motley crew is responsible for keeping Houston in touch with the spacecraft and linking the broadcast signal from outer space to Australia and the rest of the world.

Of course, even the best-laid plans can go wrong, and during a power outage Mitch temporarily loses sight of Apollo 11. The staff, including NASA representative Al Burnett, must work together to cover up the mistake and preserve Parkes' civic pride.

The Dish manages to co-opt a story that is universally seen as American and put a nice, original spin on it. Instead of focusing on the moonwalk, Sitch takes a more human approach and centers the story on the characters. In a Hollywood film there would be stirring music, technology galore, and a nagging sense of being manipulated into feeling patriotic. In Sitch's film, by the time we get to the actual event we're not thinking about the "giant leap for mankind," but rather the simple steps taken by Buxton, Mitch, and Glenn that made the broadcast possible. It's a human story, and one told with a great deal of heart.

"The Apollo 11 mission ultimately became something that was not about rockets at all," says Sitch. "Instead, it transcended those television pictures live from the moon. It became about the human spirit soaring. *The Dish* celebrates achievement and striving for greatness. Those themes are universal and timeless and worth celebrating."

Sam Neill is the film's anchor. As Cliff Buxton he shows many sides of his character's personality. While the story of his wife's passing threatens to weigh the movie down with melodrama, Neill skillfully sidesteps any mawkish behavior, instead showing us a man with great courage and intelligence who occasionally slips into a veil of sadness. It is a quiet but fully realized performance.

On *Seinfeld* Patrick Warburton played Puddy, a thickheaded suitor of Jerry's ex-girlfriend Elaine. His monotone voice and lumbering good looks made that role unforgettable, so unforgettable that I thought I might have a hard time accepting him in another part. In *The Dish* he leaves Puddy behind to become the "ugly American," a know-it-all who has the good sense to realize that he doesn't know it all and must rely on the expertise of the small-town scientists. It's a nicely handled role, and one that shows his range as an actor.

Supporting roles are well cast, and generally used for comic effect. Taylor Kane is hilarious as the overzealous Rudi the security guard, who spends most of his time shooing away curious sheep from the telescope. Roy Billing and Genevieve Mooy bring Mayor Bob McIntyre and his wife Maisie to life, playing them for laughs, but like the entire tone of this movie they giggle *with* the characters, not at them.

The humor in *The Dish* flows from situations and character quirks, and doesn't seem forced. In one of the movie's funniest moments the local band greets the American contingent at the town hall with a surprising version of the American anthem. It's laugh-out-loud funny, but not mean-spirited like so many modern comedies.

Rent *The Dish* on DVD or VHS, and if you like the gentle humor and character-driven story check out Working Dog's previous film *The Castle*, about a man who takes on city hall and wins.

"On the southern coast of England there's a legend people tell,
Of days long ago when the great Scarecrow would ride
from the jaws of hell . . ."
— Theme song for *DR. SYN: ALIAS THE SCARECROW*

DR. SYN: ALIAS THE SCARECROW (1964)

Years before he would find fame as Number Six on TV's *The Prisoner*, Patrick McGoohan was Dr. Syn, a hero dressed like a scarecrow in an eponymously named movie. Originally made as a four-part mini-series for *Walt Disney's Wonderful World of Color* in 1962, *Dr. Syn: Alias the Scarecrow* was repackaged and released theatrically two years later.

Based on a Russell Thorndike novel first published in 1915, the story has been committed to film three times, first in a 1937 black-and-white film starring George Arliss, and twice in the early '60s by Disney and the British Hammer Films. Despite having been voted Best TV Actor of the Year by the British public in 1959, the American-born, U.K.-raised McGoohan was an unknown in America when he was signed to a three-picture deal by Disney in 1961. He had already turned down the role of James Bond (which eventually went to Sean Connery), but Disney recognized that he had the smoldering good looks and charisma to carry an action-adventure film, and molded *Dr. Syn* as a star vehicle for him.

The movie is set in 1736, and McGoohan plays Dr. Christopher Syn, a real-life English pastor who led a double life — upright citizen by day, and rogue smuggler by night. Disguised as "The Scarecrow," Syn leads a rebellion across the English countryside against the oppressive taxes of King George III. When the cruel General Pugh (Geoffrey Keen) is dispatched to the area to quell the insurgents, Syn and his underground army step up their efforts, looting the King's coffers and doing their best to avoid the ferocious press gangs that roam Romney Marsh, looking to force young men into the service of the Royal Navy. To make an already complicated situation even more complex, an escaped American revolutionary prisoner and an AWOL sailor (and son of a leading town official) both seek the help of Dr. Syn. Swashbuckling scenes abound as the legendary Scarecrow does battle against the forces of tyranny.

McGoohan ably handles the dual role of the pastor and the rebellious Scarecrow, imbuing each character with a distinctive personality. His Scarecrow isn't just the pastor with a mask, but a completely separate and well-rounded character that doesn't simply rely on a costume à la Batman or Superman to define his personality. Also look for Geoffrey Keen as the evil General Pugh. Fifteen years after shooting *Dr. Syn* he undertook his best-known role, that of M's deputy, Sir Frederick Gray, in six James Bond movies from 1977's *The Spy Who Loved Me* to 1987's *The Living Daylights*.

McGoohan's strong lead performance coupled with great historical action-adventure makes *Dr. Syn* a great romp for the family, but may be too intense for younger children.

"Death to Invaders"
— Graffiti on DOGTOWN wall

DOGTOWN AND Z-BOYS (2002)

A close-up look at the birth of skateboard culture in Southern California, *Dogtown and Z-Boys* has attitude to burn, just like the sport it documents. Directed by Stacy Peralta, one of the legends of the sport, it captures the punk-rock spirit of skateboarding and perfectly places it into the context of its time — the 1970s — and location — Dogtown, a marginal area of California including parts of Venice, Ocean Park, and South Santa Monica, described by the boys as "the last great seaside slum," and "where the debris meets the sea."

Even if you are not a fan you'll be fascinated by the story about street-wise teens who traded in their surfboards for homemade skateboards. Based at the Zephyr Surf Shop, the Z-Boys (and one Z-Girl) altered the course of modern skateboarding, redefining the sport by inventing gravity-defying stunts honed to perfection in dried-out swimming pools during the California droughts of the 1970s. Told using a combination of narration, stills, great vintage 1970s skateboarding footage, classic rock (Aerosmith, Black Sabbath, Jimi Hendrix, and David Bowie, among others), and new interviews with all the key players, the film details a small, interesting slice of Southern Californian life.

Sean Penn provides the narration, adding a flair all of his own. The opposite of stodgy, Penn speaks *to* the audience, not *at* them, sounding like someone sitting at a bar telling the tale. At one point, in mid-sentence, he coughs, pauses for a moment, and then continues. It's this kind of approach that gives this movie its edge.

> "Meet the Blands! They're square . . . They're in LOVE . . .
> AND they kill people."
> — Advertising tagline for *EATING RAOUL*

EATING RAOUL (1982)

"I'm very interested in doing eccentric individual low-budget films," said director Paul Bartel early in his career. And so he did. After making several cutie nudies in the late '60s, he hit his stride in 1975 with *Death Race 2000*, a campy sci-fi exploitation flick starring a then-unknown Sylvester Stallone. A series of drive-in movies followed, but it was a small no-budget film that made him a cult star. He wrote, directed, and starred in *Eating Raoul*, a dark look at suburban life.

Bartel conceived the idea for *Eating Raoul* while serving on the jury at the 1979 Berlin Film Festival. Working independently, he cobbled together a modest budget from friends, family, and credit cards, and shot the film bit by bit in Los Angeles when he could afford it. "I wanted to make a film about two greedy uptight people who are not so unlike you and me and Nancy and Ronnie [Reagan]," he said, "and to keep it funny and yet communicate something about the perversity of these values."

In the film, the aptly named Paul and Mary (Paul Bartel and Mary Woronov) Bland dream of owning a house and restaurant in the country, but can't come up with the $20,000 down payment. Paul has just lost his job as a wine merchant for refusing to sell crappy wine to a customer. Money is tight, and the couple are desperately looking for a solution to their problem. Late one night a swinger from a party next door enters the Bland apartment and attacks Mary. Wielding a frying pan, Paul kills the intruder. When they discover $600 on the man, the couple forms a deadly plan.

Paul and Mary take out an ad in the personals section of the local newspaper to entice sex-seekers to their home. Mary, posing as a prostitute, indulges their erotic demands before Paul kills them and takes their money. To dispose of the bodies they sell the corpses for dog food. Their plan is double pronged: because of their disgust for the "johns" and their sexual perversions, the couple feels that they are cleaning up society, while at the same time the money they make finances their dream home. According to Paul their clients are "horrible, sex-crazed perverts that nobody will miss anyway."

All is going well until a locksmith named Raoul (Robert Beltran) uncovers their scheme and demands a cut of the action. Raoul transports the bodies, but is ultimately expendable . . . and edible.

To write off *Eating Raoul* as a cannibal movie is not accurate. There are elements of cannibalism in the script, but they are a means to an end. Bartel needed something taboo to show the lengths that "normal" people can go to to achieve their slice of the American dream. The unsavory

Richard's Favorite Movie Quotes

1. "Love means never having to say you're ugly." – Dr. Anton Phibes (Vincent Price), *The Abominable Dr. Phibes* (1971)
2. "Honey there's a spider in your bathroom the size of a Buick." – Alvy Singer (Woody Allen), *Annie Hall* (1977)
3. "Normally both of you would be as dead as fucking fried chicken by now, but since I'm in a transitional period I don't want to kill either one of your asses." – Jules (Samuel L. Jackson), *Pulp Fiction* (1994)
4. "The hideousness of that foot will haunt my dreams forever." – Emilio (John Turturro), *Mr. Deeds* (2002)
5. "This is my happening and it freaks me out!" – Ronnie 'Z-Man' Barzell (John Lazar), *Beyond the Valley of the Dolls* (1970)
6. "I once thought I had mono for an entire year. Turns out I was just really bored." – Wayne Campbell (Mike Myers), *Wayne's World* (1992)
7. "Her insides were a rocky barren place where my seed could find no purchase." – H.I. (Nicholas Cage), *Raising Arizona* (1987)
8. "I hate Illinois Nazis." – 'Joliet' Jake Blues (John Belushi), *The Blues Brothers* (1980)
9. "I was trying to suggest something about the duality of man, sir." – Private Joker (Matthew Modine), *Full Metal Jacket* (1987)
10. "Look at me – I'm a prickly pear." – Ben (Nicholas Cage), *Leaving Las Vegas* (1995)

situations in the film are used to amplify the farcical elements of the story, and maybe tickle your funny bone by shocking you a little. *Eating Raoul* is Bartel's finest achievement as a director and writer, and represents the point at which underground and mainstream cinema meet.

Bartel and Mary Woronov (see *Chelsea Girls*), who were previously paired in 1979's *Rock and Roll High School*, play the Blands with dead-pan perfection. Their expressionless delivery illustrates their stupefying suburban existence and adds to the humor of the situation as the body count rises and things seem to spin out of control. Woronov went on to star in many more films (and write several books) but *Eating Raoul* remains her best performance on screen. Paul Bartel went on to direct several lackluster films, including *Lust in the Dust* (starring Divine) and *The Class Struggle in Beverly Hills*, and act in some good ones, like *The Usual Suspects*, *Basquiat*, and Ethan Hawke's *Hamlet*, before passing away of liver cancer in May 2000.

In 1982 the gallows humor of *Eating Raoul* pushed the frontiers of bad taste, but despite itself is a very likeable black comedy.

"That's my girl. Her father is Robert I. Miller, writer of all those adventure books. They live up at the club. You oughta see her swim!"
—TOMMY (ARCH HALL JR.) in *EEGAH!*

EEGAH! THE NAME WRITTEN IN BLOOD (1962)

Most filmmakers would do anything to stay off the bottom of the bill at the drive-in. Arch Hall Sr., the maverick mini-movie-mogul and president of Fairway-International Productions, was not like most filmmakers. He spent a few glorious years pumping out B-movies best seen just after dusk through the windshield of your dad's car.

By the early 1960s Arch Hall Sr. (real name: William Watters) was an established B-movie wheeler-dealer, distributing schlocky low-budget films and documentaries. In 1961 he attained notoriety as the subject of *The Last Time I Saw Archie*, a comedy directed by Jack Webb and co-starring Robert Mitchum as Archie.

Like many doting parents, Senior was convinced that his son, Arch Hall Jr., could be a movie star. That Junior was supremely untalented was of little consequence. Hall Sr. gave his son a guitar and a shiny suit and paraded him through a series of rock-and-roll exploitation flicks. "He always used to say, 'Gee, Pop, I can't sing,'" said Hall Sr. "But I told him that a lot of people had done well who didn't know how to sing."

Their first outing, 1962's *Wild Guitar*, featured Junior singing his own songs . . . badly. The film was directed by Ray Dennis (a.k.a. Cash Flagg), who would later direct and star in the most clumsily-titled drive-in classic ever, *The Incredibly Strange Creatures Who Stopped Living and Became Mixed-Up Zombies*. Not surprisingly, *Wild Guitar* lost money; even red ink wasn't enough to keep Hall Sr. from trying to turn Junior into the next Ricky Nelson.

The elder Hall conceived *Eegah!* after meeting the 7'2" Richard Kiel, who was a bouncer in a cowboy bar. Hall Sr. sensed that Kiel's unusual looks and 300-pound size could make a commanding if not unusual film presence, and began working on a script that would co-star Arch Jr. and Kiel. Kiel had appeared on television, usually as an extra, and was willing to give the lead role a try as long as Hall supplied a place for him to stay.

Hall Sr.'s script added his own special twist to the *Beauty and the Beast* fable, set to the rock-and-roll beat of Arch Jr.'s compositions. Keil was cast as a caveman who has survived from pre-historic times by drinking sulfur-infused water in a secret desert cave. He is discovered by Roxy Miller (played by Marilyn Manning, who in real life was a receptionist for a chiropractor who had rented an office from Hall), when she almost runs him over on a desolate desert road. Unhurt, she rushes home to tell her father of her discovery. Robert Miller (Arch Hall Sr.) is a distinguished author of adventure books who dons his pith helmet and investigates his daughter's outrageous story. He disappears. Roxy and her boyfriend Tommy (Arch Hall Jr.) set off in a dune buggy to rescue doddering old Dad. They have no luck and decide to bed down for the night (in separate sleeping bags, of course). During the night the caveman looms over Roxy, but is scared off when Tommy rolls over and inadvertently switches on his transistor radio. The next day, while Tommy explores the area with a shotgun, the mysterious cave-dweller grabs Roxy. They return to the cave to find her father safe and in good spirits. The perfect prehistoric gentleman treats his company well and offers Roxy a meaty bone, grunting affectionately while rubbing his nose against her arm. Sparks fly between the two, and it is apparent that Roxy is falling for her superannuated captor. She dubs the ancient Lothario Eegah because he keeps saying that word over and over.

Tommy discovers the underground love nest and picks a fight with Eegah. Amazingly the slight city slicker opens up a 40-ounce can of whoopass on the giant, Davey and Goliath style, before beating a hasty retreat with Roxy and Mr. Miller in tow. The rest of the film sees Eegah out of his element, pursuing Roxy through the travails of the modern world.

To say *Eegah! The Name Written in Blood* was cheaply produced is like having a 500-pound hippo in your bedroom: it's so apparent you don't even have to mention it. Hall Sr. was desperate to make back the money he lost on *Wild Guitar*, so he cut corners everywhere he could on this film. With no money in the budget for a director, he helmed the film himself (under the pseudonym Nicholas Merriwether), even though he had never been behind a camera. He also cooked for the crew and cast himself in one of the major roles. Everyone, including his son, basically toiled for no money. "He worked for peanuts," said Senior. "He was only 16."

Even with doubling up on duties and underpaying his actors, Hall still had to raise $15,000, the kind of money that was scarce after the failure of his previous effort. "I had to sell my own car, borrow money, make exchanges, offer pay-you-laters to finance the thing," he said. "When I think of all the special deals — it was just Mickey Mouse all the way through."

You get what you pay for. Shot on location in Palm Desert, California, with additional scenes shot on Harpo Marx's property, most days the temperature reached an astronomical 115°F. Crewmembers were dropping from sunstroke, and some just went crazy from the heat. An inexperienced soundman repeatedly switched the recorder to Playback rather than Record during production of some scenes, failing to record sound; the problem wasn't discovered until after shooting had wrapped. During post-production they tried to dub the missing dialogue, but because the actors had ad-libbed so much no one could remember what the lines were supposed to be. They fixed the problem, and while bad dubbing is better than no dubbing, when you hear the dialogue, you have to wonder why they bothered. Another rookie crew member on the desert shoot loaded as much sand into the camera as he did film, ruining many takes and wasting hours of production time.

The editing, or what passes for editing, is of home-movie caliber. Scenes end suddenly, there are inappropriate close-ups . . . it's just a mess. Probably the best example of the haphazard post-production comes in a scene as Mr. Miller walks toward the cave, when suddenly a crewmember's voice shouts, "Watch out for snakes!"

Now, there is Grade B acting, and then there is Arch Hall Jr. The way Arch Sr. flaunts his son in front of a camera in this way is almost cruel, and in some countries could probably be considered child abuse (or at least audience abuse). It is a testament to a father's love that Arch Sr. was so blind to his son's shortcomings that he would continue to parade him around in these pictures. Hall Jr. is a wooden actor, and the songs . . . oh, my, the songs. He warbles three tunes in *Eegah!*, including one love ballad recycled from *Wild Guitar*. "Vitamins are good they say," he sings in "Valerie," "And so's a calorie, but I feel like a tiger on one kiss from Valerie." A sunny sentiment to be sure; too bad his girlfriend's name is Roxy. The father-and-son team went on to make several more films together, including *The Nasty Rabbit*, about Russian spies who wreak terror on the United States with a diseased rabbit. Arch Jr. found his true calling when he retired from motion pictures and became a commercial pilot.

To recap, *Eegah!* features terrible acting, bad sound, a lame story, and atrocious editing. Why do I love this movie? Because it dares to be bad. In a business where everyone craves respectability and prestige Hall Sr. was a self-made man who didn't care what anyone thought of his films. He didn't concern himself with reviews, only the bottom line. He figured out what audiences wanted to see — in this case rock and roll, dune buggies, and an unusual creature — and shamelessly gave it to them. He's the kind of independent character that could only come out of Hollywood. Did he make good films? No, but he sure knew how to entertain.

"I used to get teased about *Eegah!* quite a lot," he said. "It was always sort of a subject of laughter that the darned thing did so well." Hall laughed all the way to the bank; by the time of his death in 1978 the film had grossed over one million dollars.

"It must be terrible to lose your most precious possession."
— EMMA'S MOTHER on hearing of the LINDBERG BABY KIDNAPPING

EMMA'S SHADOW (Skyggen at Emma) (1988)

This Dutch film is the kind of thing that is becoming harder and harder to find — a movie that the whole family can enjoy. Set in the 1930s, the story revolves around 11-year-old Emma (Line Kruse), the only child of wealthy Danish parents. Her father is a businessman who has very little time for his daughter, while the mother is self-centered and barely acknowledges her offspring. When little Emma overhears a conversation about the Lindbergh baby kidnapping she hatches a plot to earn some attention from her parents — she stages her own abduction and runs away.

While her chauffeur is distracted, Emma bolts, disappearing into a poor section of Copenhagen. She meets a crude but kind sewer worker, Malthe (Borje Ahlstedt), an ex-convict who agrees to hide her after she tells him a ridiculous story about how she is on the run from Russian Bolsheviks who shot her nanny. "Actually, they shot my whole family," she fibs. She concocts a scheme to squeeze money out of her parents, who believe that they are paying evil kidnappers. Instead Emma uses the money to improve her and Malthe's living situation, getting a room and decent food for her gullible new friend and two young neighborhood boys.

The dirty sewer worker and the upper class little girl form a bond based on respect — a new experience for both of them. Emma teaches Malthe about self-assertiveness, while he showers her with affection. Tension mounts as the simple-minded Malthe mistakes the detectives who are searching for Emma for Bolsheviks. The final, wordless scene is a triumph of emotion without slipping into manipulative sentiment.

At the soul of the film is Line Kruse's wonderfully intelligent performance as Emma. Her loyalty to Malthe tugs at the heartstrings because their brief relationship contains more love than her parents could muster in a whole lifetime. Veteran actor Ahlstedt, best known as the uncle from *Fanny and Alexander*, is masterfully understated as the slow-witted Malthe, a man who is capable of much more than the hand life has dealt him.

Emma's Shadow was an international critical success, earning a Bodil Award — the Danish Oscar — for Best Film in 1989, and a Best Actress award for Kruse and a Special Jury Prize at the 1989 Paris Film Festival. Presented in Danish with English subtitles.

> "It's about role-playing in a prison-like situation. You'll be randomly divided into groups of guards and prisoners. If you take part in the experiment as a prisoner, you'll be required to give up your private life and your rights as a citizen."
> — DR. JUTTA GRIMM (ANDREA SAWATZKI)

THE EXPERIMENT (2002)

This German film is based on *Black Box*, a novel by Mario Giordano, which drew on the famous Stanford Prison Experiment for inspiration. In 1971 the university began a planned two-week experiment into the psychology of prison life by dividing a group of students into prisoners and guards. The whole thing had to be scuttled after only six days when the guards became sadistic and the prisoners showed signs of extreme depression and anxiety.

Director Oliver Hirschbiegel effectively translates the psychological horror of the experiment, skillfully peeling away the layers of acceptable behavior until the grisly third act of the film. "Every good story tells us something about people," says the director. "In all my films, it's been important that in the development of the characters, people go through learning processes and apply what they've learned and that they're in a situation that forces them to take a stand. This is required of many of the people in the novel."

A study in what happens when you strip away the power from one group and give it to another, *The Experiment* casts stereotypes — the rebel, the submissive, and the sadist — in easily definable roles. It's no surprise that Tarek Fahed, Prisoner Number 77 (Moritz Bleibtreu, the Tom Cruise of Germany) is the rebel: he has the look of a troublemaker. What is surprising is the idea that by simply changing their clothes to shapeless prison smocks or dark blue guard uniforms you can change the personality of the characters. The prisoners' dress-like smocks strip away their masculinity, making them subservient to the sharply dressed authority figures.

The Experiment packs many ideas into its 114-minute running time, and by the end you'll be questioning the nature of all relationships, not just institutionalized ones. German with English subtitles.

"I put my whole self into everything I do."
– LONESOME RHODES (ANDY GRIFFITH)

A FACE IN THE CROWD (1957)

Three years before he would charm television audiences with his gentle portrayal of corn-pone sheriff Andy Taylor, Andy Griffith made his big-screen debut in a very different kind of role. Although he had no training as an actor, he had earned a reputation as a stand-up comedian, and was nominated for a Tony award for his role in the Broadway comedy hit *No Time for Sergeants*. Elia Kazan, the director of such hard-hitting dramas as *A Streetcar Named Desire* (1951), *Viva Zapata!* (1952), *Man on a Tightrope* (1953), *On the Waterfront* (1954), and *East of Eden* (1955), saw something in Griffith that made him the perfect choice to head up *A Face in the Crowd*, a brutal indictment of television.

Lonesome Rhodes was a role that required Griffith to put aside his likeable persona and become a ruthless egomaniac. "In the character of Lonesome Rhodes I wanted to show the ambivalence in someone who was almost evil, but who said and believed many things that were right at the same time," said Kazan. "I wanted him to be seductive and say out loud things that other people didn't." Allegedly inspired by the spectacular rise to fame of Arthur Godfrey, *A Face in the Crowd* tells the story of Lonesome Rhodes (Griffith), a philosophical country and western singer discovered in a small town drunk tank by radio reporter Marcia Jeffries (Patricia Neal). In Rhodes, she sees a good human interest story. In Jeffries' microphone, Rhodes sees a possible meal ticket. Soon his songs, homespun stories, and country wisdom land him a television spot and instant celebrity. His aw-shucks on-stage personality make him a modern day Will Rogers, attracting millions of fans and dozens of endorsements. Although loved by his public, off-stage Lonesome isn't so loveable. As his fame grows, so do his political aspirations, turning him into a power-hungry schemer, who discards people who get in his way. Morally corrupt, it seems that there is no stopping his megalomania, until Marcia engineers his comeuppance.

The pre-Mayberry Griffith is remarkable as the Machiavellian television host, displaying an acting range — from pathetic to frightening — that he would never again draw upon in his long career. Many familiar faces turn up in supporting roles. Lee Remick makes a strong debut as Lonesome's baton-twirling child bride. As the socially-conscious writer Mel Miller, Walter Matthau becomes the movie's voice of reason, lecturing Rhodes on the evil of his ways. Patricia Neal makes the best of *On the Waterfront* writer Budd Schulberg's stinging script, giving a touching, layered performance.

Despite a good cast and a compelling story, *A Face in the Crowd* didn't do well in the theaters. Audiences, relatively new to the medium of television, weren't ready for a harsh exposé of their small-screen idols. Viewed through today's eyes, however, the movie's message of never accepting anyone at face value is as timely today as it was in 1957.

"We should always believe children.
We should even believe their lies."
— AUGUST ZABLADOWSKI (PETER LIND HAYES)

THE 5000 FINGERS OF DR. T (1953)

This sadly neglected gem sprang from the delightfully twisted mind of Theodore Geisel (a.k.a. Dr. Seuss) in 1953. During his long and distinguished career he wrote 44 books, created several classic television specials, and won three Academy Awards for writing short wartime documentaries, but *The 5000 Fingers of Dr. T* is the only feature film Dr. Seuss was ever directly involved in.

Set in suburban America, the fanciful story begins with young Bart Collins (Tommy Rettig — remember him from *Lassie*?) asleep at the piano. His dreams take us to a castle ruled by an evil piano teacher, the peculiar Dr. Terwilliker (Hans Conried), who is hatching a nefarious plot to establish his "Happy Fingers Method" of teaching piano as the best in the world. To this end, the evil Dr. T has banished all other instruments to the dungeon and enslaved 500 boys (with their 5000 nimble fingers) to perform in unison on a colossal piano. It is his wicked plan to make them rehearse "24 hours a day until they are perfect."

Shot in Technicolor, *The 5000 Fingers of Dr. T* features mind-blowing production design — huge colorful sets dominate the dream sequences, while the Dali-esque dungeon for non-piano-playing musicians is a frenetic set piece that clearly shows Seuss's influence.

This kid's movie didn't do much business in its first run, but it found another, unexpected life when it was rereleased in the '60s as *Crazy Music* and was embraced by hippies who better understood the stream of consciousness storyline and psychedelic undertones. Fans of *The Simpsons* will note some similarities — the television show's adolescent hero is named Bart and his sworn enemy is Robert "Sideshow Bob" Terwilliger. Coincidence? I think not.

> "I came 4,000 miles to get a story. I get shot at like a duck
> in a shooting gallery, I get pushed off buildings,
> I get the story, and then I've got to shut up!"
> **– JOHNNY JONES (JOEL MCCREA)**

FOREIGN CORRESPONDENT (1940)

Alfred Hitchcock's name has become synonymous with suspense, his famous pudgy profile a screen icon almost as recognizable as that of Mickey Mouse. He began making films in Britain in 1920, first working as a title-card illustrator on a dozen films before working his way through the ranks as an art director, assistant director, editor, writer, and director. As early as 1926 he was a name director in Europe, and had begun his lifelong habit of making a cameo appearance in his films.

In 1939, with a string of hits under his belt, he answered Hollywood's beckoning call, winning respect and an Academy Award for Best Picture with *Rebecca*, his first American film. Next up was *Foreign Correspondent*, a story of global intrigue that was nominated but failed to win any Academy gold. It's one of the lesser-known films on Hitchcock's resumé, but ranks with the best of his British work.

Set in Europe in 1939 just before the outbreak of World War II, the story involves Johnny Jones (Joel McCrea), a hard-nosed but inexperienced crime reporter who witnesses a fake political assassination on a rainy Amsterdam street and becomes embroiled in an international spy ring. Billed at the time as the "Thrill Spectacle of the Year," *Foreign Correspondent* still packs a wallop, and Hitchcock's visual flair is abundantly clear in several set pieces that are pure eye candy. In the aftermath of the assassination Jones trails the shooter through the streets, pushing his way through a sea of bobbing black umbrellas in a suspenseful dance that is both eye-catching and intense. Brian De Palma was so taken with the shot he recreated it in 1990's *Bonfire of the*

Vanities for a scene where the main character Sherman fights his way through a group of savage reporters.

Foreign Correspondent's best sequence takes place during a trans-Atlantic flight on a plane that is about to crash. Hitchcock shoots the scene over the shoulders of the pilots as the plane plummets towards the water. On impact, water floods the cockpit as passengers tussle to escape the sinking aircraft. Only six survive, finding refuge on the plane's wing. Hitchcock is pitch perfect in this scene, building incredible suspense amid the terror of the inevitable destruction of the airplane. It is snippets of film like this that explain what the director meant when he flippantly said, "I enjoy playing the audience like a piano." He toys with the viewer in this scene, delaying the expected collision until the audience is literally on the edge of their seats wondering who will survive and who will perish.

Even at this early juncture in his career Hitchcock was making films that pleased audiences and stand the test of time. *Foreign Correspondent* came out in 1940, the same year as *Rebecca*, and the two films earned a combined 17 Academy Award nominations (six for *Foreign Correspondent*, 11 for *Rebecca*). While *Rebecca* has gone on to become a classic, *Foreign Correspondent* has been largely forgotten. It's a shame; this is classic Hitchcock with fine performances from George Sanders in a heroic role, and a nominated turn from German actor Albert Basserman, who spoke no English and learned his lines phonetically.

Richard's Favorite Cameos by Directors

1. Alfred Hitchcock is the granddaddy of the self-cast cameo, popping up in no less than 34 of his films, beginning with *The Lodger* in 1927. His best moment occurs in the airport scene in 1969's *Topaz*. We see him moving through the airport in a wheelchair, when he suddenly stops, gets up, and walks away.

2. M. Night Shyamalan can be seen in 2000's *Unbreakable* as a football fan, and plays a doctor in *The Sixth Sense*. He promoted himself to main character status in 2002's *The Signs*.

3. Does the disgruntled Wonderland theme park worker in *Beverly Hills Cop III* look familiar? He should — it's *Star Wars* creator George Lucas.

4. In 1980's *Raging Bull* director Martin Scorsese is visible as a stagehand, and can be heard (but not seen) as the voice of a dispatcher in 1999's *Bringing Out the Dead*.

5. Steven Spielberg has never appeared in one of his own movies, but made his film debut as the Cook County Clerk in *The Blues Brothers*.

6. Frances Ford Coppola briefly plays the director of a television crew in *Apocalypse Now*.

7. John Landis frequently turns up in his own movies, but also was a doctor in Sam Raimi's film *Darkman*.

8. Barry Levinson makes a cameo in *Rain Man*, playing a doctor.

9. Roman Polanski cast himself as the man who slices Jack Nicholson's nose with a knife in 1974's *Chinatown*.

10. In 1991 Jonathan Demme gave his old boss Roger Corman a small role as an FBI agent in *Silence of the Lambs*.

"Only demons should fear me, and you're not a demon . . . are you?"
— DAD (BILL PAXTON)

FRAILTY (2001)

This is a hatchet job. Literally.

Bill Paxton, in his feature film directorial debut, presents an eerie story involving would-be demons, religious fanaticism, fatherly love, and ax-wielding serial killers. "I really saw this as a neo-classical piece," Paxton said, "and a lot of people in Hollywood recognized that it was a great piece of work, but they wouldn't touch it with a barge pole. I thought the way to do it was to imply it, not to show it, like Alfred Hitchcock or Robert Aldrich. We've become such a society of exploitation that we're desensitized to violence. But the mind's eye, and that which is implied, is so much more powerful than explicit gore."

Paxton and screenwriter Brent Hanley crafted *Frailty* to disturb without the use of gore and keep you guessing right until the end. "I looked at a lot of Hitchcock films when I wrote *Frailty*," says Hanley. "I watched *Night of the Hunter* and listened to music by Leonard Cohen. *Frailty* even references the Bible, offering a modern take on the story of Isaac and elements of the Old Testament."

Here's the outline: Suffice to say life is turned upside down for a single parent family when Dad (Paxton) makes it known to his two sons (Matthew O'Leary and Jeremy Sumpter) that he's on a mission from God to kill demons. "Killing people is wrong," Dad says. "Destroying demons is good." It wouldn't be fair to give away any more plot details — thrillers rely on the element of surprise — but be assured, there are more twists and turns here than on any winding mountain road.

Texas native Matthew McConaughey turns in his strongest performance in years as the narrator. "I really enjoyed this story," he said. "It is a classic Gothic horror picture and I enjoyed trying something a bit darker. *Frailty* is my brand of scary in that it is a very human story about someone taking something literally, and doing something for the sake of righteousness, and that's an interesting part of the human mind." Both McConaughey and Powers Booth (as the FBI agent who listens to McConaughey's story) shine, but it is Paxton as the well meaning but insane father who really impresses. His "everyman" approach to the character is chilling, displaying the ordinariness of evil; the kind of evil that could live next door to you or me. "Today, if someone says 'God spoke to me,' we think they're crazy," says producer David Kirschner. "Yet, the Old Testament is based on God's conversations with Moses. We want to believe it happened then, but we can't accept that it might happen today. That's what is so fascinating about *Frailty*. It suggests that the impossible is possible."

> "Turn up the good! Turn down the suck!"
> **– DEAN MURDOCH (PAUL SPENCE)**

FUBAR (2002)

You probably went to school with some of them. Or maybe when you see them on the street, you cross to the other side. They are headbangers, also known affectionately as bangers. You know the type: long greasy hair with heavy metal t-shirts, who can usually be seen shot-gunning beer and yelling "Just give'r!" at the top of their lungs.

Fubar is a fabulous über-low-budget mockumentary about two bangers, Dean (Paul Spence) and Terry (David Lawrence), who live in Calgary — think Bob and Doug McKenzie with electric guitars. To paraphrase KISS, these dudes want to rock and roll all night and party every day. "We're not making fun of bangers," says director Michael Dowse.

"I'm actually in awe of them. This is a celebration of the banger. I was never really a banger because I was a couple of years behind the big metal thing."

"After high school I worked up on the pipeline for six months as a welder's helper. I really absorbed these guys from day to day," adds Lawrence. Lawrence used his experiences to write some of the more colorful language in the film, including the classic banger term, "just give'r." These guys are easy targets for ridicule, but Dowse doesn't go for the easy jokes. Instead he lets us get involved with the characters and get to like them before dropping a bombshell about one of them, one of the several unexpected turns that *Fubar* takes.

Fubar blurs the line between fact and fiction by casting several real life non-actors playing themselves. For instance, Dr. S.C. Lim, who is actually Michael Dowse's physician, plays himself in the film. In addition many of the "extras" in the fight scene were actual bar patrons who thought they were taking part in a real documentary.

This film was a favorite at 2001's Sundance Film Festival, and it's not hard to see why.

"Fun is king!"
— BONNIE (ALICIA WITT)

FUN (1994)
▬ ▬ ▬ ▬ ▬

Fun is divided into two time lines — the present, filmed in bleak monochromatic 16 mm, and flashbacks to the afternoon of "fun," shot in vibrant, clear color.

In the current day, two 15-year-old girls, the solemn Hillary (Renee Humphrey) and the raucous Bonnie (Alicia Witt), have been tried, convicted, and sentenced for the cold-blooded murder of a trusting old woman. The flashback scenes all take place on one hectic day when the two met, fell in love, and brutally stabbed the elderly woman. Why did they do it? "It was fun. Fun is number one!"

This is a chilling peek into the minds of disaffected youth, one that recalls cinematic thrillers like *Rope*, *Heavenly Creatures*, and *Butterfly Kiss*. It's not preachy, but the filmmakers subtly suggest that by allowing young people from dysfunctional families into an impersonal, violence-soaked society that doesn't care about them, their resulting behavior will be anti-social and possibly violent.

Anchoring the movie are the powerful performances of the two female leads. Alicia Witt, who got her start at age nine in the movie *Dune* (and whose mother holds the *Guinness Book of World Record* title for the having the longest hair), is particularly effective. Her mile-a-minute take on Bonnie is disturbingly real — she's a thrill seeker who killed someone just for the adrenaline rush, a drug-free high. Renee Humphrey is eclipsed by Witt, who has the showier role, but she delivers an effective portrait of a haunted, introspective soul. The two women believably display how opposites can attract, how in this case two damaged people became one whole — no longer individuals, but one lethal identity. The two actresses were awarded a special recognition from the Sundance Film Festival.

Directed by Rafal Zielinski — best known for helming teen sex comedies — *Fun* maintains a high emotional pitch for its 105 minutes and contains images that will not soon be forgotten.

> "Fiction is real — what you see in the movies is what you see literally."
> — PAUL (AMOS FRISCH)

FUNNY GAMES (1997)

This violent Austrian film isn't for everyone. In fact, one critic so reviled the movie he wrote, "After watching *Funny Games* the Jonestown suicides will appear to be a viable option." I guess Frank Zappa's idea that it doesn't matter *what* kind of reaction you get, as long as you get a reaction, holds true in this case.

The darkly provocative *Funny Games* is an art-house film that explores the use of violence in the cinema. A well-heeled young family's summer vacation turns into a nightmare when Paul and Peter (Amos Frisch and Frank Giering), two seemingly well-mannered young boys who are friends of the neighbors, drop by to borrow some eggs. Soon the family is held hostage and subjected to a night of torture and degradation by the two psychopaths.

Director and screenwriter Michael Heneke keeps the audience off guard from minute one. To make the point that the young bullies have been influenced by violence in the media he has them call one another Beavis and Butthead and speak directly to the audience in several self-aware moments in the film. In one scene they note that they can't kill the family quickly because "we're not up to feature length yet." In another extraordinary sequence the wife Anna (Susanne Lothar) gets her hands on a gun and shoots and kills Peter. Paul, the second sadist, decides he didn't like that scene, so he grabs a remote, rewinds the scene, and takes the gun from her before she can shoot.

Such touches add a sense of humor to the grim proceedings, but also make a comment on how we as an audience watch extremely violent material as entertainment. Heneke seems to be saying that by watching films like this we are complicit in creating a society that could create the two monsters we are watching on screen. It's an interesting thesis on film violence, one that seems at once to embrace and then reject its subject. A fine ensemble cast and skillful direction keep the themes in check, finding a balance between the humor and the violence, keeping the film on track and elevating it above the level of an average slasher flick. German with English subtitles.

"It's Moet and fucking Chandon all the fucking way . . ."
— GANGSTER (PAUL BETTANY)

GANGSTER NO. 1 (2001)

Gangster No. 1 feels like a continuation of one of the most disturbing movies of the 1970s. Malcolm McDowell became a star playing the hoodlum Alex DeLarge in *A Clockwork Orange*, a study of ultra-violence that shocked audiences with graphic depictions of rape and brutal behavior. McDowell's Alex was a young scowling punk with a passion for savagery. Thirty years later McDowell revisits the twisted world of the London underground. Little Alex is all grown up now, and *Gangster No. 1* is the logical conclusion to his life of crime.

Set in London in 1968 and the present day, *Gangster No. 1* is a simple character-driven story about a power struggle played out between mob boss Freddie Mays (David Thewlis) and his protégé, a vicious punk simply known as Gangster. We first meet Gangster (Malcolm McDowell) at age 55 at a swank dinner with other shady characters in an upscale hotel. When he learns that his old mentor, Freddie Mays, is about to get out of prison after doing a 30-year stretch for murder, a flood of emotions envelops him, pushing him to a very dark place.

Turn the clock back 30 years to the end of the summer of love.

Jacqueline Kennedy had just married Aristotle Onassis; Valerie Solanas tried to kill Andy Warhol; and Freddie Mays is the king of the London underground. Mays is reverentially known as the "Butcher of Mayfair," a nickname he picked up after killing a corrupt policeman. He is feared and respected by all, especially the young Gangster (Paul Bettany). Gangster desperately wants in on the action and will do anything to earn his way into the mob's inner circle.

His ruthlessness impresses Mays, who makes Gangster his righthand man. Gangster is fiercely loyal to Mays and cold-bloodedly protects his boss's position of power within the organization. He develops a psychotic admiration for Mays born out of allegiance and envy. He wants what Mays has: the red E-type Jaguar, the kitted-out apartment with Italian leather chairs and gold fixtures, and the clothes — *especially* the clothes. Mays wears handmade suits from Jermyn Street, Italian shirts, silk socks, ruby cufflinks, a white-gold watch, and a beautiful tie pin. When he is near Mays, Gangster feels "arseholed on the smell of success."

For a time they are unstoppable. Their unholy alliance propels them to the top of the underworld, but the good life starts to unravel. Gangster's insane jealousy gets the best of him when Mays falls for a local singer named Karen (Saffron Burrows). As Mays devotes more and more of his time to making wedding plans with his new girlfriend, Gangster feels left out. He feels his world is crumbling and must do something about it. When a plot is uncovered to assassinate Mays, Gangster keeps the news quiet and sets up his boss to take a fall.

Thirty years later the two meet again. Gangster wants to confront Mays to find out where it all went wrong, but first he must face up to his own demons as he grasps that his ascent to the top was ultimately a pyrrhic victory.

Gangster No. 1 is a taut, bloodthirsty genre picture that offers a well-constructed peek into a brilliant but warped and cruel personality. Both Bettany and McDowell as the young and senior Gangster respectively lend a palatable air of menace to the character. Like Alex DeLarge in *A Clockwork Orange*, Gangster seems capable of anything, a monomaniac who will do anything to hold all the aces.

McDowell's portrayal of the older Gangster bookends the film. We meet him in the twilight of his criminal career, looking back at his life, where we see that even now, Mays remains out of his league. Mays was a class act, stylish and charming, whereas Gangster is simply a barbarian. McDowell plays him as an animal, feral, a creature of pure instinct. "He's a monstrous person," McDowell said of the character. "I've never met anyone remotely like Gangster, and I wouldn't want to."

The real star turn in *Gangster No. 1* is Paul Bettany as the young thug. He's a modern day Richard III, a soulless man who only understands rage. His feelings for Mays range from envy to hate and very possibly love. He reacts like a spurned lover when Mays falls for Karen, and responds the only way he knows how, with extreme fury and violence. "Gangster seeks some sort of fulfillment," says Bettany, "but he has a hole inside him that gets bigger as the violence gets more pornographic."

Bettany is a powerhouse, fleshing out Gangster's monstrous behavior with a mixture of wit and menace. He's at his most dangerous when he smiles, as he does when Karen spits in his face. It's a frightening scene because we learn that his reactions can never be counted on. He's a loose cannon and completely unpredictable. Director Paul McGuigan calls Bettany "a wild card, incredibly wired. He has the elegant menace of a young James Bond. Very manly, very watchable."

McGuigan allows most of the violence to play off-screen, allowing the brutality to play itself out in the viewer's imagination, but in one of the most terrifying scenes in this film, or any gangster film, we see young Gangster commit an unspeakable act of violence against a mob rival. After breaking down the door to Lennie Taylor's flat and disabling him by shooting him in the knee, Gangster carefully removes his coat, undoes his tie, and takes off his shirt and pants to prevent them from becoming soiled in the events that follow. Then he methodically arranges the tools of his trade: a hatchet, a chisel, and a hammer. Stripped to his underwear, Gangster savagely attacks Taylor, and we see the action from Taylor's point of view as he shifts in and out of consciousness. The image of Gangster gleefully chopping his victim to bits is one that will not soon be forgotten.

Gangster No. 1 is a timeless crime saga that horrifies, thrills, and enthralls.

"He has no friends and never talks to anybody . . ."
– NEIGHBOR OF GHOST DOG

GHOST DOG: THE WAY OF THE SAMURAI (2000)

"Ghost Dog is an imagined character that follows the *Hagakure*, the code of the samurai," says writer/director Jim Jarmusch. "He's sort of a Don Quixote character really. He follows a spiritual warrior code that is from another century and another culture that doesn't really interface with the world he lives in, and yet it becomes his guide. He *is* a samurai because he follows the code of the samurai."

The Akron, Ohio-born Jarmusch is almost as well known for his bushy shock of white hair as his films. He is a critic's darling, and has a shelf full of awards to prove it, but he's never really made a commercial film. His work in the 1980s came to define a certain school of minimalist, art-house, high-concept, low-production-value, indie cinema. His 2000 big-screen release *Ghost Dog* is as close to a mainstream action movie as Jarmusch has ever come.

Forest Whitaker is Ghost Dog, a self-styled samurai who works as a hit man for the mob. He fell into that line of work after his life was saved by a mafia don named Louie (John Tormey), and by samurai law Ghost Dog must now dedicate his life to his Mafioso master. Ghost Dog is a man of mystery, even to his employers. He receives his instructions by carrier pigeon, and, in an annual tribute, is paid only once a year for his services, on the first day of the fall.

This becomes a complication after a hit gone wrong. Ghost Dog assassinates a rogue member of the crime family, but is seen by the victim's daughter (Tricia Vessey). He spares her life because she is reading one of his favorite books, *Rashomon*. Louie is unhappy with this turn of events and orders Ghost Dog eliminated; trouble is, no one knows where he lives because their only contact with him is through the pigeons. Ghost Dog deals with the death warrant in the manner of a true samurai warrior — he attacks.

This is an extremely offbeat movie. Virtually every piece of the puzzle makes no sense. Is it possible for a hit man to be completely anonymous, and only communicate through carrier pigeons? I would think not, but that's not the point. Jarmusch uses this device to accentuate the alienation of the character. Ghost Dog is a man completely shut off from the rest of the world, a person with virtually no contact with others — his best friend is a Haitian ice cream vendor Raymond (Isaach De Bankole) who doesn't speak English, and Ghost Dog doesn't speak French — who is ultimately left sad and alone.

The study of alienation works so well here because of the work of Forest Whitaker in the title role. He gives a domineering performance that drives the entire movie, and his character can be summed up in one passage from *L'ours*, read by his Haitian friend Raymond: "The bear is a solitary animal adaptable to all sorts of climates, environments, and foods. In groups they share food when quantities are abundant, despite their limited social interaction. The bear is a formidable adversary with no predatory instincts at all. But when surprised or wounded, a bear may attack and become very dangerous." The viewer always knows that underneath Whitaker's sleepy eyes is a coiled snake ready to strike, and it lends a tension to his character that few actors could pull off with such subtle élan.

"In the very beginning of *Ghost Dog* I was trying to think of a character that I could write and work with Forest on," says Jarmusch. "So that came before the story, before he was a samurai.

"I like the fact that he is physically imposing and yet has that face," says the director of his leading man. "His face, those eyes, there is a kind of poignancy that is very soft. There is a kind of gentleness. It is kind of contradictory. I've seen a lot of characters that he has created on screen. Very often they are shaded more toward that vulnerable side. I wanted to get a balance where he was very strong, stoic, a man of few words, and let that softness that is in his features and spirit kind of be present and not be pushed in any way. We were trying to make a character that would use both sides of Forest."

For the film to work the bizarre character of Ghost Dog would have to be completely credible. Jarmusch thinks that Whitaker hit all the right buttons: "A samurai uses his sword as an extension of his body," said the director, "and his body is an extension of his spirit. Forest took that further because Ghost Dog knows guns — it's modern — as well as he knows sword technique. The guns are an extension of his body, and therefore his spirit, as is the way he puts a CD into the CD player or the way he crouches or walks or moves. Forest really brought a beautiful physical translation of the soul of the character to the screen."

Gone are two of the trademarks of Jarmusch's previous films: the long takes and silent passages. *Ghost Dog* has the energy of a squirrel, and the fast, edgy cuts are combined with a harsh hip-hop soundtrack by the RZA of the Wu-Tang Clan. Jarmusch has long recognized the power of music in his films, and chooses soundtrack material carefully. Whether it's Screamin' Jay Hawkins, Tom Waits, or Lounge Lizard John Lurie, Jarmusch has a knack for matching his images with effective music. *Ghost Dog*'s nervy edge is perfectly suited to RZA's abrasive hip-hop, with the music lending a jittery inner-city feel to the film.

"Music always starts really early for me," says Jarmusch discussing the soundtracks of his films. "In the case of my previous feature film *Dead Man*, even while I was writing my dream was to get Neil Young to do the music, and it happened. In this case it was the same thing. While I was still collecting fragments of ideas I had this dream that I would get the RZA to do the music. I was a fan of the Wu-Tang and of a certain percentage of hip-hop that I think is really amazing. Also the Wu-Tang philosophy was really interesting to me before I met the RZA or any of the Wu-Tang, so I had this dream that maybe I could get the RZA to do the music. I listened to a lot of his music while writing, and I was able to find people I know that knew people that he knew, and was able to get to meet and talk to him about it. My dream came true again."

Ghost Dog is a unique animal, a strikingly new examination of urban crime drama (although I wish Jarmusch had freshened up the characters of the mob guys a tad), that explores not only the physical act of killing, but the metaphysical as well.

> "I'm a goddamn force of nature. I feel like
> I could do just about anything."
> **— GINGER (KATHARINE ISABELLE)**

GINGER SNAPS (2000)

In 1944 the screen's first female werewolf, Princess Celeste LaTour (Nina Foch) terrified moviegoers in *Cry of the Werewolf* as she murdered everyone who knew her terrible lycanthropian secret. Fifty-six years later the beastly tradition of women doomed to shape-shift into horrible creatures continued with *Ginger Snaps*, the story of a teenage girl and "the curse." It's funny, feminist horror.

If you follow the news, chances are you may have read about *Ginger Snaps* before it even went into production, but not because it had a cast of superstars or was being directed by an A-list Hollywood talent. No, *Ginger Snaps* hit the headlines in the wake of the Columbine and Taber, Alberta, school shootings. The *Toronto Star* ran a sensational (although untrue) story describing the as-yet-unmade film as a slasher movie featuring the toxic combo of teens and violence. In a knee-jerk reaction to the hot-button topic an onslaught of press followed, criticizing the filmmakers and one of the movie's main backers, Telefilm Canada.

Luckily the government-funded Telefilm didn't buckle under, and continued to support the project, although the negative press made it difficult to find a casting agent willing to take on the film; several casting agents refused to even look at the script, much less send it to their clients. It took six months to cast the leads, with auditions being held in Toronto, Los Angeles, and Vancouver. Eventually every role was cast and production began just a few days before Halloween 1999 in the Toronto suburbs of Brampton, Scarborough, and Etobicoke.

The fictional suburb of Bailey Downs is home to 15-year-old Brigitte Fitzgerald (Emily Perkins) and her soon-to-be-sweet-16 sister Ginger (Katharine Isabelle). They are pariahs in the small bedroom community, clinging to each other as best friends, bound by a childhood pact. They are so desperately unhappy and bored they vow to commit suicide together. In preparation they assemble a school art project — a series of gruesome photos of Ginger in various death scenes. On the night of Ginger's first period the duo are cutting through the woods on the edge of town when Ginger is ferociously attacked by a mysterious creature.

Ginger survives, her wounds miraculously healing in no time flat. She may be mildly physically scarred from the attack, but the psychological scars seem much deeper. She becomes prickly and in denial. Brigitte is the first to realize what is happening. The sudden appearance of little silvery hairs on the scars and a tail budding from the base of her spine point in only one direction — Ginger is becoming a werewolf.

"I've got this ache," says Ginger, referring to her unnatural cravings, "and I thought it was for sex, but it's to tear everything into fucking pieces." Ginger is no longer an outsider, but a predator using her sexual charms to seduce victims who will unwittingly satisfy her new-found blood lust. Brigitte searches for a cure for her sister's malady, turning to Sam (Kris Lemche), a local drug dealer and amateur botanist. They search for a holistic remedy to cure the infection that has overtaken Ginger.

As Ginger loses her battle with the dark side she begins to behave and think more like a beast. Brigitte, blinded by the love of her sister, becomes an accomplice to Ginger's vicious crimes, and the whole thing comes to a crescendo on Halloween night.

Ginger Snaps adroitly plays against the usual horror movie conventions when it comes to portraying teenagers. The nubile scream queens of *I Know What You Did Last Summer* and *Urban Myth* are nowhere to be found. Ginger and Brigitte are late-bloomers, goth girls who are entering adulthood and experiencing all the traumatic transformations that go along with it. The film's best piece of dark teenage humor is the use of menstruation as a metaphor for turning into a werewolf. How many hack comics have joked about the beastly effects of PMS? *Ginger Snaps* takes those jokes one step further in a wickedly funny allegory.

A movie like this hinges on the performances of its leads. Director John Fawcett wisely chose to play it straight, avoiding the camp that mars so many teen horror flicks. Emily Perkins shows real depth as Brigitte, moving her character through an arc from the timid little wallflower you might see in an Edward Gorey cartoon to an independent powder keg à la *Buffy the Vampire Slayer*. "I was drawn to the fact that she doesn't belong anywhere," says Perkins, "I think teenagers can relate to that. She's a strange, strange girl."

Katharine Isabelle is a bottle rocket as the hormonally unbalanced Ginger. The character almost threatens to career off the rails, but Isabelle keeps her on track in a performance that shows great skill. "Ginger is an exaggeration of my bad side," says Isabelle. "She's not too much of a stretch for me. Except all the being a werewolf and killing people stuff. That's a bit of a stretch."

Both actresses glide through the material, bringing realism to an unreal situation. Ginger and Brigitte are nihilistic, fighting the pressures to conform and fit in with a society they have no use for. Add boys to the mix and you've got a potentially explosive situation. These are the kind of teens who give high school guidance counselors ulcers.

It's clear that screenwriter Karen Walton remembers her high school years very well. Her snappy script never talks down to the teens, instead addressing their problems as legitimate issues without a hint of condescension. The sensitive handling of the lead characters gives this film a feeling of authenticity that works very well whether you choose to look upon this more as a horror flick or a clever commentary on the pain of becoming an adult.

Ginger Snaps may take itself seriously, but it washes the premise down with a spoonful of sugar. The metaphors are quietly woven into the fabric of the piece, which bristles with genuine frights and a great deal of humor built around the characters and situations, unlike the postmodern "look at me, I'm so ironic" humor of the *Scream* series. Mimi Rogers as the girls' mother, Pamela, is the main source of laughs. She's a guileless Mrs. Cleaver type (if Beaver's mom had taken too much acid in the '60s). To celebrate her daughter's first period and her ascent into womanhood, Pamela inappropriately bakes a large strawberry cake for the whole family to enjoy. She's thrilled; the girls, of course, are mortified.

Ginger Snaps is a welcome addition to the werewolf genre.

LESSON SEVEN: Cultivate hatred: It's your greatest asset.
– *THE GREAT ROCK 'N' ROLL SWINDLE*

THE GREAT ROCK 'N' ROLL SWINDLE (1980)

The making of the Sex Pistols' film *The Great Rock 'N' Roll Swindle* was almost as chaotic as one of their concerts. The original director quit, one of the stars died, and the whole thing seemed ready to fall apart. Only the tenacity of a young guerrilla filmmaker saved the movie from the scrap heap. Julien Temple stepped in and made a movie about a band that had already broken up, putting together something he called "a vandalized documentary," and in the process made a little-seen but classic rock-and-roll movie.

The Sex Pistols were the most reviled people in England; a series of outrageous publicity stunts had turned the foul-mouthed foursome into the tabloids' favorite whipping boys. Public reaction to them was so strong they had to tour under the name SPOTS (Sex Pistols On Tour Secretly) to sidestep various bans and potential protests. It was while they were on their cloak-and-dagger tour that the idea of making a movie first came up — manager Malcolm McLaren wanted to find a cheap, safe way to promote the band in other territories, and with the band banned in so many European cities, a film was the only way for most people to see them.

McLaren had approached a number of well-known English comics to write a script, including Peter Cook, the legendary improv master and former partner to Dudley Moore. Cook considered the project, but never put pen to paper. McLaren ruled out another likely candidate after a night of drinking at a pub. A meeting was set up with Monty Python co-founder Graham Chapman. Many drinks later Chapman performed his favorite party trick: dipping his penis into a pint of beer for the pub dog to lick. While one would think that the display might appeal to McLaren, a man who encouraged the Pistols to vomit in public and was often interviewed wearing a full S&M rubber suit, he was actually so disgusted by the show he crossed Chapman off the list of potential writers.

Running out of options in England, McLaren and the band turned their eyes to a cult, soft-porn filmmaker in the United States. Russ Meyer's subversive take on the entertainment industry in *Beyond the Valley of the Dolls* appealed to Johnny Rotten, who called Meyer "an absolute nutcase." Meyer agreed to make the film on the condition that he could bring some of his own people, including his stripper girlfriend Kitten Natividad and screenwriter Roger Ebert.

The hard-boiled Meyer didn't know what to make of McLaren or the band. When McLaren showed up at one meeting wearing bondage pants Meyer insisted on sitting on the aisle. "If we have to evacuate he'll get those goddamned straps tangled up in the seats," he said.

Ebert and Meyer set to work on a script that was due to start shooting on Halloween in 1977. Writing and rewriting over the course of three months, they cobbled together a piercing indictment of the music business called *Who Killed Bambi?*. In keeping with the punk rock ethos the film explored themes of debauchery, corruption, anarchy, and the death of innocence.

In the surreal title sequence an aging rock star known as MJ (probably Mick Jagger) is threatened by the popularity of the Sex Pistols and pulls a Robin Hood stunt. "Jagger — we don't call him Jagger — goes out in hunting garb and crossbow and shoots a deer on the queen's reserve," Meyer told *Search and Destroy* in 1978. "He straps it on the Rolls and drives careening through the countryside. He picks a suitable thatched-roof cottage to give it to the poor and throws it down on the porch. A little girl comes out and says, 'Mommy! They've just killed Bambi!'"

An eclectic group of actors was assembled. Along with the Pistols — Johnny Rotten, Sid Vicious, Steve Jones, and Paul Cook — Mick Jagger's ex-girlfriend Marianne Faithfull was cast as Sid's incestuous mom and a motley crew of Pistols' fans were brought in for color.

Shooting on the Meyer's film ended abruptly after only a day and a half, and no one seems to be able to agree why production was shut down. Ebert claims work came to a halt when it became apparent that the crew was not going to be paid for their work. According to McLaren the project was killed by its main financier, 20th Century Fox, who pulled out under the pretext that, "We are in the business of making family entertainment." Apparently several shareholders, including Grace Kelly, were outraged by the film's subject matter. Either way, the movie seemed as dead as the deer in the opening scene.

With just a few feet of film from the Meyer project, McLaren tried to salvage the film and turned to British director Pete Walker, best known for a string of exploitation movies with titles like *Die, Beautiful*

Marianne and *Asylum of the Insane*. Cameras never even rolled on his version, as the band weren't interested in learning the reams of lines set out in the script. Later that year the band fell apart when Rotten escaped to Jamaica, Cook and Jones went to Rio to hang out with Great Train Robber Ronnie Biggs, and Sid took refuge in Paris.

In Paris a young film student who had been filming the Pistols since their early days was hired to shoot some footage of Sid. Julien Temple came complete with a cinematic sense and an attitude. His plan was to show the seamier side of the music business, so he arranged a set piece with Sid, by this time ravaged by heroin, singing "My Way" in front of a respectable upper-class audience. On a set originally built for French superstar Serge Gainsbourg, Sid wears a dinner jacket and motorcycle boots and mumbles his way through rewritten lyrics that were part Frank Sinatra, part Joey Ramone. In the end Sid pulls out a revolver and shoots members of the audience. It's pure punk rock, and Sid plays it perfectly. "We saw Sid as the first monster child of the hippie generation," said Temple.

In the absence of the band Temple pieced together a mockumentary broken into 10 sequences — lessons on how to sell a band. Using clips and animation he cynically outlines McLaren's modus operandi of artist management, everything from "How to Manufacture Your Group" to "How to Become the World's Greatest Tourist Attraction."

The film came out in 1980, two years after the Pistols played their last gig. The band, particularly Johnny Rotten, hated it, as did most reviewers at the time. To me, though, it represents a unique time capsule of one of the most exciting movements in popular music. Punk rock was a short-lived, but wildly influential period that has informed hundreds of bands, and *The Great Rock 'N' Roll Swindle* is the unruly blueprint.

"That whole gay thing is just like a hobby."
— **WAYNE WAYNE WAYNE JR. (STEVE ZAHN) in *HAPPY, TEXAS***

HAPPY, TEXAS (1999)

Happy, Texas is a hard movie to define. Think *The Fugitive* if it had starred Tim Conway and Harvey Corman, or maybe *Tootsie* set in a small rural town. How about *Drop Dead Gorgeous* without the crazy mother? This much is for sure: *Happy, Texas* is a screwball comedy about two convicts on the lam who go to great lengths to avoid detection.

Mark Illsley and Ed Stone were old friends struggling to make it in the film business. After reading the Robert Rodriguez's how-to memoir on the making of *El Mariachi* called *Rebel Without a Crew*, the duo were inspired to make a film on a shoestring budget. They set out to write a film that they could shoot in their backyard using just a few friends as actors. As the script took shape both men realized they were writing something a little more ambitious than a patio epic that they could shoot over a long weekend. The script eventually fell into the hands of producer Rick Montgomery, who convinced the fledgling filmmakers to set their sights higher and shoot the story as a feature film. When Academy Award winner William H. Macy signed on to play the gay sheriff of Happy, Texas, the funding and the rest of the cast fell into place.

The story of Wayne Wayne Wayne Jr. (Steve Zahn) and his partner-in-crime Harry Sawyer (Jeremy Northam) begins as they escape from an overturned police van and steal an RV from a gas station to make their getaway. When the sheriff of Happy stops them they think they have been caught. "There's a lot of people looking for you," says the cop with a smile. Busted.

Or are they? What they don't know is that the vehicle they took belongs to two gay men who travel through the small towns of Texas consulting on beauty pageants. They haven't been arrested, they've just been handed a new identity.

In town they pose as the pageant producers, coaching a group of small girls who dream of one day being Little Miss Fresh Squeezed. No one from Happy has even qualified in 25 years, so the pressure is on. The small-town folks take this pageant very seriously, something screenwriter Ed Stone learned through personal experience. He was a disc jockey at a radio station just a few miles from Happy, Texas. In his daily news reports he often had to read stories about the Happy High School sports teams and Happy pageants, and was always amused by the name.

"Like most every small town in Texas, Happy's citizens were just mad when it came to pageants," he says. "As a disc jockey from another part of the world I'd sometimes go on the sir and poke a little fun at this obsession with pageants, and you wouldn't believe the angry calls that came in. It was really surprising to find out how seriously the Texas population takes their pageantry."

Harry, the slicker of the two, coaxes the thickheaded Wayne into teaching the girls ballet and poise while he cases the bank. His plan to crack the safe is foiled, or at least sidelined when he falls for the bank manager Jo (Ally Walker). She thinks he is gay, a ruse he maintains to get closer to her. Meanwhile, love is in the air as Wayne develops a crush on a local schoolteacher Ms. Schaefer (Illeana Douglas), and Sheriff Chappy Dent (William H. Macy) eyes Harry. Despite living a lie and running from the police Wayne and Harry find happiness in the small town, a happiness neither of them has known before.

Happy, Texas is supported by two great comic performances. As the kind-hearted dolt Wayne Wayne Wayne Jr., Steve Zahn is over-the-top hilarious. As he tends to the young pageant hopefuls he discovers that he really likes this work and cares about the kids, even if he's not sure how to behave with them (his idea of bonding with them is to offer them cigarettes or teach them to sing *99 Bottles of Beer on the Wall*). With his walrus moustache and hangdog expression, Zahn brings a manic energy to the movie but never crosses the line into sentimentality as Robin Williams has so many times in similar roles. Even when Zahn is being endearing — as in the scene where he wonders aloud about the best way to sew a sparkly heart on a costume — he still has an edge. The critics saw it too, and he picked up a special jury prize for Best Comedic Performance at the Sundance Film Festival.

William H. Macy's take on the gay sheriff of this small town isn't nearly as showy as Zahn's character, but is funny and touching at the same time. Macy can do more with a glance than many actors can with several pages of dialogue, and he demonstrates his talent here, rising above the farce aspects of the story and breathing real life into his role. Even though Chappy is a comic character being played for laughs, the audience still feels for him; you can't help but be saddened for Chappy when Harry doesn't return his affections.

"Chappy undergoes a transformation in this film," says Macy. "At the start he's so protected that he couldn't be available to anyone. But eventually his heart gets big and vulnerable. For me this film is ultimately about love. Love is truly a rare thing. If you can find it, then go for it. Don't miss your chance."

Romantic lead Jeremy Northam is strong. Until *Happy, Texas* Northam was best known for period dramas like *The Winslow Boy* and *Emma*. Here he drops his English accent in favor of a midwestern American drawl, and leaves the waistcoats in the dressing room. Northam breezes through the movie, coasting on his considerable charm and good looks.

Happy, Texas is a funny little charmer that takes a sitcom-like plot and entertainingly stretches it to feature length. The screenwriters may use homosexuality as a plot device, but they never resort to homophobia as a source of humor.

THE HARDER THEY COME (1973)

If not for *The Harder They Come*, you might not have that copy of Bob Marley's *Legend* CD on your shelf wedged between Marilyn Manson and Martha and the Vandellas. In 1973 reggae music was virtually unknown outside of Jamaica, but when the low-budget, rags-to-riches gangster flick became a hit on the midnight movie circuit, it helped to introduce a whole new audience to the music's lilting island rhythms.

Shot on a shoestring budget of $400,000, *The Harder They Come* tells the story of Ivan Martin (Jimmy Cliff), a young man from rural Jamaica who comes to Kingston to seek his fortune. Hoping to find fame as a musician, he tries to peddle a handful of original reggae songs. Naive to the ways of the record business, he is conned by music industry sharpies and winds up penniless and disillusioned. With his dreams of stardom shattered, he takes a job working for a local minister, but trouble in the form of a relationship with a ward of the preacher, Elsa (Janet Barkley), forces him to flee. While on the run Martin auditions for a producer (Bobby Charlton) by singing the movie's title tune. Impressed, the producer offers $25 for the rights. He refuses the paltry offer, and soon finds work as a ganja dealer.

In the mean streets of Kingston, the marijuana traffic is under the dominion of the police. Martin double-crosses the local drug lord (Carl Bradshaw), and is attacked by several police officers. Then an interesting thing happens: while on the run he becomes a folk hero when a record company cashes in on his notoriety by releasing his old audition tapes. His records top the charts as he has one final showdown with the corrupt cops.

The first thing that stands out about *The Harder They Come* is the music, which accentuates and propels the film's action. Three decades since its release the soundtrack still stands as the perfect introduction to Jamaican pop music. With the notable exception of Bob Marley, most of Trenchtown's biggest stars are represented here — Cliff, Toots and the Maytals, the Melodians, the Slickers, Scotty, and Desmond Dekker. Culled from a selection of Jamaican singles from the late '60s and early '70s, these songs represent the birth of reggae, a point at which the music was finding its feet, adding a slower, more complex rhythm to the traditional sounds of ska and blue-beat.

There is a wide berth of reggae represented here. Toots and the Maytals' "Pressure Drop" provides the soul, while the socially conscious "Shanty Town" by Desmond Dekker is true to the origins of reggae. Cliff's four selections — including the title track and "You Can Get It If You Really Want" and the Melodians' "Rivers of Babylon" — add a dash of syncopated pop. The music's harder edge is present in the songs of the Slickers and Scotty. It's a superb compilation, a cornerstone of West Indian music that earned an international audience for reggae, paving the way for Bob Marley and others.

The film itself probably won't win any awards from Jamaica's tourist bureau. Grim and violent, it eschews any clichés of Kingston as a laid-back island paradise. This is a raw film that delves into the frenzied street world of Trenchtown. Director Perry Henzell places much of the action in the city's decaying black ghetto, an immense tableau of rusted corrugated tin roofs and filth where people pick through garbage for food. Corruption and ruthlessness are ubiquitous, with violence around every corner. It's a bleak vision of Jamaica's emerging identity, breaking ground in its honest portrayal of Kingston's urban existence. Life imitated art when two of the film's actors were violently killed in Kingston shortly after the movie's release.

Whatever Jimmy Cliff's deficiencies as an actor, he more than makes up for in charisma. His scenes crackle with energy and authenticity. It's hard to take your eyes off him, even when the going gets grim, as when he carves up a man's face while snarling the line, "Don't ... fuck ... wid

. . . me." It's a gory scene (too much fake blood seeped through the actor's fingers, but with no money in the budget for a second take, the grisly sequence was left in the completed film), but is made more gruesome by the intensity of Cliff's acting. He's a better singer than actor, to be sure, but as Ivan Martin he brings a spirited amateur screen performance to life.

After the film's completion director Perry Henzell found that his vision of life in urban Jamaica was a tough sell to theater owners. Popular in Jamaica, *The Harder They Come* took several years to catch on outside of the Caribbean. Henzell hawked his film around the world only to be told, "nobody here is interested in reggae." It took six years for the film to be shown in Italy, but when it did, reggae took off immediately there. "Bob Marley came in a year later and played to 100,000 people," he said. That same scenario happened many times before the film found its mainstream audience. Part of the sales problem may also have been cultural. Foreign buyers had a hard time understanding the dialogue. Although it is in English, the heavy Jamaican patois proved daunting for some audiences, so Henzell added English subtitles to certain parts of the film. It remains one of the very few English movies to have English subtitles.

To date *The Harder They Come* is the only film from Jamaica's burgeoning motion picture industry to find an international cult audience. "It's two different films really," Henzell says, explaining its appeal. "In North America, Europe, and Japan, it's for college-educated people who want to glimpse the other side. In places like Brazil and South Africa, it plays like *Kung Fu* for illiterate audiences."

Richard's Favorite Soundtracks

1. *The Girl Can't Help It*, Various Artists (1956 reissued 1992). Standout cuts: "Be Bop A Lula," Gene Vincent; "You Got It Made," Bobby Troup

2. *What's New Pussycat?*, Burt Bacharach (1965 reissued 1998). "What's New Pussycat?," Tom Jones; "My Little Red Book," Manfred Mann Group

3. *Enter the Dragon*, Lalo Schifrin (1973, reissued 2001). "The Big Battle"; "The Human Fly," Lalo Schifrin

4. *In the Heat of the Night*, Quincy Jones (1967, reissued 1998). "In the Heat of the Night," Ray Charles; "Whipping Boy," Quincy Jones

5. *Once Upon a Time in the West*, Ennio Morricone (1968, reissued 1990). "Once Upon a Time in the West"; "The First Tavern," Ennio Morricone

6. *Trouble Man*, Marvin Gaye (1972, reissued 1998). "Poor Abbey Walsh"; "Break In (Police Shoot Big)," Marvin Gaye

7. *The Great Rock 'N' Roll Swindle*, The Sex Pistols (1979, reissued 1992). "My Way," Sid Vicious; "Friggin' in the Riggin'," Steve Jones

8. *One From the Heart*, Tom Waits and Crystal Gayle (1981, reissued 1990). "Is There Anyway Out of This Dream?," Tom Waits; "Picking Up After You," Crystal Gayle

9. *Pulp Fiction*, Various Artists (1994). "Misirlou," Dick Dale & His Del-Tones; "Son of a Preacher Man," Dusty Springfield

10. *The Harder They Come*, Jimmy Cliff (1972, reissued 2001). "Many Rivers to Cross," Jimmy Cliff; "Pressure Drop," The Maytals

> "My sex change operation got botched
> My guardian angel fell asleep on the watch
> Now all I got is a Barbie doll crotch
> I've got an angry inch!"
> — HEDWIG (JOHN CAMERON MITCHELL)

HEDWIG AND THE ANGRY INCH (2001)

A frumpy German woman divorced from her American GI husband was the inspiration for John Cameron Mitchell's best-known character. "She had a trailer we went to and she'd give us drinks," he remembers. "She had a lot of dates and I couldn't figure out why she was so popular, because she was not overly attractive, although she did have a certain pose. In retrospect, I realized she was a prostitute." Mitchell expanded on that woman's unhappy story when creating the "internationally ignored song stylist" title character for *Hedwig and the Angry Inch*.

Hedwig creators Mitchell and Stephen Trask met because of a bad movie. They were seated next to one another on a plane and both hated the inflight film. Instead of watching the movie or falling asleep the strangers began to talk, hitting it off immediately as they traded work stories from their respective fields, theater and music. Post-flight the duo kept in touch and were soon collaborating on a project, a rock-and-roll musical. "I had become bored with doing the usual guest-star sitcom work and was interested in doing a solo piece incorporating rock music," says Mitchell. "And then I met Stephen, who is an amazing composer."

With Mitchell writing the monologues and Trask and his band Cheater providing the music, they soon whipped together an early version of *Hedwig* that played on drag nights at Squeezebox, a Manhattan rock-and-roll bar. Over the next few months the show changed and grew, as did its fan base. Soon they had to move to larger quarters, an actual theater in the West Village, and Mitchell's rowdy off-Broadway performances as the "girly-boy" Hedwig were garnering rave reviews and attracting attention from film companies.

Mitchell leapt at the chance to present *Hedwig* on the silver screen. "When I started writing for stage, I actually saw it more cinematically," he says. "There were jokes or visual cuts I had in mind. And I thought, 'Oh it would be so much easier if we could just show an image.' You know a picture is worth a thousand words."

Killer Films, the company behind Todd Solondz's *Happiness* and the Academy Award-winning *Boys Don't Cry*, was chosen to produce the film, which was shot in Toronto.

The search for stardom and love begins with a German boy named Hansel who undergoes a sex change operation and switches his name to Hedwig, in order to marry an American GI and escape to the freedom of the United States. "To walk away," he says, "you gotta leave something behind." Unfortunately the operation is bungled, leaving only a small deformed lump between his legs, the "angry inch" of the movie's title. The marriage doesn't work out, and Hedwig finds herself divorced and living in a trailer in Kansas with dreams of rock and roll stardom. "I scraped by with babysitting gigs and odd jobs," Hedwig explains in the movie, "mostly the jobs we call blow." She forms a band, and begins a relationship with one of her fans, a young boy named Tommy Gnosis (Michael Pitt). Together they write songs and yearn for a better life, and Tommy becomes Hedwig's protégé.

Tommy begins to have doubt in the relationship and finally abandons her when he discovers that she was born a man. "What's that?" asks Tommy, feeling an ever so slight bulge in Hedwig's pants. "It's what I got to work with, honey," she says. He forms his own band and becomes a big time rock star based on songs he has stolen from Hedwig. "From this milkless tit you have sucked the very business we call show," she says.

We learn all this through flashbacks, animation, and songs. The film begins in the present with Hedwig performing behind the salad bar at a chain restaurant called Bilgewater's. She and her band, The Angry Inch, are shadowing Gnosis's tour; while he plays the stadium in town,

Hedwig, bitter and a little worse for the wear and tear, can be found around the corner singing for dumbstruck restaurant patrons who don't know what to make of her. As she stumbles through her tour, trying to capitalize on the fame of her ex-lover, she discovers the true origins of love.

The whole film is about duality and healing. Hedwig is the product of a broken home in communist East Berlin, a divided city. He reluctantly agrees to a sex change operation that leaves him split once again — not fully male or female. Hedwig's search for love and acceptance is the result of feeling like a divided person her entire life, so she makes it her quest to heal herself and become whole. That philosophy — that everyone is looking for something — drives the movie but doesn't weigh it down.

"Everything Hedwig does is to gain some kind of wholeness," says Mitchell. "Everyone is seeking something and trying to make him or herself whole, including Hedwig and Tommy Gnosis as well. In the end it is Tommy who gives Hedwig the knowledge she needs to move on, to realize that she is whole in a way she didn't expect."

It's a strange and sometimes sordid story, but is brought to sparkling life by Mitchell in the lead role. His Hedwig is a tour de force performance that hits all the right notes — the style, the sound, the fury, and the pain. There isn't a hint of parody in Mitchell, even when he is wearing some of Hedwig's more outlandish costumes and wigs. He plays it straight (no pun intended), and that is the beauty of the performance: the audience must feel for Hedwig or the whole thing will fall apart. Mitchell makes her lovable and keeps her interesting. Hedwig is all heart, especially when she is being self-deprecating. "I had tried singing once and they threw tomatoes at me," she says, "so after the show I had a nice salad." She's part vaudeville, part heartbreak.

Overall, *Hedwig and the Angry Inch* works extremely well as a rock-and-roll musical. Mitchell, who doubled as director, injects a fast and furious energy to the musical numbers, particularly one glam rock tune performed in a trailer home that transforms into a stage. Rock-and-roll musicals are a bit of a minefield, and rarely ever work on the big screen, but Mitchell's in-your-face style of directing is the perfect complement to his "post-punk, neo-glam" material. *Hedwig* rocks out with a fierce power rarely found on the silver screen.

"A picture different from anything ever screened before!"
— Advertising tagline for *HERE COMES MR. JORDAN*

HERE COMES MR. JORDAN (1941)

As a film critic who sees several hundred movies a year, there are a couple of words that strike fear into my heart. The word "sequel" usually means that I'm going to spend a couple hours of my day sitting in a theater watching a bunch of Hollywood types thrashing away at a warmed-over concept. Another word is "remake" — I dread the inevitable ache of witnessing Guy Ritchie bungle *Swept Away* or watching a dead-eyed Sly Stallone in *Get Carter*.

Of course, not all sequels and remakes are train wrecks. *Godfather 2* is arguably a better film than the original, and Steve Martin's *Dirty Rotten Scoundrels* vastly improves on the 1964 version of the same tale, *Bedtime Story*. The 1941 romantic fantasy *Here Comes Mr. Jordan* has been remade several times, with varying degrees of success. Six years after the original was nominated for a Best Picture Oscar the story resurfaced as a flashy Technicolor musical titled *Down to Earth* and earned favorable reviews for its star Rita Hayworth. In 1978 Warren Beatty retooled and retitled the story, scoring his biggest hit to date with *Heaven Can Wait*. In 2001 comedian Chris Rock took another kick at the can, but with far less satisfying results. His *Down to Earth* took a critical drubbing, with one noted critic calling it an "astonishingly bad movie." It's time then to go back and have a look at the first and best version of the story.

Based on a popular stage play, *Here Comes Mr. Jordan* starred Robert Montgomery (father to *Bewitched* star Elizabeth Montgomery) as saxophone-playing boxer Joe Pendleton, who perishes in a plane crash on the way to his next fight. In Heaven he is told that there has been a mistake — he had been taken by an overzealous Heavenly Messenger (Edward Everett Horton) 50 years before his time. Looking for a way to right this wrong, angelic pencil pusher Mr. Jordan (Claude Raines) sends Pendleton's soul back to Earth. Unfortunately they are too late, and his body has already been cremated. The solution? Give him a new body.

Eventually they settle on the form of Oliver Farnsworth, a millionaire who has just been murdered by his wife. A new love and the scheming of the murderous wife complicate his new life as he prepares to win the prize fight he missed in his old body.

There are plot holes, some feel-good dramatics, and the occasional overwrought performance — check out Horton's contrite blubbering — but the light tone and breezy comic dialogue rise above the movie's shortcomings. So what if Robert Montgomery looks more like a matinee idol than prizefighter? This is a Hollywood screwball comedy, not *Raging Bull*. Taken for what it is, a charming romantic comedy without an ounce of irony or cynicism, *Here Comes Mr. Jordan* is a classic of its genre, and bears up to repeated viewings.

HIGH SCHOOL CONFIDENTIAL (1958)

The credit sequence of *High School Confidential* kicks off with wildcat rocker Jerry Lee Lewis pounding out the title song while being driven through town on the back of a flatbed truck. He plays as though he has a fire in his belly, setting an unrestrained tone for the rest of the movie. Fasten your seat belts, daddy-o, it's gonna be a wild ride.

Tony Baker (Russ Tamblyn), a hip-talking transfer student, wastes no time in stirring things up at his new school, Santo Bello High. "I'm looking to graze on grass," he tells a fellow pupil on his first day, making it known that he wants to score some marijuana. Baker is the epitome of hipster cool, a fast-talking juvenile delinquent who lives on the edge. He proves his juvie street cred by pulling a switchblade on his classmates and inviting his teacher Jan Sterling (Arlene Williams) back to his place to "live it up." But there is something amiss: he also drinks milk, and refuses a toke from a joint.

After declining Baker's offer, Sterling attends a staff meeting with a federal agent. "In the language the addicts use, marijuana is referred to as Mary Jane, pot, weed, or tea," the agent deadpans, before warning that a plague of drug use has happened in other schools and "it can happen here."

Baker, meanwhile, has discovered an off-campus junkies' paradise, the local coffeehouse. A beatnik "doll" recites ridiculous rhymes — "We cough blood on this earth / Now there's a race for space / We can cough blood on the moon, soon / Tomorrow is dragsville, cats / Tomorrow is a king-sized drag" — while he tries to buy "some H, some coke, and some goofballs." He meets the local drug kingpin, Mr. A (Jackie Coogan), who also runs a jukebox empire.

Okay, so far there are drugs and rock and roll, but where's the sex? That's where the randy Aunt Gwen (Mamie Van Doren) enters the picture. She's a torpedo-breasted sex kitten who tries to seduce her nephew Tony every chance she gets. Baker is too intent on buying drugs to have anything to do with his lascivious landlord, and her advances go unheeded.

Near the end of *High School Confidential* there is the inevitable showdown between good and evil, before a high-toned narrator tells us, "You have just seen an authentic disclosure of conditions which unfortunately exist in some of our high schools today. The job of policemen will not be finished until this insidious menace to the schools of our country is exposed and destroyed."

High School Confidential was produced by Albert Zugsmith, a journeyman journalist, producer, and director. "I don't make movies without a moral," he said, "but you can't make a point for good unless you expose the evil." To this end he made films (and fistfuls of money) about male impotence, racial bigotry, juvenile delinquency, sexual promiscuity, alcoholism, and of course, drug addiction. It may be hard to justify the contradiction of exploiting the lurid details of the human condition while at the same preaching against them, but Zugsmith is unrepentant. He fills *High School Confidential* with more hot-rod races, busty blondes in tight clothes, hip jargon, and drugs than any drive-in crowd could hope for, while at the same time bashing them over the head with a moral. *High School Confidential* outdoes other "just say no" movies like *Reefer Madness* for the sheer hilarious bludgeoning force of its anti-drug message.

While most of the ideas seem hopelessly outdated — one toke can lead to harder drugs; heroin, when thrown in the eyes, can cause blindness — I think the film makes one point that was years ahead of its time: the idea that bad kids can come from good homes. Even today, the topic is still viewed with bewilderment when shown on tabloid talk shows. *High School Confidential* suggests that everyone is susceptible to temptation, even middle-class kids who should know better.

Zugsmith lays it on thick, but also offers some ridiculous solutions.

Drug addiction can apparently be dealt with quite easily, once the problem is identified. Ms Sterling snaps a joint in half, forever curing teen pothead Diane Jergens of her habit. (If it were that easy, jails would be a lot emptier. Just ask Robert Downey Jr.)

The actors manage to be convincing, although the script doesn't do them any favors. Littered with proto-hip lingo, the dialogue was designed to sound foreign to the average viewer, but today it sounds ridiculous because it is so obsolete. It's hard to imagine the actors keeping a straight face delivering lines like, "You're dragging your axle in waltz time." There is a certain nostalgic appeal in these words, but mostly they sound crazy, man, *crazy*.

Russ Tamblyn, despite being way too old for the role, hands in a nice performance, and is quite believable as the freckle-faced juvenile delinquent, but it is Mamie Van Doren that steals the show. She's the poor man's Jayne Mansfield, a Marilyn Monroe also-ran, but she is spunky and lights up the screen in her sexy scenes, especially when she takes a large, longing bite out of Tony's apple in the seduction scene.

High School Confidential was banned in several countries upon its initial release — apparently there were some nervous nellies who didn't think Zugsmith went far enough with his anti-drug preaching — but luckily it is available on DVD and video.

"Well, there's just two ways to get outta here: work out and die out."
— BOMBER (EDWARD ELLIS)

I AM A FUGITIVE FROM A CHAIN GANG (1932)

The success of early 1930s prison films such as *The Big House*, *The Criminal Code*, and *Ladies of the Big House* exposed the rough state of affairs of America's prisons. These socially aware movies led to an equally popular, but more hard-hitting subgenre known as chain gang films. The first of these was RKO's *Hell's Highway* in 1932, starring the square-jawed Richard Dix. That same year Warner Brothers jumped on the bandwagon with a high quality melodrama called *I Am a Fugitive from a Chain Gang*.

Based on the real life experiences of Robert E. Burns, the movie starred Paul Muni, hot off the success of the ultra-violent *Scarface: The Shame of the Nation*. He plays James Allen, a returning veteran who dreams of becoming an engineer, but can find employment only in a shoe factory. The day-to-day drudgery of the job bores him, and he soon finds himself unemployed, a drifter who is reduced to unsuccessfully trying to hawk his war medals for money. When he witnesses another man commit a crime, he is mistakenly arrested and sentenced to 10 years on a chain gang. Beaten savagely by a sadistic guard, he vows to escape.

With the aid of a fellow inmate he makes a break, eventually landing a job with a successful construction company in Chicago making $14 a day as an assistant superintendent. His past comes back to haunt him when his needy girlfriend Marie (Glenda Farrell) threatens to expose his shady past unless he marries her. Rather than risk being found out, he enters into a loveless marriage with Marie, who fritters away his hard earned money and cheats on him. His tenuous grip on his carefully constructed new life begins to disintegrate when he meets and falls in love with Helen (Helen Vinson), a beautiful society woman.

The final third of the movie is a depressing medley of blackmail, arrest warrants, and broken promises. An unforgettable last scene between James and Helen is shot in shadows, reportedly because the studio's klieg lights failed just as Muni uttered the film's final and effective line. Director Mervyn LeRoy had the good sense to incorporate the technical difficulty into the film, as it provides an abrupt but unexpected closing image for the story of James Allen.

Paul Muni's acting style owes much to the stage, and while he occasionally dips into a broad theatrical style, his portrayal of a man who has been betrayed by the justice system brims with bewilderment and loathing. LeRoy keeps things moving at a good clip, condensing 10 years of Allen's life into a quick and breezy 92 minutes. He also kept a tight rein on the preachy quality of the material, coating the movie's prison reform politics with a compelling human drama.

The story rings true, in part due to the contribution of Burns, who consulted on the movie while still on the run from Georgia state officials. He smuggled himself into Los Angeles, working on the film before nervously running away after a few weeks. The film didn't win any fans in Georgia. Upset with the representation of their penal system, the state banned the film from theaters, and two wardens from the state prison unsuccessfully tried to sue Warner Brothers for defamation. The rest of the country, however, embraced the film, making it one of the biggest box office successes of the year.

"*Incubus*, ah jes, as we'd say in Esperanto, the language employed in this thot-lost supernatural thriller. How lucky that Vilhelmo Shatner played in it. I attended the 100th anniversary of the creation of the universal language and for 10 tagoj (days) was amongst 7000 personoj (people) from 60 different landoj (countries) and if only they'd had a print of this picture, everyone could have understood it!"
— FORREST J. ACKERMAN,
founder and former editor of *FAMOUS MONSTERS OF FILMLAND*

INCUBUS (1965)
■ ■ ■ ■ ■ ■ ■

On the surface *Incubus* doesn't seem to offer up much to the modern moviegoer. It's 35 years old, in black and white, stars a pre-*Star Trek*

William Shatner, and to boot, it's in Esperanto. Film buffs, however, will tingle at the chance to see this film, once believed to be lost forever.

Incubus was written and directed by Washington, D.C.-born Leslie Stevens, the creator of the science-fiction program *The Outer Limits*. His interest in fantasy extended back to his early childhood. At age 15 Stevens wrote a play about robots titled *The Mechanical Rat*, which he entered in a contest sponsored by Orson Welles' Mercury Theatre. He won, and his prize was the opportunity to meet the Mercury Players. He parlayed that lucky break into a six-month stint on the road with Welles, soaking up knowledge and reinforcing his love of show business. After a stint in the army he returned to the theater, penning several more plays including *Champagne Complex*, which ran on Broadway.

By 1955 he had made inroads in the more lucrative business of writing scripts for television and film. By 1959 he was writing and directing, and looking to expand his repertoire. He created Daystar, Hollywood's first "free-independent" production company (that is, no soundstages or lot), which he named after a line from Shakespeare. He ran his company by keeping in mind the lessons he learned from Orson Welles. "Basically, I'm a writer," he said at the time. "I became a director to protect the writer, and I became a producer to protect both of them, and a company owner to protect them all. The artist is in serious danger in this business."

Apart from *The Outer Limits*, Daystar's output remains obscure. Their first feature film, *Private Property* (1961), was a psycho-pathological thriller starring Warren Oates that has been unavailable since its initial release. *Stoney Burke* (1962-63), a rodeo series with Jack Lord in the lead role, has disappeared without a trace. Their next project, a pilot for a show called *The Unknown*, was scrapped and later re-edited as an episode of *The Outer Limits*. *The Haunted*, another pilot that featured Martin Landau as a psychic investigator, failed to get picked up. Nineteen sixty-two's feature-length *Marriage-Go-Round* met with less than enthusiastic reviews, and can occasionally be seen on late night television.

None of Daystar's productions has created so much speculation as

1965's *Incubus*. Shot after the cancellation of *The Outer Limits*, Stevens admitted that he was "broke and out of it" as production began. Soon after he began writing the script about demonic women who "lure tainted souls into final degradation," he also penned a second version called *Religious Legends of Old Monterey*. The second script was a treatment for a fake documentary, and was used as a diversion to keep any of the town's religious leaders from blowing the whistle that Big Sur Beach and the Mission of San Antonio were being used as locations for a film with a diabolical theme.

Kia (Allyson Ames), a young, beautiful succubus, has grown tired of tempting weak, degenerate souls to the "Gods of Darkness." She wants a challenge. "I'm weary of luring evil, ugly souls into the pit," she complains to her sister. "They'll find their own way down to the sewers of hell."

She chooses Marc (William Shatner), a virtuous young man who lives with his sister Ardnis (Ann Atmar). Marc is an injured soldier who recently saved his comrades from a horrible fate. Kia tells her sister that she will "cut him down, corrupt him, crush him, put my foot on his holy neck, and make him rave and howl and bleed and weep." Marc, of course, has no idea that Kia is evil. He believes his new friend is human, and takes her to a church while she is asleep.

Kia wakes up understandably upset, and runs screaming from the church. She seeks revenge by summoning an incubus (Milos Milos), a young, buff male demon. He avenges Kia's "holy rape" by ravishing Marc's sister, who dies as a result of the attack. The climax of the film is the inevitable showdown between good (Marc) and evil (everyone else).

Stevens wrote the script in English, only to have it later translated into Esperanto. "Esperanto was [Leslie's] new thing," explained associate producer Elaine Michea, "and I desperately tried to talk him into shooting it two ways so he'd at least have something to market. But he's pretty stubborn when he makes up his mind."

Esperanto (translation: One Who Hopes) was first presented in 1887 by Polish oculist Ludwig L. Zamenhof as a universal second language, based on roots of several European languages. Despite opposition from

Hitler, Stalin, and Joseph McCarthy, over 30,000 books have been published in Esperanto. All of the signs in Charlie Chaplin's *The Great Dictator* were printed in the artificial language, a song written in it appeared in *The Road to Singapore*, and more recently the liner notes to Elvis Costello's album *Blood and Chocolate* were in Esperanto.

While the language has never enjoyed wide use, Stevens was taken with the global village conceit, and insisted that the cast of *Incubus* take a weeklong crash course in Esperanto before shooting commenced. Even with the lessons, the actor's pronunciation is pretty awful (don't worry, it's subtitled), but the language adds an otherworldly feel to the film that lends weight to the strange story.

The film was shot in just 10 days, but the cast and crew made the best of the hurried schedule. Cinematographer Conrad L. Hall (winner of Academy Awards for *Butch Cassidy and the Sundance Kid* and *American Beauty*) remembered the Big Sur setting as "a windswept forest of eucalyptus trees with gnarled limbs that looked like monsters looking down at you." He took advantage of the moody landscape, often shooting through, or moving past foliage, adding a depth of feel within the frame.

Another imaginative shot takes place in the Mission. The camera tracks a running man and does a rollover into an upside-down POV, all without a cut. Given the no-budget nature of the film, no expensive equipment was available, so Hall had to improvise to get his vision on the screen. For the upside-down shot he used a handheld camera, placing the cameraman on a blanket and dragging him across the floor. Hollywood is rarely that inventive. Hall's work intrigues, making *Incubus* visually exciting, given that there are no special effects, just tricks with light and smoke.

Upon release the film was greeted with favorable reviews at several film festivals. In 1966 the San Francisco Film Festival program described the scene where the incubus emerges from the earth as "one of the most splendid pieces of horror since the late James Whale conceived the idea of Frankenstein's electronic monster." More raves came from France. "The best fantasy film since *Nosferatu*," said *Paris Match*. But despite good notices, nobody seemed to know what to do with the film. In the days before video, low-budget movies (other than drive-in fare or pornos) didn't have much of a chance against the major studios. Especially a strange horror film in an even stranger language.

The film was placed into storage and forgotten. *Incubus* became known as a cursed film, and not just because of its poor financial showing. "Who knows if there's a curse or not," producer Tony Taylor told *Salon.com*, "but a lot of stuff happened to a lot of people."

Ann Atmar, the former pin-up girl who played Shatner's sister, was the first to fall victim to the film's streak of bad luck. Just weeks after the shooting wrapped, she committed suicide.

Next was the Hollywood Babylon-esque story of the Yugoslavian actor Milos Milos. Less than a year after playing the incubus he murdered his girlfriend, Barbara Ann Thompson Rooney (Mickey Rooney's estranged fifth wife), before taking his own life.

Next came the kidnapping and murder of elder sister succubus Eloise Hardt's daughter. Taken from her driveway, her body was discovered weeks later decomposing in the Hollywood hills.

While those were the sensational stories that set tongues wagging about the *Incubus* curse, there were more strange occurrences that suggested a hex, or just bad luck.

At the film's premiere at the San Francisco Film Festival the print arrived sans sound. A last minute version had to be found, keeping the audience waiting for over an hour. Guests included Roman Polanski and his date Sharon Tate, who would later be the most famous victim of the most talked about killings of the 1960s — the Manson family murders. Later, due to the failure of the film in theaters, Stevens lost his company, Daystar. Perhaps the most bizarre manifestation of the evil eye was the story of music editor Dominic Frontiere, who was arrested and did prison time for scalping thousands of Super Bowl tickets.

But for film fans there is a happy ending to this story. In 1993 producer Tony Taylor decided to take *Incubus* out of storage for a possible release on video. He was told that the print had disappeared during its

20-odd years in limbo. He sued and was awarded a large settlement, but really just wanted his film back. In 1996 a print surfaced at the Cinémathèque Française in Paris. It turned out that the film had been screening there regularly for the past 30 years.

Taylor had a copy of the print made, and now for the first time since its initial release, *Incubus* is available on video and DVD. While the print isn't perfect (French subtitles are simply covered by black bands containing an English translation), it is back where it belongs — in front of an audience.

"What is the law?"
— From the Sayer of the Law scene, *ISLAND OF LOST SOULS*

ISLAND OF LOST SOULS (1933)
- - - - - - - - - - - - - -

One of the most compelling horror films ever made, 1933's *Island of Lost Souls* features memorable performances, a perfect villain, and great makeup effects, and was the inspiration for a classic new wave song in the 1970s.

Paramount Studios brought this project together in 1932, under the direction of a former Mack Sennett comedian named Erle C. Kenton. Born in Montana in 1896, Kenton first made his mark in films appearing in pre-Hayes Code fare such as *A Bath House Blunder*, *The Surf Girl*, and *His Speedy Finish*. Throughout his career he was a jack-of-all-trades, performing, writing, and directing in everything from two-reel comedies to feature films, most notably Abbott and Costello's *Pardon My Sarong* and *Who Done It?*. *Island of Lost Souls* was his first and best attempt at horror, although he later revisited the genre with *House of Dracula* and *House of Frankenstein*.

With a few small additions, the screenplay is a faithful adaptation of the H.G. Wells' novel *The Island of Dr. Moreau*, a book deemed so horrifying that it was banned in some countries, including parts of the United States. Charles Laughton plays Dr. Moreau, described in the book as "a benign-looking doctor who lives and works on his own private South Seas Island." The doctor's creepy world and strange experiments are discovered by Edward Parker (Richard Arlen), a traveler lost at sea who is picked up by a ship heading for the uncharted island.

At first Moreau is an accommodating host and offers Parker a shuttle back to the mainland the next day. The doctor even offers up some "feminine" companionship for his visitor in the form of Lota (Kathleen Burke), a panther-woman. You see, Moreau is playing God on his island, creating a race of half-human, half-animal creatures. Parker's arrival allows the evil doctor to fulfill his plan — to couple Parker and Lota and produce the world's first human/animal child. The matchmaking falls flat when Parker notices that Lota has claws rather than fingers. Spurned, Lota cries on Moreau's shoulder. Far from being sympathetic, Moreau takes delight in her pain, impressed that his experiment has such emotional depth.

Later, Parker investigates the island and discovers the building where Moreau performs his cruel work, The House of Pain, and a band of rebels (look for Buster Crabbe, Alan Ladd, and Randolph Scott under heavy makeup) led by Bela Lugosi, in a brief but memorable performance. The film's final moments are chilling.

There are several elements that put this film on par with the horror films Universal was producing around the same time. The Universal movies — *Frankenstein*, *The Mummy*, and later, *The Wolf Man* — have become classics of atmospheric horror and favorite Halloween rentals at the video store. *Island of Lost Souls* deserves to be placed alongside these films for several reasons.

First, the performances. Charles Laughton, fresh from shooting *The Old Dark Horse*, delivers the perfect villain in Dr. Moreau. Elegant and evil, Laughton shows us a man with a God complex who is ultimately destroyed by his self-loathing. Laughton says he based his portrayal on an oculist, and "has not been able to visit the zoo since."

The role of Lota the Panther Lady is the emotional core of the film; like the Frankenstein creature, she is a character that inspires pity rather than fear. Lota's character does not appear in Wells' book. Screenwriters Waldemar Young (*The Unholy Three*) and Philip Wylie (*When Worlds Collide*) added her to pump up the sex appeal of the film and add a dash of romance. Kathleen Burke won the role after Paramount staged a publicity-grabbing, nationwide "Panther Woman of America" contest. Burke acquits herself well, and parlayed this performance into a career that included 21 movies over the next five years.

Bela Lugosi (covered only with a wig and beard) provides the real horror and the film's scariest scene. He plays The Sayer of the Law and in the film's most famous sequence lays down the "manimal" law — Not to run on all fours, not to eat meat, not to spill blood — followed by the question, "Are we not men?" It is a chilling scene, wonderfully shot by Karl Struss.

The scene made a big impression on musician Mark Mothersbaugh. Four decades after its release, *Island of Lost Souls* became the source for the line "Are we not men?" made famous by Devo in 1978's "Jocko Homo." "Fucking amazing movie," said Mothersbaugh.

The idea for the song had occurred to Mothersbaugh several years before, after watching the late, late show on television. "I had a little handheld tape recorder that I would use to tape off my little black-and-white 11-inch TV," he said. "We didn't have video recorders in 1972, so in my apartment, I would tape the soundtracks to movies I liked. *Island of Lost Souls* was one that just kind of hit at the right time."

The climax of the movie has a beautifully rendered scene as the sub-humans run through the jungle, casting eerie shadows on the House of Pain. "They don't want to go to the House of Pain," continued Mothersbaugh, "which is [Laughton's] laboratory where he is doing these experiments that are not working out quite they way he was hoping they would. When the shadows went by, I just remember going 'Holy shit,' because it reminded me of the factories in downtown Akron, just a couple of blocks from where I lived. The old factories that were built during the Industrial Revolution. I just remember thinking, 'I know these people.' I watched all the shadows go by. 'I live here. I live on the *Island of Lost Souls*. I work at the House of Pain.' That was obviously the chorus and the rallying theme behind the song." "Jocko Homo" was never released as a single, but nevertheless remains one of Devo's best-known tunes.

Island of Lost Souls is a classic example of 1930s' horror, and despite its showy performances and lack of a background musical score, for sheer thrills it far surpasses the two subsequent attempts at remaking the story.

"The epic story that was destined to stand as a colossus of adventure!"
– Advertising tagline for *JASON AND THE ARGONAUTS*

JASON AND THE ARGONAUTS (1963)

Stop-motion master Ray Harryhausen created unique worlds and monsters on film one frame at a time. His work on film, inspired by seeing *King Kong* at the young age of 13, was honed by making stop-motion training films for the navy in World War II before creating Dynamation, a process that combined live action with live-action backgrounds.

His first feature, *The Beast from 20,000 Fathoms*, led to work on a series of eye-popping films based on Greek and Arabic myths that would redefine movie magic. The best known of these, 1958's *The 7th Voyage of Sinbad*, was a box-office hit, leading to a series of sci-fi films like *The 3 Worlds of Gulliver* and *Mysterious Island*. In 1963 he returned to mythology, creating his greatest film, *Jason and the Argonauts*. In 1992 actor Tom Hanks gave tribute to Harryhausen, saying, "some say *Citizen Kane* is the greatest movie of all time, others say its *Casablanca*, for me, the great picture of all time is *Jason and the Argonauts*." It's easy to see why the film would have captured Hanks's imagination, as it is a near-perfect blend of storytelling mixed with Bernard Herrmann's rousing score, manly-men Argonauts, and (for the time) mind-blowing special effects.

The story centers on Jason and his efforts to regain his kingdom by traveling on a death-defying expedition to acquire the Golden Fleece. He gathers the greatest heroes of all time, including Hercules, and sets out on a ship with the assistance of the gods. On the way they encounter a seven-headed Hydra; Titan Talos, a giant bronze statue come-to-life; and the evil winged Harpies.

The Hydra provides the film's greatest sequence, when Jason must battle the skeleton soldiers that grow from her teeth. It's a jaw-dropping scene that brings the film to an exciting climax. In the original myth the skeletons were the rotted corpses of the Hydra's victims, but the filmmakers decided that would be too gruesome an image for their film. Instead Harryhausen choreographed the live-action actors swinging the weapons at imaginary adversaries, and later, using his Dynamation technique, spent four-and-a-half months adding in seven sword-wielding skeletons. "The dueling scene in *Jason* with the skeletons had to be very carefully laid out," he told *Animation World* in 2000, "because the touching of the swords and all that had to be perfectly synchronized or it wouldn't be convincing."

Harryhausen went on to make films until 1981 — including *One Million Years BC* (1966), starring the genetically blessed Rachel Welch, a special effect all her own — when his stop-motion technique fell out of vogue. In his golden years the animation maestro found a second career when modern filmmakers paid tribute to him by casting him as an extra in films like *Beverly Hills Cop III*, *Spies Like Us*, and *Mighty Joe Young*. In 1992 Harryhausen's gifts to the art of special effects were rewarded with an honorary Oscar.

THE KID STAYS IN THE PICTURE (2002)

Robert Evans is the last of a dying breed. The kind of Hollywood mogul who calls women "broads" and hands out his phone number with the caveat "I'm only seven digits away, baby." In other words, a real character. "Robert Evans is a Zelig-like figure of the latter half of the 20th century," says director Brett Morgen. "He has dated some of the most glamorous women of the last 50 years, from Ava Gardner and Lana Turner to Kathleen Turner — you name them. His best friends over the past 50 years have been Jack Nicholson, Warren Beatty, Al Pacino, and Henry Kissinger. He has written speeches for four presidents. There is no iconic figure that has lived over the past 50 years who Evans does not have an incredible story about — and it's not just 'I met them at a party.' Beyond that he is responsible for bringing to the screen some of the greatest films made in the last 30 years."

Evans' life is the subject of a documentary directed by Brett Morgan and Nanette Burstein, based on his autobiography. It's a stirring tale. "There are three sides to every story. My side, your side, and the truth," he says in the film. "And no one is lying. Memories shared serve each one differently." He tells of how he was offered his first movie role by actress Norma Shearer because she liked the way he looked in a bathing suit as he lounged by the pool at the Beverly Hills Hotel. How he rose from B-actor status to become head of production for Paramount Pictures, putting films like *The Godfather*, *Love Story*, and *Chinatown* into production. He led a fairy-tale life — married to a movie star, living in a Beverly Hills mansion, hanging out with Jack Nicholson — until bit by bit his Hollywood dream turned into a nightmare.

His films started losing money; he was kicked off his beloved Paramount's lot; his wife left him for Steve McQueen; and he started using drugs. His high-rolling life unraveled and it seemed he'd never eat lunch in Hollywood again. But to paraphrase the title, the kid stayed in the picture, and has lived to tell the tale. Evans narrates the film without a hint of self-consciousness, and entertainingly mimics everyone from Ali MacGraw to Roman Polanski. It's an absorbing look at a complicated, resilient man.

> MIKE: Oh Shit! This is bizarre, it's like, uh . . .
> DEBBIE: A circus tent.
> MIKE: What's a circus tent doing all the way out here,
> a real lousy place for a show . . .
> — dialogue from *KILLER KLOWNS FROM OUTER SPACE*

KILLER KLOWNS FROM OUTER SPACE (1988)

Clowns are creepy. Their grotesque shiny red lips, baggy suits, and weirdly colored tufts of hair really disturb some people. While most of us see Ronald McDonald as a nice corporate symbol, the 8% of the population that suffers from clownophobia (more properly called coulrophobia) view him as evil incarnate. The mere mention of the Insane Clown Posse — a mix of bad gangsta rap and grease paint — is enough to inspire nightmares in the clown challenged (and most music critics too, actually). Silent-screen horror legend Lon Chaney Sr. tried to explain the fear. "A clown is funny in the circus ring," he said, "but what would be the reaction to opening a door at midnight and finding the same clown standing there?"

There is a history of disturbing clowns haunting the movies. Among the stand-outs in the sub-sub-subgenre of "clown horror" are Tim Curry as Pennywise the Dancing Clown in *Stephen King's It*, and *The Clown At Midnight*, wherein a number of attractive youngsters get hacked to death by a psycho in a Bozo costume. But the coolest clowns to terrify audiences didn't come from the circus — they came from outer space!

Fans of '50s horror will recognize the opening moments of *Killer Klowns from Outer Space* as a tribute to *The Blob*. Both movies begin with a young couple at the local make-out point spotting a shooting star and deciding to follow it. It is soon discovered that it wasn't a shooting star, but something much worse, something that the teenagers decide they must investigate. Here the two movies part ways.

Our lovebirds, Mike Tobacco (Grant Cramer) and Debbie Stone (Suzanne Snyder), discover their shooting star is actually an intergalactic circus tent filled with murderous mirth-makers. These Killer Klowns have come to the tiny town of Crescent Cove armed with circus-inspired weaponry — killer balloon animals, perilous puppet shows, and popcorn guns — to wreak havoc. Officer Mooney (John Vernon) believes the reports of homicidal clowns wrapping people in cotton candy cocoons are a prank and refuses to investigate. Meanwhile it is up to Mike and Debbie, armed with an ice cream truck, to save the town and their friends.

Killer Klowns from Outer Space will definitely scare the hell out of coulrophobics. The alien Klowns are beautifully realized creations, reminiscent of the outrageous puppets from the British television satire *Spitting Image*. Beneath large painted-on grins are rows of yellowed sharp teeth, topped off with beady jaundiced eyes, oversized ears, and wildly colored hair. Every feature is madly exaggerated until you have a living caricature of a clown — something funny, but weird and scary at the same time.

That feeling is the film's greatest asset. The creative minds behind *Killer Klowns*, the Chiodo brothers — Charles, Edward, and Stephen — manage to strike a balance between camp and seriousness by playing it straight. The situation is bizarre and some of the dialogue is downright cheesy, but the actors never wink at the camera. Hamming it up would have made *Killer Klowns* just another jokey sci-fi take-off, a self-conscious look at a genre that is easy to poke fun at.

So when Grant Cramer as Mike says, "They're not clowns, they're some sort of animal from another world that look just like clowns. Maybe their ancients came to our planet centuries ago and our idea of clowns just comes from them," he plays it straight, and his intensity makes the line funnier than it reads on the page.

The real scene-stealer here, the only human actor that can hold his own against the Klowns, is John Vernon. Trained at London's Royal Academy of Dramatic Arts, Vernon has had a varied career working with some of the greatest directors in Hollywood — Alfred Hitchcock, George Cukor, and John Boorman — but is probably best remembered as Dean Wormer in 1978's *Animal House*. How he ended up in this low-budget cult film is anyone's guess; I'm just glad he's here. His Officer Moody is a treat, and his deadpan delivery creates some of the film's best lines.

B-movie composer John Massari supplies a great score, but it is the Dickies performing the title track that really kicks butt. It's a great slice of mid-'80s punk rock from a band best known for songs like "I'm Stuck in a Pagoda (With Tricia Toyota)" and "Where Did His Eye Go?"

There aren't many scary moments in *Killer Klowns*, although a scene involving a little girl and a Klown with a mallet is pretty intense. The film's mood is more light-hearted, and keeps the nudity and gore down to a minimum. Director Charles Chiodo keeps the pace up, and at an economical 88 minutes, *Killer Klowns* leaves you wanting more.

The Chiodo brothers never made another feature film, although they have supplied the special effects for everything from *Critters* to the Power Rangers movies.

Italian painters Alfredo Cifarello and Nando Bernardini in *Annigoni: Portrait of an Artist*. "I thought it was incredible that nobody had ever made a film on this painter," says director Stephen Peter Smith.

Annigoni: Portrait of an Artist Director of Photography Duilio Ringressi and Director Peter Smith on location in Rome.

"Once you hear the story you can't get it out of your mind," says *Atanarjuat: The Fast Runner* producer Norman Cohn. (PHOTOS COURTESY KATRINA SOUKUP)

Wrestler New Jack and *Beyond the Mat* director Barry W. Blaustein: "It's hard to get funding for a documentary in the States. You can get a government grant if your film is about black lung disease among coal miners in West Virginia, but not for a movie about wrestling." (PHOTO COURTESY BARRY W. BLAUSTEIN)

Elvis (Bruce Campbell) and JFK (Ossie Davis) in *Bubba Ho-Tep*. "It was the weirdest script I had ever read," says Campbell. (PHOTO COURTESY STARWAY INTERNATIONAL)

Elvis (Bruce Campbell) and his boys in *Bubba Ho-Tep*. (PHOTO COURTESY STARWAY INTERNATIONAL)

The author and *Biggie and Tupac* director Nick Broomfield. "I think documentaries are about entertainment . . . but I don't think that means they can't be about something at the same time." (PHOTO COURTESY *REEL TO REAL*)

Carnival of Souls star Candace Hilligoss only made one more film after this one, a 1964 chiller called *Curse of the Living Corpse*. (ILLUSTRATION COURTESY THE CRITERION COLLECTION)

Cyberman's Steve Mann. Think of Mann as the bastard child of Bill Gates and Inspector Gadget. (PHOTO COURTESY CBC'S *NATURE OF THINGS* AND PETER LYNCH)

Movie fact: *Dementia 13* features the first decapitation by ax on the silver screen. (PHOTO COURTESY TROMA ENTERTAINMENT)

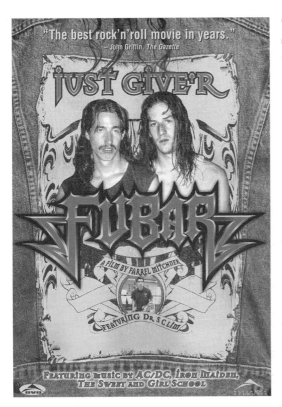

"We're not making fun of bangers," says *Fubar* director Michael Dowse. (PHOTO COURTESY ODEON FILMS)

Ginger Snaps director John Fawcett and actress Katharine Isabelle. "Ginger is an exaggeration of my bad side," says Isabelle. (PHOTO COURTESY 49TH PARALLEL)

Great Rock 'N' Roll Swindle director Julien Temple. "We saw Sid [Vicious] as the first monster child of the hippie generation. . . ."

"There are three sides to every story," says Robert Evans in *The Kid Stays in the Picture*, seen here on the set of *The Sun Also Rises* in 1957, "My side, your side, and the truth."

Stephen, Edward, and Charles Chiodo and the Killer Klowns. Scientific fact: Eight percent of the population suffers from coulrophobia, or a morbid fear of clowns. (PHOTO COURTESY THE CHIODO BROTHERS)

Connor Widdows, seen here as Will in *Mile Zero*, made his big screen debut in *A Feeling Called Glory* in 1999. His bit part character was listed in the credits as "Little Shirtless Boy." (PHOTO COURTESY ANAGRAM PICTURES)

The Minus Man director Hampton Fancher wrote the screenplay for 1982's sci-fi classic *Blade Runner*.

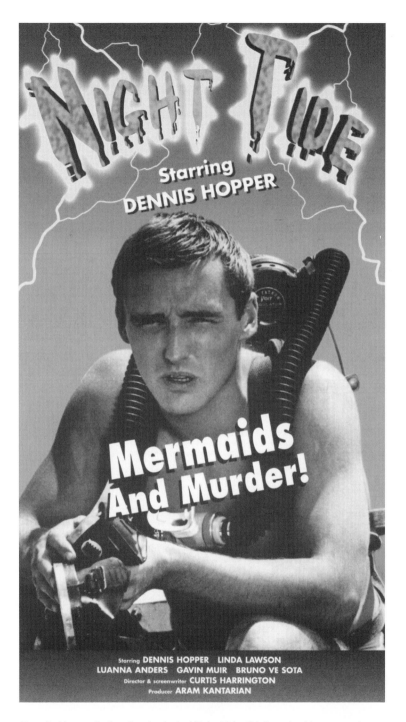

Starring
DENNIS HOPPER

**Mermaids
And Murder!**

Starring **DENNIS HOPPER   LINDA LAWSON
LUANNA ANDERS   GAVIN MUIR   BRUNO VE SOTA**
Director & screenwriter **CURTIS HARRINGTON**
Producer **ARAM KANTARIAN**

Dennis Hopper's first lead role in *Night Tide* didn't make him a star, but it did make *Time*'s Ten Best of the Year list in 1961. (PHOTO COURTESY RHINO HOME VIDEO)

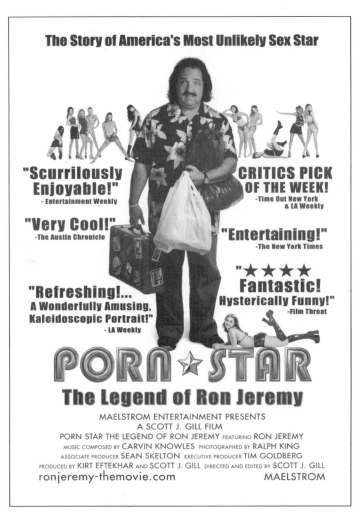

Theatrical poster for *Porn Star: The Legend of Ron Jeremy*. "Porn's the purest form of acting," says Jeremy. (PHOTO COURTESY MAELSTROM ENTERTAINMENT)

Ron Jeremy and the author (PHOTO COURTESY *REEL TO REAL*)

"Except for the Disneys, there is very little in film houses during the season that kids can recognize and call their own," said *Santa Claus Conquers the Martians* producer Paul Jacobson.

Troma Films co-founder and president Lloyd Kaufman. "We're the jalapeno peppers on the cultural pizza." (PHOTO COURTESY TROMA ENTERTAINMENT)

"*The Toxic Avenger* is the only movie in the history of cinema where a kid's head is crushed under the wheel of an automobile to be made into a children's environmentally correct Saturday morning cartoon show," says Lloyd Kaufman. "That's pretty cool." (PHOTO COURTESY TROMA ENTERTAINMENT)

Actors Clé Bennett and Carter Hayden mock their prisoner in *Treed Murray*. Actors Kevin Duhaney and Jessica Greco are in the background. (PHOTO BY L. PIEF WEYMAN, COURTESY BILL PHILLIPS)

Actor David Hewlitt is stuck in a tree in *Treed Murray*. "Putting a man up a tree turned out to be quite difficult," says director Bill Phillips. (PHOTO BY L. PIEF WEYMAN, COURTESY BILL PHILLIPS)

"What is interesting about the twist is that it became a metaphor for everything of the period," says *Twist* director Ron Mann. (PHOTO COURTESY SPHINX PRODUCTIONS)

The Twist director Ron Mann.
(PHOTO COURTESY SPHINX PRODUCTIONS)

> "It is so difficult to make a neat job of killing people
> with whom one is not on friendly terms."
> — LOUIS MAZZINI (DENNIS PRICE)

KIND HEARTS AND CORONETS (1949)

Alec Guinness is probably best known in North America as Jedi knight Obi-Wan Kenobi, a role he regarded with contempt. He reportedly thought George Lucas's script was nonsense and claimed that Obi-Wan's death was his own idea as a way to get out of his contract. "What I didn't tell him was that I just couldn't go on speaking those bloody awful, banal lines," said Guinness. "I'd had enough of the mumbo jumbo." As beloved as that character may have been, it was just one role in a long and distinguished career that dates back to the years immediately following the Second World War. Despite his first acting couch's opinion that "You'll never make much of an actor, Mr. Guinness," he began making films in 1946. Acclaimed performances in two Charles Dickens' adaptations, *Great Expectations* (1946) and *Oliver Twist* (1948), led to a string of comedies made for the now legendary Ealing Studios. The first of these was *Kind Hearts and Coronets*, an acerbic farce that made him a star. Years before Eddie Murphy or Mike Myers would take on multiple roles in films, Guinness played an astounding eight (count 'em, eight) roles, including a woman.

The movie opens with Louis Mazzini (Dennis Price) in prison penning his memoirs. He's an elegant, well-dressed fellow, who tells his story through a series of flashbacks. Born to the disowned daughter of a duke and a destitute Italian singer, Louis is raised in poverty. When he is denied permission to bury his mother in the ancestral vault, he vows revenge on the well-bred family who turned their backs on him and his mother. Once they are gone he'll be able to take his rightful place as the next Duke. One by one he offs members of the d'Ascoynes kin — the

Duke, the Banker, The Parson, the General, the Admiral, Young d'Ascoynes, Young Henry, and Lady Agatha — all of whom bear an uncanny resemblance to, you guessed it, Alec Guinness.

When not plotting revenge, Louis is pursuing a complicated love life. On one hand there's Sibella (Joan Greenwood), a childhood love who spurned him to enter a loveless marriage with a wealthy man; on the other, Edith (Valerie Hobson), the widow of one of his victims, and his true love. A twist at the end is unexpected and hilarious.

Even though the story is told in flashback — usually the kiss of death for any narrative — the movie flies along at a gallop. Slick, witty dialogue cuts through the heavy English accents and is buoyed by fine performances all round. As the vengeful cool-as-a-cucumber heir, Dennis Price brings charm, wit, and elegance to his role. Similarly the two women in his life, Greenwood and Hobson (the latter of whom would later marry British Secretary of State for War John Profumo and become embroiled in the call-girl scandal that led to his resignation), hand in lively quintessentially English comedic performances.

It is, however, Guinness in the flashy multi-role routine that brings the house down. While easily recognizable in each part, he doesn't repeat himself from character to character, carefully constructing each d'Ascoynes from the happy-go-lucky young photographer to the window-smashing suffragette Lady Agatha. Even though some are only on screen for a few minutes, he inhabits each persona, including subtle mannerisms that add up to fully rounded portrayals. It is an acting tour de force — comedic or otherwise. Guinness stayed with Ealing until 1951, making two more comedy classics, *The Lavender Hill Mob* and *The Man in the White Suit*, before branching out to an international film career. He later won a Best Actor Oscar and Golden Globe for his performance in *Bridge Over the River Kwai* and earned a reputation as one of Britain's best actors of all time.

THE KRAYS (1990)

A mother's love is a beautiful thing. Someone to love you unconditionally. Someone to tell your secrets to. Someone who'll make you tea and biscuits after a hard night of terrorizing London and extorting honest businessmen out of their hard-earned money.

Yes, a mother's love is a beautiful thing, especially if you are the Kray boys, identical twin brothers who ruled London's East End in the 1960s. *The Krays*, a film by Peter Medak, may be a one of a kind: the only Oedipal gangster movie ever made.

Based on the book *The Profession of Violence* by noted English criminologist John Pearson, *The Krays* tells the story of Ronald (Gary Kemp) and Reggie (Martin Kemp), twin brothers bonded by a fierce devotion to their mother Violet (Billie Whitelaw) and an even more ferocious predilection for violence and control.

In England's swinging '60s the siblings owned a number of nightclubs in London's East End. They were café society types, palling around with celebrities and posing for photographs with the elite. Several scenes of the 1963 British film *Sparrows Can't Sing* were shot at one of their clubs, and director Peter Medak, an assistant director on that film, remembers the immaculately dressed brothers hosting an elaborate wrap party for the cast and crew.

When not climbing the social ladder they were cutting a swath of a different sort through the streets of London. Using their favorite weapon, a sword, they maintained their underground empire with bloodletting and violence. To paraphrase Willie Nelson, the nightlife ain't no good life, but it was their life.

The contradiction of the Kray brothers lies in their lives after the nightclubs rang last call. The twins would return home to their modest, semi-detached East End home, hang up their Savile Row suits, and wish Violet, their Cockney mother, sweet dreams. This dichotomy lies at the heart of *The Krays* — the violent killers as mama's boys. Although the brothers had romantic interests — Ronnie with men, Reggie with women — their mother was their great love. Violet doted on her sons, making them afternoon tea while they plotted their reign of terror. As the maternal Kray she became something of a celebrity herself, enjoying royal treatment — born out of the fear of her sons — wherever she went.

While Violet enjoyed the spillover notoriety of her sons, not all the people in their lives were as lucky. Ronnie's life was filled with a string of good-looking but disposable young men. Reggie's love life had more devastating effects on the object of his affections. Following a long courtship, he married Frances Dawson, who cracked under the pressure of marriage to the viciously controlling gangster. Initially attracted to Reggie's power and glamour, she soon realized that she had given up her life. In despair, she attempted suicide before finally descending into madness.

The Krays is propped up by several great performances. Billie Whitelaw shines as Violet Kray. Onscreen, she's a dynamo. As the mother who affectionately refers to her sons as her "little monsters," Whitelaw builds a character of strength whose only weakness is the unconditional love of her sons. Tom Bell and Steven Berkoff are suitably venal as rival mobsters, while Kate Hardie lends Frances a heartfelt sensitivity that is particularly touching.

"I see things in your eyes," Frances tells Reggie.

"What things?" he asks.

"Monsters," she replies, with a mix of fear and wonder.

Gary and Martin Kemp, the leaders of the foppish Spandau Ballet pop group, are the movie's real revelation. They're not twins, but convincingly pass as mirror images with an almost psychic bond. What could have been stunt casting — hiring two pop star brothers who bear an uncanny resemblance to one another — pays off for director Medak. They embody the glamorous Krays, looking smart in their high-priced suits and spit-polished shoes, but the performance is more than window dressing. They convincingly portray an air of cold-blooded evil, especially apparent in the boxing scene where they beat one another senseless, snarling and grinning all the while. In another scene Ronnie, the more violent of the two, carves a smile in a rival's face. Gary Kemp is particularly effective as the psychopathic Ronnie, the instigator of the hard-core violence, although it is Martin who has gone on to huge success on the small screen in Britain, playing Steve Owen on *East Enders*.

The Krays is sketchy at times, glossing over details of the twins' lives, but more than makes up for its plot deficiencies in atmosphere and style. It's the rare kind of gangster film that doesn't dwell on violence, instead choosing to examine the reasons behind the violence. Buoyed by good performances and the folkloric appeal of the real life Ronnie and Reggie, *The Krays* is one of the most original crime dramas in years.

ADRIENNE: Do you fall in love with all of your clients?
MARLOWE: Only the ones in skirts.
— Dialogue from **LADY IN THE LAKE**

LADY IN THE LAKE (1946)
— — — — — — — — — — — —

Gumshoe Philip Marlowe, Raymond Chandler's most famous literary creation, has been played by a variety of hard-boiled actors. Dick Powell first introduced moviegoers to the character in 1944's *Murder, My Lovely* (a.k.a. *Farewell, My Lovely*, the book's title). The movie was a hit and led to a series of Marlowe films. Humphrey Bogart put his indelible stamp on the role in 1946's classic whodunnit *The Big Sleep*, but that didn't stop George Montgomery, James Garner, Elliot Gould, and Robert

Mitchum from donning Marlowe's distinctive overcoat and busting heads on the mean streets of Chandler's Los Angeles.

Perhaps the most original take on the sleuth came in 1946 with actor/writer/director Robert Montgomery's *Lady in the Lake*. Based on a 1943 novel, the labyrinthine plot involves the disappearance of the wife of a magazine publisher (Leon Ames). It is assumed that she has run off to Mexico, and Marlowe is hired to track her down. Seems simple enough, but when bodies start piling up the plot thickens. The story is typical Chandler, populated with tough-talking dames, hard-edged police detectives, and Marlowe's unconventional methods.

What distinguishes *Lady in the Lake* from other Marlowe films is the use of the subjective camera. Director Montgomery (who also plays Marlowe) shot everything from the detective's point of view. *Everything*. The only time the viewer actually gets a glimpse of Marlowe is the odd time he passes by a mirror. This technique leads to some wildly inventive moments, such as the scene where a severely beaten Marlowe crawls from a phone booth. We see the world from his point of view, on his hands and knees. Other shots aren't as successful: each time Marlowe lights a cigarette smoke swirls around the camera lens, obscuring the image.

The rhythm of the film takes a few minutes to get used to because of the structure of the film. Scenes are played out in long, uninterrupted takes, with the characters directly addressing the camera. This method flies in the face of the conventional wisdom that calls for rapid editing in thrillers and gives the movie a wonky tempo, but as the scenes play out the unusual first-person POV technique becomes less noticeable and adds to the intrigue of the film. Strong dialogue (most likely cribbed directly from Chandler's book) propels the action, while a bizarre musical score adds to the experimental feel of the movie.

Chandler was not overly impressed with this film, and refused to have his name included in the credits. "Old stuff," he said dismissively. "'Let's make the camera a character'; it's been said at every lunch table in Hollywood at one time or another." After the box office failure of *Lady in the Lake* Robert Montgomery never again directed for a major studio, although he went on to have a successful acting career and to direct a handful of films in the next dozen years. *Lady in the Lake* stalled in the theaters, but remains a brave attempt to redefine the film noir genre.

"There is a pattern emerging. I must keep track of every second."
— **ALEXANDER LUZHIN (JOHN TURTURRO)**

THE LUZHIN DEFENCE (2000)

Despite his stature in the world of letters, less than half of Vladimir Nabokov's novels have been adapted for the screen. Only eight works have made their way to the movie house, although his most famous book, the controversial *Lolita*, has been filmed twice. *The Luzhin Defence* is based on *The Defence*, a novella literary critic Martin Amis called "the nearest thing to pure sensual pleasure that prose can offer."

Set in 1929 the film tells the story of Alexander Luzhin (John Turturro), an awkward, introverted chess Grand Master who travels to a Northern Italian lakeside resort to participate in a world championship match. People from all over the world have congregated here, including the Russian debutante Natalia (Emily Watson) and her aristocratic mother Vera (Geraldine James). Vera has brought her daughter to the tournament to meet a suitable husband. She has her eye on the perfect candidate, Comte Jean de Stassard (Christopher Thompson), a gifted chess amateur.

Natalia is aware of her mother's motives, but isn't attracted to Stassard. Instead she falls for the unconventional genius of Luzhin and his erratic behavior. The feeling is mutual, and after only one meeting he proposes. "I want you to be my wife," he says, "I implore you to agree." Disobeying her mother she begins a whirlwind romance with the man she describes as the most "fascinating, enigmatic, and attractive man" she has ever met.

As Luzhin's world with Natalia is flourishing, another person arrives who will make any newfound happiness in his life shrivel. Valentinov (Stuart Wilson) is Luzhin's childhood schoolteacher, a corrupt and vicious man who exploited his student's talent while at the same time resenting his protégé's genius. He guided Luzhin's chess career for a decade until it seemed that he had lost his touch. Valentinov then abandoned his client in Budapest, taking on a fresher talent. Now that Luzhin has made it to the Grand Championship, Valentinov has resurfaced.

It seems that everyone save for Natalia is conspiring to keep Luzhin from finding happiness. The evil Valentinov turns up the pressure on Luzhin, hoping to shatter his delicate grasp on sanity, while Vera tries to undermine his new relationship. Even the film's setting, which was the site of one of his childhood matches, seems to stoke his internal trauma. His first true love, chess, the only thing he truly understands, now threatens to destroy him and his chance at happiness.

The Luzhin Defence is a costume drama that uses chess as a metaphor. From a marketing point of view, this is a lethal combination that spelled certain box office death. While the film fared poorly financially, it is rich in artistic merit. Director Marleen Gorris (best known for directing the Academy Award-winning film *Antonia's Line*) skillfully mounts the story in two distinct pieces. We see Luzhin in the present and, through well-timed flashbacks, we also learn how the events of his life shaped him. These flashbacks provide crucial information. "Luzhin is a very hard character," says Turturro, "although the flashbacks help to show from where he has developed. As a listless, apathetic boy he couldn't connect with his parents, but once he got his chess pieces it was love at first sight and he found a way out."

The success of *The Luzhin Defence* depends on the believability of the characters, particularly Luzhin and the ability of the audience to get inside of the head of the troubled genius. Gorris and her cast sell the unusual premise and give the love story a ring of truth.

The film is driven by the performance of John Turturro. He portrays Luzhin as a child-like being, almost incapable of dealing with the world around him. Luzhin is tortured by past demons, but is not without humor. Turturro finds a balance between pathos and comedy and, in doing so, finds the humanity of his character. Like other angst-ridden-genius movies like *Shine* and *A Beautiful Mind*, the central character, fuel the film and, as they descend into their own personal hell, they must be compelling enough to take the viewer along for the ride. Turturro gives a powerhouse performance that is part Groucho Marx, part Bobby Fischer.

Turturro looked to the original source material to help him build his character. "The book is about the inside of his mind," he said. "It's more of a chess game, less dramatic, but there were some useful ideas for me in there since it's a very well drawn character." He also studied the game of chess. "I'm now at a beginner's stage and it's a great game, but so complex. I think the fact that I have had experiences other than acting has helped me. Certainly directing and editing a film ensures that you deal with a number of processes at the same time, putting all the pieces together to make this big breathing body. Chess Grand Masters know so many games and they can see so many moves ahead that when you play as a novice you realize how limited you are, unable to think in such a free, conceptual way."

Emily Watson has the thankless job of playing against the showier Turturro role. She holds her own, giving an emotional depth to Natalia, a woman who is beguiled by Luzhin's manic lust for life. "It was a departure for me in that I'm the one watching somebody having a nervous breakdown," says Watson. "It's a very sane, centered, amused, and healthy character, which is unusual for me to play."

The Luzhin Defence is a thoughtful, old-fashioned movie that relies on the emotional punch of the story to provide the fireworks.

"Who knows what it's like to be me? How I'm forced to act . . . how I must, must . . . don't want to, must! Don't want to, but must! And then a voice screams! I can't bear to hear it! I can't go on! I can't . . . I can't . . ."

– HANS BECKERT (PETER LORRE)

M (1931)
■ ■ ■ ■

This is a film of firsts. It was legendary German director Fritz Lang's first experiment with sound, Peter Lorre's debut as a lead actor, and is credited with being the original serial killer/police procedural committed to celluloid.

Set in 1931 Berlin, this melodrama chronicles a police department's efforts to capture a mysterious child murderer. Frustrated in their attempts, they begin to round up every criminal in town. "There are more cops on the streets than girls," says one disgusted pimp. Tired of being rousted, Berlin's underworld characters decide to find the killer themselves. They succeed where the police have failed, rounding up the baby-faced killer Hans Beckert (Peter Lorre), putting him on trial for his life in their own kangaroo court. He breaks under the pressure, screaming that he is unable to manage his homicidal tendencies. "Ghosts pursue me — ghosts of mothers, ghosts of daughters . . . I can't help myself," he cries in a dramatic speech. "I haven't any control over this evil thing that's inside me. The fire. The voices. The torment." Before a verdict can be reached, the police raid the impromptu trial, rescuing Beckert from certain death, so he may seek justice under more "respectable" circumstances.

M was originally titled *Murderer Among Us*, but was changed when members of the Nazi party objected, assuming it was a critique of their heavy-handed politics. At the center of the film is a career-making performance from Peter Lorre as the gnome-like killer who lures children with candy and companionship. He is invisible for most of the film, hidden in shadows, but when we do see him the effect is chilling. Often his ghostly presence is signaled by his eerie whistling of *Peer Gynt* (Lang did the whistle as Lorre never learned how), a tune that becomes a musical motif for the murders.

The role made him a star in Europe, paving the way to Hollywood, where he fled to avoid Germany's growing Nazi threat in the 1930s. An unauthorized picture of Lorre from the movie would later be co-opted by the Nazi's as an example of the "typical Jew" on the posters for their anti-Semitic propaganda film *The Eternal Jew*.

Lang (who would also leave Germany in 1934) uses creative cinema language to frame the murders. In the first 10 minutes of the film he sets up the horror of the situation without showing any violence, instead using clever editing and the implication of terror to build a feeling of dread. When Beckert abducts his first victim, we see a young girl named Elsie bouncing a ball against a kiosk with a "Wanted" poster plastered to its side. He approaches the girl, buying her a balloon. Lang cuts to her mother, sitting at a table set for two. As she calls out for her daughter to come inside she is greeted with silence. Cut to Elsie's ball on the sidewalk and the balloon trapped in some utility wires. The scene is spare — there's virtually no dialogue — but it packs an emotional hit. Elsie is gone without a trace, and Lang creates terror without resorting to graphic violence or bloodshed.

Lang has stated that *M* is his most fully realized film. In fact, when Lang plays himself in the 1963 Jean-Luc Goddard film *Contempt*, there is a scene where Brigitte Bardot's character Camille remarks that her favorite film of his was *Rancho Notorious*. "I prefer *M*," he says. It's easy to see why; it is a commanding masterpiece of style and suspense.

MAD MONSTER PARTY (1967)
■ — ■ — ■ — ■ — ■ — ■ — ■

This is a feature-length "Animagic" stop-action jewel from Rankin/Bass, the people best known for creating the Christmas claymation perennial *Rudolph the Red-Nosed Reindeer*. Featuring monster stop-motion figures designed by *Mad Magazine* artist Jack Davis (who cut his teeth drawing the EC horror comics of the '50s) and voice work by Boris Karloff, *Mad Monster Party* is a gothic gas. Designed to cash in on the late '60s monster-mania, *Mad Monster Party* took its lead from *The Addams Family* and *The Munsters*, mixing slapstick with classic bad guys. It's an irresistible blend, but despite the popularity of monster movies, TV shows, and the Aurora Model kits, it didn't do well on its theatrical release. It later won a cult audience when it started appearing on Saturday afternoon "Creature Feature" television shows.

Here's the story: With his life's work behind him — the development of a secret formula capable of destroying all matter — Baron Boris Von Frankenstein (Karloff) decides to hang up his test tubes. He invites all the world's great monsters — Frankenstein's monster and his Bride, the Werewolf, Dracula, the Invisible Man, and a Peter Lorre-esque character called Yetch — to join him for a farewell dinner. Also on the guest list is the Baron's bumbling nephew Felix Flankin, a human whom the Baron names as his successor to run the Worldwide Organization of Monsters. This doesn't sit well with the creepy conventioneers who scheme to do away with Felix.

Along the way there are plenty of swinging jazz tunes (written by Maury Lewis and Jules Bass), a Beatle-wig-wearing skeleton rock-and-roll-band called Little Tibia & the Phibbeans, and some cool special effects. Best of all, *Mad Monster Party* is utterly devoid of the sentimental morality that weighed down the Rankin/Bass Christmas specials — this bristles with good fun and bad puns.

It's clear this film left an impression on a generation of filmmakers. Jim Henson's "Count" puppet for *Sesame Street* bears an uncanny resemblance to Davis's Dracula, and I'd bet Tim Burton referenced an old *Mad Monster Party* print more than once when he was making *The Nightmare Before Christmas*.

"I would like to take advantage of my little time left to tell you a story . . ."
— **The FISH in the opening scene of** *MAELSTRÖM*

MAELSTRÖM (2001)

You know you're in for a long strange trip when the narrator of the film you're watching is a fish being scaled and butchered in a fish market. It's a surreal touch from director Denis Villeneuve in a stylish French-Canadian movie about how life can take an unexpected turn and kick you in the ass. "*Maelström* is about extremes," says the Quebec-based director. "You have very dramatic moments with humor, and you have ultra-realistic moments with fantasy."

The main character in *Maelström* is Bibiane Champagne (Marie-Josee Croze), a beautiful, 25-year-old Montreal woman whose life is unraveling. Early in the film she has an abortion, followed by a brush-off from the man responsible. In response she hits the nightclubs. Numbed by drugs and alcohol, she accidentally hits a man with her car, and panicked, leaves him lying on the road as she flees the scene. The next day she returns to the scene of the crime, only to discover the man died.

Racked with guilt, she tries to commit suicide by driving her car into a river. Emerging alive, metaphorically baptized in the water, she stares destiny in the face and tries to come to grips with her chaotic life.

Maelström is a dark movie that explores the mysterious nature of fate and how seemingly unrelated events add up to form a whole. Bibiane is leading an accelerated life where one bad relationship leads to abortion, a drinking binge, and the death of an innocent person. While the film has a surrealistic feel, every tragic event in the movie is realistic and could actually happen. Bibiane is a victim of her own bad judgment, and not a particularly sympathetic character, but she isn't a monster. She is, like so many people, a person who refuses to acknowledge her shortcomings and mistakes. It's a nervy move to build a movie around a character like this, and an even harder job to cast it.

"Marie-Josée is very talented," says Villeneuve, "and this was a very, very difficult role for her to do because she doesn't have a lot of tools. Very often [the character] is alone, and the emotion has to come when she is alone and doing nothing. When she is with others she is trapped and doesn't communicate."

Croze is marvelous to watch onscreen. Since her feature film debut in 1993, she has worked extensively in both English and French, in Quebec-shot Hollywood fare like *Battlefield Earth*. Her Bibiane is totally believable, a multi-layered character that is both fragile and confused, but resilient. Her greatest feat is to make Bibiane likeable, and by the end of her rebirth to actually have the audience root for her. As she sorts out the mess she has made of her life, finding love and meaning along the way, Croze imbues Bibiane with a humanity that is hard to deny.

Villeneuve pieces the story together with aplomb. The abortion scene that opens the film is meant to grab the audience, and let them know they are not on safe ground. This is a movie that takes chances, one that keeps you off balance as it untangles Bibiane's anguish. The abortion is controversial, but absolutely necessary to the film's fabric.

"The abortion scene is the most important scene in the film," says Villeneuve. "I think it is the most important scene I have ever shot. You always make a film in reaction to the film you made before, and *August*

23rd on Earth was not raw enough, not close enough to life. I wanted to add authenticity, according to my point of view. I didn't want the abortion to be disgusting, but I also didn't want it to be safe. I tried to find the right emotional impact that I think abortion is about. There is a relationship that I see between abortion and responsibility."

Villeneuve pumps up the impact of the scene with music. As the doctors perform the cold, antiseptic procedure, the song "Good Morning, Starshine" from the peace and love musical *Hair* chirps cheerfully on the soundtrack, at stark odds with the pictures on the screen. It's an ironic choice that displays how life in the outside world will always continue despite whatever angst is playing out in your personal life.

"I like songs that are not in sync with the images," says Villeneuve. "When there is a gap between the mood of the song and the mood of the scene it creates an emotional response, a tension, and a poetry that I think is more creative than just underlining the emotion."

The abortion sequence might be shocking, but the tragicomic talking fish that narrate the tale are a memorable image that won't soon be forgotten. Sitting atop a bloody butcher block, a series of fish are about to meet their doom under the fishmonger's cleaver. Before they are filleted they try to articulate the movie's existential undercurrent of destiny and fate. In gruff voices they give us insight into the action onscreen.

"When I decided to write a movie in which several fish would tell the story I was expecting a lot of questions about that," says Villeneuve. "It came from a nightmare, and I respect that a lot. In cinema I like a dream quality. Sometimes you might have a strong subconscious response, but sometimes you have difficulty explaining them. I'm not expecting people to get it. For me the fish is about my relationship with cinema. It's about the relationship with storytelling. I like the idea that those fish are close to death, but still trying to tell a story. For me it is like the storytellers from different backgrounds from the beginning of humanity who try and tell the same story, and then stop dead. Then someone else has to continue.

"It was a big casting when you make a little fish," he continues, "because it is going to come alive with the voice. I had to find a very specific voice. Pierre Lebeau is an actor at home [Quebec] that has this beautiful voice and can bring humanity to this plastic fish."

Maelström is an intelligent, disturbing movie that is bound to spark thought about the vagaries of everyday life, and how one selfish or ill-conceived action can directly affect the lives of many people — simple cause and effect. It is a playfully cautionary story that advises the viewer to be careful and responsible.

> "You have to believe it to see it."
> — Advertising tag line for *THE MAN WHO FELL TO EARTH*

THE MAN WHO FELL TO EARTH (1976)

Someone much smarter than me once said that there are only two types of stories. In the first a person goes on a journey. In the second, a stranger comes to town. *The Man Who Fell to Earth*, a spacey 1976 Nicolas Roeg thriller combines both premises with a science-fiction twist. David Bowie, in his feature film debut, plays a visitor from the planet Anthea who comes to earth in search of water.

As a cinematographer, Nicolas Roeg lent his expert visual style to the films of Clive Donner, David Lean, Richard Lester, and Francois Truffaut. His resumé as a director begins with a surreal 1970 movie that examined the nature of identity. *Performance* starred James Fox as Chas Devlin, a gangster on the run who moves in with Turner, a reclusive, androgynous rock star played by Mick Jagger. At first Devlin is disgusted by Turner's excessive existence, but soon their strange lifestyles become intertwined. Devlin spirals downward into Turner's world of drug-induced decadence, and his refuge becomes a hell as his own sense of reality starts to disappear.

Performance baffled critics, who objected to the graphic violence, sex, and drug taking, with one critic asserting that it was "the outcome of an over-developed visual sense and an under-developed moral one." Battles with censor boards in Europe and North America delayed the film's release for two years, and killed its chances of finding an audience. This commercial flop was followed by two critically acclaimed, but financially unrewarding films, *Walkabout* and *Don't Look Now*.

In the early development stages of his fourth film, an adaptation of the Walter Tevis novel *The Man Who Fell to Earth*, Roeg had considered Mick Jagger for the role of Mr. Newton, the alien, but decided that he was "too strong, too positive." "I want somebody who looks as if he has no bones in his body," he said. One night he happened to catch a BBC documentary featuring David Bowie called *Cracked Actor*. "Watching that film," Roeg told writer Jerry Hopkins, "he was my film's character, Mr. Newton. My reaction was, 'That's him alright, all wrapped up and done.'" Roeg was attracted to Bowie's otherworldly appearance, saying that he "exudes such a wonderfully perverse non-human quality." Like Jagger before him, Bowie had been cast to play a part that was molded to create echoes of his existing public persona.

From his end, Bowie admired *Don't Look Now* and was excited to work with Roeg, although he forgot about their initial February 1975 meeting, and kept the director waiting for eight hours. The movie's story was familiar ground to Bowie, who had created the musical outer-space character Ziggy Stardust in 1972. "Ziggy really set the pattern for my future work," Bowie said. "Ziggy was my Martian messiah who twanged a guitar. He was a simplistic character. I saw him as very sim-ple . . . fairly like the character Newton I do in [*The Man Who Fell to Earth*] later on. Someone who's dropped down here, got brought down to our way of thinking, and ended up destroying his own self."

The Man Who Fell to Earth begins at the end of the visitor's long journey, as his space vehicle enters the Earth's atmosphere. We follow the vehicle's strange visitor as he assumes the identity of Thomas Jerome Newton, a British expatriate, and pawns gold rings brought from his planet to finance a trip to New York. In the Big Apple he hires patent attorney Oliver Farnsworth (Buck Henry) to form a company to sell his inventions, which are actually products from his home planet. They create a wildly successful communications company and generate millions of dollars, which Newton plans to use to launch his own space program for the dual purposes of returning to his family and saving Anthea by bringing back water. On his Bill Gates-like journey he meets Nathan Bryce, a lecherous college professor, and begins an affair with Mary-Lou (Candy Clark), a drunken motel maid. Suspicion grows in tandem with his sudden rise to prominence. Betrayed by friends, his extraterrestrial origins are uncovered. An enigmatic government agency kidnaps him and carries out a battery of tests to ascertain who, or what, he is. Newton's space program is dismantled, and he is cut loose. Alone and frustrated, with no means to return home, he turns to drink.

Capturing *The Man Who Fell to Earth* on film presented some unusual challenges for the rock star. The three-month shoot, mostly on-location in New Mexico, was an exhausting affair, with Bowie having to rise at 4 a.m. to attend a five-hour makeup call each day. The long shoot did have one upside, however — the remoteness of the location cut Bowie off from his usual drug dealers, and by the end of the shoot he was almost free of the debilitating drug habit that had plagued him in recent years.

One peculiar story from the production log begs for an explanation, although it seems not to be drug related. While shooting on an old Aztec burial ground, something inexplicable happened. Bowie was drinking a glass of milk on set when he noticed "some gold liquid swimming around in shiny swirls inside the glass." Production had to be shut down for the next two days when the actor fell ill. After running tests, doctors could not determine any cause for the ailment, even though six witnesses testified that they had seen a foreign substance in the bottom of the glass. Powerless to explain the story, Bowie chalked up the entire experience to "very bad Karma."

The Man Who Fell to Earth isn't a typical science-fiction film. Roeg doesn't rely on special effects to dazzle; he doesn't have to, he already has David Bowie. As Newton, Bowie is an organic special effect — otherworldly, androgynous, and mysterious. But it is the unspoken emotion, the heart and soul of his character that shines through in his performance. In the book Newton has no fingernails, has a waist that measures only five inches and is over six feet tall. No amount of makeup could perfectly reproduce that effect, but Bowie's physicality is ideal; he's pallid, gaunt, with a bone structure that is reminiscent of the popular, large-eyed image of aliens. Trying to imagine anyone else in the role is like trying to nail Jell-O to a wall. It just can't be done.

If you want action, rent *Independence Day* or *The Terminator*, but if you like idea-based sci-fi check out Newton's story. *The Man Who Fell to Earth* is a parable showing the clash between decadent Western culture and Newton's simple, innocent alien life, and how he ends up losing his purity of heart. This was a particularly potent message in the mid-'70s, hot on the heels of Vietnam and at the beginning of globalization. Newton's Icarus story is a warning — fly too close to the sun, and you'll fall to Earth in flames.

Don't worry if you feel ashamed
It's been around for years
And thousands more that can't be named
Are interested in rears
Don't worry about hell
No harm will come to your soul
We're not a Pentecostal
And everybody's got an asshole
Sodomy!
— The "Sodomy" song from *MEET THE FEEBLES*

MEET THE FEEBLES (1989)

"It's a nasty little piece of work, and people should know that," says Kiwi director Peter Jackson about one of his early "lost" films. Originally conceived as a 24-minute television show, *Meet the Feebles* is the most disgusting, ribald, and funniest film to feature puppets as lead actors. It's the *Muppet Show* on acid. The movie revolves around the puppet cast of the soon-to-air *The Fabulous Feebles Variety Hour*. Cheerful characters on television, off-screen the Feebles are drug addled, sex-starved psychopaths. Backstage drama flourishes as Sid the elephant tries to avoid a paternity suit from his ex-lover, a chicken named Sandy; Harry, a sex-crazed rabbit, feels woozy and is concerned that he has contracted AIDS after years of unprotected sex; the uncouth producer of the show *Walrus Bletch* is involved in drug deals, while his partner Sebastian the fox becomes completely obsessed with buggery, going so far as to include a song called "Sodomy" in the show; Wynyard the frog knife thrower is a full-blown heroin addict who has frequent flashbacks to his days as a POW in Saigon; Trevor the rat dresses in a Nazi uniform and films underground porn; while Heidi the hippo, the show's star attraction, is told, "I've heard better singing from a mongoose with throat cancer." The tension backstage spills onto the air, and the show's audience finally sees the Feebles for who they are.

It's pretty dark stuff, and Jackson leaps at the chance to offend, including as much carnage, sex, and bawdy humor as 94 minutes will allow. The finished film is so unhinged that the major investor, the New Zealand Film Commission, refused to put its name in the credits. The movie is a disgustingly graphic piece of work, but there is more to it than just cows engaging in S&M, if you can dig past the layers of bodily fluids, unnatural sex, and curse words.

"I'd like to view it as a satire of human behavior," said Jackson. "Imagine a scenario where the Muppets have just finished a TV show. What would happen if they went backstage and behaved like normal people, smoking, drinking, and having sex? That's what we were aiming at." It is also a cautionary tale of the pitfalls of celebrity, or as Russ Meyer once put it, "the oft-times nightmarish world of show business."

Ten years before Jackson would begin shooting his masterpiece, the *Lord of the Rings* trilogy, his visual flair was very much in evidence. He uses handheld cameras to shoot musical numbers and very hectic scenes, perfectly choreographing the 90 rubber-faced "actors."

The "story" is basically a series of fart, urine, and porn jokes strung together, but like any great musical, the songs are the glue that bind the whole thing. Composer Peter Dasent, who would also score Jackson's next two films, *Braindead* and *Heavenly Creatures*, penned a full score for the movie, including the "Feebles Theme," which includes the obvious line, "we're not your average ordinary people," Heidi's signature song "Garden of Love" and "One Leg Missing," a blues tune sung by a Rastafarian bandleader with a chorus of poodles. The real showstopper is "Sodomy," an elaborate set piece involving a giant erect penis that literally serves as the climax of the film.

The movie has become a cult classic, but don't expect a sequel. A disclaimer that no puppets were killed or maimed during the production of *Meet the Feebles* turns out to be a fib, as Jackson cheekily noted in a press interview at the time. "The way we abused them I doubt whether they would want to work with us again."

MILE ZERO (2002)

Mile Zero is a film about male vulnerability. Michael Riley (the London, Ontario-born actor best known for small roles in *Amistad* and *French Kiss*) plays Derek Ridley, a psychologically brittle man who lets jealousy devour him, eventually pushing him to break the law. He is still deeply in love with his ex-wife (Sabrina Grdevich) despite the fact that she has moved on and is involved with another man. Unable to let go, he desperately tries to reunite his family with a series of inappropriate actions that soon escalate into the realm of stalking. He unexpectedly shows up at his wife's home to prepare her breakfast in bed, roots through her garage, and secretly installs video surveillance in his eight-year-old son Will's (Connor Widdows) bedroom.

When all else fails he convinces the boy to go on a bizarre father-and-son "adventure" into the wilderness of British Columbia, on the promise that the trip will help reunite the family. The deeper into the utopian backwoods they travel, the darker the story becomes. Derek slowly descends into madness, behaving recklessly, endangering himself, his son, and those around them. Will soon figures out that what he thought was a family outing is turning into a life-threatening situation. His confidence in Derek shattered, Will's reticence to accept his father's love forces Derek to face the truth about his own failures and the meltdown of his marriage. It's a family drama about a family gone wrong.

As the deluded dad, Riley delivers a powerhouse performance, at once both pathetic and scary. Widdows also excels as Will, a young boy caught between the love of his father and the realization that the man he idolizes is seriously disturbed. Will is wise beyond his years, and Widdows strikes the perfect tone, never becoming precocious. He is simply a kid with good observational skills, who is nonetheless vulnerable to the manipulations of his parent.

Mile Zero is strong material, crafted by a director who understands Derek's plight. "The reason I made the film is because I am a single parent," director Andrew Curry told the *Georgia Straight* in 2001. "Some years ago, when I got separated, I sometimes wasn't seeing my son for four or five weeks at a time. His mum started a new relationship, which is normal and healthy and everything, but because I was so far away, it encouraged me to feel a lot of, um, irrational things about what was going on. The film is an expression of my fears, what I imagined. The idea of being replaced by another man is terrifying to anyone. I don't want to overplay what I went through. I was working at the time with Michael Melski, who had already written a short screenplay for me called *Fragile X* about a man who's just too fragile for this world."

I could have used a little less of the home movie flashback scenes, but they did reinforce the sense of loss Derek was experiencing after his wife kicked him out of the house. It's heart-rending stuff, and while you can't condone Derek's actions, Riley makes him human enough that the viewer can at least understand his behavior.

"Some people die in less than a minute, others it takes 10. I guess it's what they call metabolic. If it wasn't closed I'd go to the library and get clear on this."
— VANN SIEGERT (OWEN WILSON)

THE MINUS MAN (1999)
— — — — — — — — — —

"He was such a polite guy." "He seemed like such a nice quiet young man." That's what Vann Siegert's neighbors would say about him. That's what the neighbors of serial killers always say after the police have taken away the suspect in chains. Vann Siegert is a mass murderer, and *The Minus Man* is a study of a broken psyche.

Hampton Fancher is best known as the screenwriter of the 1982 science-fiction classic *Blade Runner*, but the native Los Angelian had already had a long and bizarre career before that movie was released. He quit school as a teen and moved to Spain, where he became a well-known flamenco dancer under the name Mario Montejo. Upon returning to the States he worked as an actor, playing everything from a zombie in the 1958 cult-horror flick *The Brain Eaters* to Adoptive Parent #3 in the 1974 TV weeper *The Stranger Who Looks Like Me*. Tired of being offered less-than-stellar roles, he turned to writing, penning *Blade Runner* and the Denzel Washington film *The Mighty Quinn*. The inspiration for his next script would come while reading a book review.

Fancher was first exposed to author Lew McCreary's book *The Minus Man* by novelist Anne Rice's review of it in the *New York Times*. He thought the book sounded interesting and clipped the column. He carried it around with him for years, until one day he stumbled across a copy of the out-of-print novel in a used bookstore.

"I read it that night," he says, "which is unusual because I'm generally not a fast reader, but this book was a page-turner. I was so fascinated that I couldn't stop until the sun was up and the book was on the floor. I realized in the morning that this story encapsulated a theme that had always interested me — the idea of a person who is essentially very good but who does things that are very bad. I'd always wanted to do a movie about this concept."

The finished script was a darkly comic exploration into the mind of an unconventional serial killer — a likeable guy who is also a terrible threat to those around him.

The film begins with Vann Siegert (Owen Wilson) offering a ride to an inebriated young woman (Sheryl Crow) he has just met in a tavern. At a rest stop he discovers her in the bathroom shooting up. He's not shocked by the drug use, and offers the woman a drink from his flask.

Next we see him propping her dead body against the bathroom wall, making it look like she overdosed. Is he a guy who just doesn't want to get involved in the death of someone he just met, or is there something in that flask besides amaretto?

Vann stops in a rural Pacific Northwest coastal town looking for a place to live. He rents a room from an older couple, Doug (Brian Cox) and Jane (Mercedes Ruehl), whose marriage is falling apart after the disappearance of their daughter. Jane is wary of Vann and wants Doug to keep his distance from the lodger. "Don't make a boarder your guest," she warns. Of course he doesn't listen, and the two men become as tight as two peas in a pod.

With Doug's recommendation Vann gets a job at the local post office and begins to date a fellow worker, Ferrin (Janeane Garofalo). Ferrin is a free-spirited young woman who Garofalo describes as a "townie who lives in this suburb and doesn't really have many aspirations beyond the confines of the post office." Despite her best efforts, Ferrin can't penetrate Vann's wall of secrecy.

Outwardly Vann appears to be the model citizen, but internal forces are eating away at him. Most nights he is visited by imaginary hard-boiled detectives Blair (Dwight Yoakam) and Graves (Dennis Haysbert) — his nightmare morality police — who carry on surreal conversations with him. "Blair and Graves are the basement of Vann Siegert's mind," Fancher explains, "the nightmares within. There is nothing really cruel or twisted in this movie — except these two characters. They are detectives but they are also devils and angels."

When the locals start to mysteriously disappear, suspicions arise.

The Minus Man is a look at what lies just beneath the surface of normality. Fancher — who wrote and directed the film — has created a striking character in Vann. He's the serial killer next door; a man so painfully normal it is almost inconceivable that he could ever have a nasty thought, let alone kill. Owen Wilson is effective because he is disarming, and his matter-of-factness about his murderous urges is chilling. "I never make a plan," he says. "It just happens." His easy grin and all-American-guy demeanor reveal very little about him. Almost everyone likes him because he tells people what they want to hear. He's a seductive charmer with a dangerous hidden edge.

"I think Vann is someone who through really listening to people can become whatever they want him to be," says Fancher. "He is the perfect confidante, the perfect reflection, the perfect love. But meanwhile he actually has this blankness inside of him. He is nothing; the man who fell to earth. Vann is so pure and kind, like a child, not murky or diluted or filled with ambiguities. You feel you can look right into him, and yet he is a stranger."

The supporting roles are nicely cast. Brian Cox was an ironic choice to play the disturbed Doug in a movie about a mass murderer; trivia buffs will remember Cox as the original Dr. Hannibal Lector in the 1986 film *Manhunter*. Cox lends heft to the picture with his portrayal of Doug as an odd, tortured man. Janeane Garofalo as Ferrin is stretching her acting wings here in a different kind of role. She nails Ferrin's naiveté in romance, letting her body language and mannerisms do the talking in a nicely understated performance.

Fancher has made a strikingly original film that defies the usual conventions of the genre. It is a serial killer movie with virtually no violence. The killer is a likeable guy, and is never revealed to be a monster. There aren't even any Hitcockian-type thrills and chills, just a probing camera and a cerebral approach. This is *Blue Velvet* without the ether, a smart serial killer movie that explores the mind, not the actions of a murderer. *The Minus Man* will leave you feeling unsettled as you slowly get into the head of a man you never thought you'd know.

MONSOON WEDDING (2001)

In *Monsoon Wedding*, director Mira Nair expertly knits together a joyous, sprawling story about a wedding, an affair, and a lovesick wedding planner. Nair aims her camera at life in modern day India, but still holds onto many of the traditions of Bollywood filmmaking. "Bollywood is very interesting," Nair told *Reel to Real* in 2001. "When I was growing up there was a slight snobbery about the high kitsch quality of it. No longer. Now Bollywood stuff is refined, slick, trendy, and hip. For the young Indian person it is the way to go. *Monsoon Wedding* is my tongue-in-cheek tribute. My family has been begging me to make Marsala Bollywood movies, and I will maybe one day, but this is sort of Bollywood on my terms, because it is all so surrealistic, but based in reality, and that allows me the fun and the high kitsch and the absolute reality of the sex appeal of the fantastic Bollywood films."

Monsoon Wedding is full of life — interesting characters, bright swirling colors, fabulous Indian music — and like one of Nair's previous efforts, the Oscar-nominated *Salaam Bombay*, is universal enough to break through the cultural marketplace and become a mainstream North American hit. "India is an extraordinary culture because we are truly about layering," said Nair. "It is a multiplicity of worlds; it is a nation of coexistence between the rich and the poor. That we know. But there are also all kinds of influences that we are open to, especially in today's modern India, which is *Monsoon Wedding*'s India. It has gone global and we have Gucci and Prada on the one hand, and traffic jams and power cuts on the other. That is just a very small part of the craziness of our existence. *Monsoon Wedding* attempts to show you that layering, in a very layered way itself, cinematically, with language, and with music and with the camera. That was my intention from the beginning."

Monsoon Wedding won numerous awards upon its release, including the Golden Lion at the Venice Film Festival and the People's Choice Award at the Toronto Film Festival, and was nominated for Best Foreign Language Film at the 2002 Golden Globe Awards.

Richard's Favorite Titles with Ten Words or More

1. *Dr. Strangelove, Or How I Learned to Stop Worrying and Love the Bomb* Stanley Kubrick's 1964 masterpiece featured Peter Sellers in three roles.

2. *The Incredibly Strange Creatures Who Stopped Living and Became Mixed Up Zombies* This 1963 horror musical was originally called *The Incredibly Strange Creatures Who Stopped Living or How I Became a Mixed Up Zombie*, but was changed after a threatened lawsuit over the similarity of Kubrick's title.

3. *Oh Dad, Poor Dad, Mom's Hung You in the Closet and I'm Feeling So Sad* This 1967 Rosalind Russell film was a precursor to *Weekend at Bernie's*.

4. *The Persecution and Assassination of Jean-Paul Marat as Performed by the Inmates of the Asylum of Charenton Under the Direction of the Marquis de Sade* Based on a successful stage play, this 1966 film is better known by its shortened title *Marat/Sade*.

5. *Those Magnificent Men in Their Flying Machines: Or, How I Flew from London to Paris in 25 Hours and 11 Minutes* Rivalries abound when a British newspaper sponsors a cross-channel airplane race in this 1965 adventure.

6. *Cafeteria, or How Are You Going to Keep Her Down on the Farm After She's Seen Paris Twice* A 1973 one-minute movie about a girl and her 26 cows.

7. *The Saga of the Viking Women and Their Voyage to the Waters of the Great Sea Serpent* A 1957 Roger Corman action/adventure about lonely Viking women who embark on a search for their missing men.

8. *I Killed My Lesbian Wife, Hung Her on a Meat Hook, and Now I Have a Three-Picture Deal at Disney* This 1993 short film was Ben Affleck's directorial debut.

9. *Went To Coney Island On A Mission From God . . . Be Back By Five* A 1998 feature which starred former child star Jon Cryer.

10. *Can Hieronymus Merkin Ever Forget Mercy Humppe and Find True Happiness?* Sixties heartthrob Anthony Newley searches for the meaning of life in this 1969 musical.

"Sensual ecstasy becomes supernatural terror!"
— Advertising tagline for *NIGHT TIDE*

NIGHT TIDE (1961)

In October 2002 I asked Dennis Hopper to tell me what scared him the most. I expected the man who played Frank Booth in *Blue Velvet*, one of the screen's creepiest characters, to give me a deep psychological answer. Instead he said simply, "Being out of work." This was coming from a man who is a Hollywood legend, having appeared in classics such as 1955's *Rebel Without a Cause*, 1969's *Easy Rider*, and 1979's *Apocalypse Now*, and continues to have a career as one of the screen's leading bad guys. Hopper is one of those Hollywood stories of great talent colliding head-on with a self-destructive streak a mile wide. His well-known drug habit earned him a reputation of being difficult, and even got him blacklisted in Hollywood for eight years. Despite his career ups and downs Hopper has made well over 100 movies, garnering two Academy Award nominations (for *Easy Rider* and *Hoosiers*) and winning a trophy case full of awards from international film festivals. He made his first film in 1954, but it wasn't until 1961 that he earned his first lead role.

In *Night Tide* (based on the Edgar Allen Poe poem *Annabel Lee*) he plays Johnny Drake, a charming young sailor who falls in love with Mora (Linda Lawson), a beautiful and mysterious woman who portrays a mermaid in a Santa Monica sideshow. As their love affair develops, Johnny learns more about her past — how she was found on a deserted island and became a sideshow attraction. Then he discovers some unnerving news. Two of Mora's previous boyfriends had disappeared, only to be found much later washed up on shore. The deaths were investigated, but no hard evidence was uncovered against Mora. Johnny is suspicious but blinded by love. When Mora tells him that "the seawater is in my veins, the tide pulls at my heart," he begins to believe the rumors that the mermaid routine is not just an act, that she is descended from man-killing sirens who customarily murder during the cycle of the full moon.

Think of *Night Tide* as a sinister version of *Splash* without the laughs or the happy ending. While it wasn't a box office success upon its release, it did collect considerable critical acclaim, even making *Time*'s Ten Best of the Year list, mostly because of director Curtis Harrington's moody handling of the material and Hopper's restrained, natural performance. In hindsight it's interesting to see a freshly scrubbed Hopper playing a nice guy after all the years he has spent playing psychos and drug-addled characters, but his performance goes beyond a mere novelty. Even though this is a genre picture with an unreal premise, Hopper plays it straight, and his enthusiasm feels very real. In one scene his gusto gets the best of him as he jumps for joy, balancing himself on a rail. It is a wonderful unforced moment that displays the childlike glee of his character. The story, strange though it may be, can't be described as a horror movie — there are no monsters or blood — but rather a psychological study that has more to do with *The Twilight Zone* than *The Creature from the Black Lagoon*. Long after the rubber-suited monsters from other films of that era have become camp nostalgia, *Night Tide* remains a seriously suspenseful story with lots of entertainment value.

"Is there anything you can do doctor, I mean, seeing as how you've lost over 200 million patients?"
– LISA (ROSALIND CASH) in *THE OMEGA MAN*

THE OMEGA MAN (1971)

Today I think of Charlton Heston as a gun totin' just-right-of-Attila-the-Hun caricature of the God-fearing super-patriot. But believe it or not, there was a time before he made it his crusade to put a gun in the hands of every man, woman, and child in the U.S. when he made movies. Some pretty good ones too. Perhaps you remember a little thing called *The Ten Commandments*. Or *Ben Hur*. Maybe *A Touch of Evil*. How about *The Agony and the Ecstasy*? In all he made over 120 movies, but there are three mid-career films that stand out from the pack.

In the late '60s and early '70s Heston made a trio of science-fiction movies in which he traded his period costumes, chariots, and religious epics for thoughtful, stirring, futuristic drama. The sci-fi trifecta begins with 1968's *Planet of the Apes*, continues with *The Omega Man*, and finishes with *Soylent Green*, a bizarre eco-cannibalism story. What sets these movies apart from modern science-fiction, or what passes for sci-fi on film, is that they are about ideas, not special effects and bombast.

My pick of the litter, 1971's *The Omega Man*, combines science-fiction, dark comedy, horror, and even a little blaxploitation. The source material, Richard Matheson's novella *I Am Legend*, is a page-turner about a man left alone in a world of vampires. Matheson was inspired to write the story after taking in a matinee of *Dracula* starring Bela Lugosi. "It occurred to me that if one vampire was frightening," he said, "then a whole world of vampires *really* would be frightening."

There have been two film adaptations of *I Am Legend*, both of which take substantial liberties with the original text. *The Last Man on Earth* (1964) sees a badly miscast Vincent Price as the eponymous hero, and disappointingly, changes the novella's ending, weakening the climax of the film. There are some genuinely creepy moments in the show, and the depiction of the zombie-like creatures seems to have been a template for George Romero's *Night of the Living Dead* movies, but this film pales in comparison to the 1971 retelling, *The Omega Man*.

In this film Charlton Heston plays Dr. Robert Neville, one of the few to survive an apocalyptic war fought with biological weapons. As a military scientist he was working on an antidote when the End came. By injecting himself with the only existing sample of the vaccine he was able to survive the bio-holocaust. The chemical combat may be over, but he is still at war. He has a new fight, a battle against a few hundred deformed, nocturnal people called The Family. They too survived the plague brought on by the chemical warfare, but just barely. Family members are sensitive to light, wear long black robes, and have an unquenchable thirst for blood.

Led by former newscaster Matthias (Anthony Zerbe), The Family hates Neville because he represents an old way of life, a life ruled by science and technology, the very things that brought about the apocalyptic war that turned them into blood-crazed zombies. Neville uses all his "old world" devices — electricity, machinery, and science — to ward off their attacks. Along the way he discovers that he is not the only person to outlive the chemical attacks.

The Omega Man has the feel of a really elaborate *Twilight Zone* episode; both novella writer Richard Matheson and director Boris Sagal (father of *Married With Children*'s Katey Sagal) were veterans of the television series. The only thing missing is the tight-jawed Rod Serling popping up to welcome us to another dimension at the beginning of the movie.

Like the television show, *The Omega Man* is thoughtfully crafted (even if it is a little ham-fisted at times) and, like the best *Twilight Zone* episodes, it bursts with social comment, in this case on racism and the dangers of irresponsible scientific research. There is even an interracial romance between Heston and Lisa (Rosalind Cash), a rare sight today on television and in movies, but even scarcer in 1971.

Sagal was a prolific director of episodic television who would occasionally take over the reigns on an Elvis movie or low-budget thriller when he wasn't making a mini-series or calling the shots on the sets of *Columbo* or *Ironside*. Like many of the creative types involved with the film, he wasn't an innovator, just a dependable craftsman. That might explain why *The Omega Man* doesn't have the visual flair of some of its innovative contemporaries like *A Clockwork Orange* or *The Andromeda Strain*.

While Sagal keeps up a vigorous pace, probably learned from directing hundreds of hours of network television, the action scenes are tepid. While they are not awful, they have a run-of-the-mill *Starsky and Hutch* quality. It's also fairly obvious that Heston didn't do his own stunts — check out his motorcycle driving stunt double, who doesn't look a thing like him. (Hey, if he is supposed to be the last man on Earth, who's driving the bike?)

Lackadaisical action scenes aside, it is bad dialogue that will usually sink a movie like this, and while there is some truly dreadful writing here, particularly in the scenes of Heston alone in his apartment, at least he seems to have a sense of humor about it. No actor wants to wander aimlessly around onscreen talking to himself, but as the last man on Earth (or so he thinks) he doesn't have much choice. Even for Heston, who was no stranger to over-the-top histrionics, it must have been difficult to deliver monologues to a bust of Caesar. "Hi, another day, another dollar. Miserable schmuck! Shut up! Why the hell can't you leave me alone?" he says to the statue. "What day is it anyway? Monday? Huh? The hell it is. It's Sunday. Sunday I always dress for dinner . . ." I'm not even sure Laurence Olivier could deliver those lines convincingly.

Heston has better luck later on when he meets Lisa. The back and forth between them has the makings of a camp classic. In one scene he tosses her a machine gun to ward off The Family. "What's this for?" she asks. "Comfort," he gruffly replies. Much of Lisa's "hip" dialogue seems ripped from the pages of an anti-establishment blaxploitation script, particularly when she refers to Neville as "The Man . . . but he's cool." Heard through today's ears the dated discourse has a retro charm that is part of the film's schlocky appeal.

Having said that, there is a lot to like about *The Omega Man*. Sagal's flashback scenes of the germ warfare are very effective and truly scary. He also takes good advantage of the deserted Los Angeles streets — the crew would shoot on location very early in the morning before people were on their way to work. The streets and buildings look lived in, but strangely barren, like something catastrophic has just happened.

The tension of the film is reinforced by veteran television composer Ron Grainer's music, a hauntingly atmospheric soundtrack that underscores the anxiety of the characters without detracting from the visuals.

The Omega Man might seem hopelessly dated and kind of cheesy — I prefer to think of it as a time capsule of early '70s American Cold War paranoia — but it is also an effective cautionary tale about the stupidity of war and the dangers of using technology irresponsibly.

"Do you know what the most frightening thing in the world is? It's fear."
— **MARK LEWIS (CARL BOEHM)**

PEEPING TOM (1960)

Peeping Tom may be one of the most reviled films ever made. British director Michael Powell was a respected filmmaker, with the critically successful *A Matter of Life and Death*, *Black Narcissus*, and *The Red Shoes* on his resumé. The release of the voyeuristic *Peeping Tom* savaged his reputation, essentially ending his long and distinguished career in film. "The only really satisfactory way to dispose of *Peeping Tom* would be to shovel it up and flush it swiftly down the nearest sewer," wrote Derek Hill in the *London Tribune*. "Even then, the stench would remain." People hated this movie so much that one outraged critic approached screenwriter Leo Marks after a press screening angrily saying, "Don't do that again," and even co-star Anna Massey called it "a horrible film to watch." The film lasted in British theaters for less than a week before virtually disappearing. Two decades later, Martin Scorsese championed it in interviews, hailing it as a masterpiece.

Peeping Tom is a deeply subversive movie that was years ahead of its time.

Mark Lewis (Carl Boehm) is a feature film focus puller with a deadly secret. In his off-hours he is a serial killer who films his victim's dying moments. He falls in love with Helen Stephens (Anna Massey), the daughter of his blind landlady, and reveals to her that he was the subject of cruel experiments by his psychologist father. The elder Lewis terrorized his son — dropping lizards on him while he slept and forcing him to grasp the hand of his deceased mother — and would film his reactions in the name of the study of fear.

Mark's unusual hobby is uncovered when he kills Vivian (Moira Shearer), on a deserted soundstage, shooting her final moments before hiding the body. When her corpse is discovered, Lewis films the horrified reactions of his co-workers. A police officer, Inspector Gregg (Jack Watson), makes the connection between the sadistic work of the well-known Dr. Lewis and the odd behavior of his son Mark, and puts a tail on him. That same night Lewis kills again, just as Helen finds the film of Vivian's murder. When she confronts him he tells her all the gruesome details as the police close in.

Ironically *Peeping Tom* would be considered a mainstream horror film today, the kind of film that Brian De Palma made early in his career, but in 1960 this subject matter really got under people's skin. Despite the fact this film showed less violence than another big hit that year, Alfred Hitchcock's *Psycho*, *Peeping Tom*'s study of the relationship between voyeurism and cinema earned ire because it wasn't a morality tale. It doesn't present Lewis as a crazed homicidal maniac, but as a sympathetic character who may be redeemable. It's a sophisticated psychological journey that may have confused and confounded audiences looking for a neat and tidy package with no gray areas.

The use of color in a horror film may also have startled viewers. Most contemporary horror films of the era were shot in black and white, thereby distancing the audience from the real life threat presented onscreen. The lurid full color presentation of *Peeping Tom* may have seemed too real, too close to home.

Whatever the reason, this underrated classic was shelved by a nervous distributor, surfacing in a butchered cut two years later that earned better notices after a brief Parisian run, but failed at the box office. Director Michael Powell was blackballed in Britain following the release of the film, and although he later found work directing series television and a handful of independent features, his well-earned reputation as a major filmmaker was irrevocably damaged. A brief interest in Powell's work occurred in the '80s, fed by the praises of heavyweight fans Frances Ford Coppola and Martin Scorsese. While he never again made important films, he did serve as senior director in residence at Zoetrope Studios and lectured at Dartmouth College in New Hampshire.

Virtually penniless at the time of his death in 1990, and his reputation in tatters, he never gave up hope of making another film. "He never became bitter," said his wife Thelma Schoonmaker, "which I think is the greatest achievement in his life aside from his wonderful films."

> "Here at the Paradise we offer you a special blend of fantasy
> and fact. Atrocity and art. Music and murder twice nightly.
> And is the horror you witness mere theatrics, or is it real?
> The only way to be sure . . . is to participate."
> — SWAN (from the liner notes of *PHANTOM OF THE PARADISE*)

THE PHANTOM OF THE PARADISE (1974)

Years before shooting Bruce Springsteen's first-ever rock video, "Dancing in the Dark," maverick director Brian De Palma made a satirical rock-and-roll musical that combined the stories of *Faust* and *Phantom of the Opera*. *Phantom of the Paradise*'s story of revenge was born out of De Palma's frustrations working with the big Hollywood studios.

Brian De Palma wrote the first draft of what would become *Phantom of the Paradise* in 1969. The story was born out of a combination of influences. De Palma had been throwing film script ideas around with a young NYU student who suggested a rock musical with the title *Phantom of the Fillmore*. The director found the idea of a contemporary opera house being haunted by a ripped-off composer very appealing in light of his own problems reconciling his artistic vision while working in the framework of the movie industry. "The problem is that even by dealing with the devil, you become devilish to a certain extent," De Palma said, expressing his distaste for the business side of show business. "You *need* the machine. And once you use it, you are a tainted human being."

He wrote and sold an early version of the script to Marty Ransohoff at Filmways, but later bought it back when Ransohoff didn't show any desire to develop it into a movie.

Ed Pressman, a producer who would go on to have everything from *Das Boot* to *Conan the Barbarian* and *American Psycho* on his resumé, bought two of De Palma's scripts, *Sisters* and *Phantom of the Fillmore*. They decided to film the horror thriller *Sisters* first, as it would be a less complicated shoot. *Sisters* proved profitable for American International Pictures, who green-lighted *Phantom of the Fillmore* but wanted drastic budget cuts. Pressman and De Palma felt the film could not be made for the kind of money AIP was offering, so the film entered development limbo.

It would take the next two years to convince studios and financial backers that a rock-and-roll parody would sell. "Studio people are so far away from the rock scene," De Palma said in 1975. "They didn't even know about things as big as Alice Cooper. . . . There's a real generation gap."

During the development period De Palma sought out a composer to write the score for his proposed rock musical. "My original conception was to get a supergroup like The Who or The Rolling Stones to write the whole score," he told *Filmmaker's Newsletter* in 1975, "but, of course, you couldn't even get them on the telephone." Instead he made what might have seemed like an unusual choice.

Paul Williams began his show business career as a gag writer for Mort Sahl. While working with Sahl he not only wrote jokes, but also dabbled in song writing. The first tune he wrote, "Fill Your Heart," wound up as the b-side to Tiny Tim's smash hit "Tiptoe Through the Tulips." Encouraged by the success of that record, he joined A&M Records as a contract writer, pumping out a series of soft-rock hits for Three Dog Night and The Carpenters. He parlayed his early '70s songwriting success into a movie career, stepping out from the sidelines to appear in a number of films (including *Battle for the Planet of the Apes*) and make the rounds on the chat shows.

With his newfound fame and easygoing nature Williams seemed on top of the world, but beneath the diminutive exterior was a growing bitterness that may have attracted the like-minded De Palma to him. Williams once said that even if he cured cancer, he would still be remembered as the guy who wrote the theme song for *The Love Boat*. That was just the attitude that De Palma was searching for. Williams' chameleon-like song writing skills also came in handy. "What is good about Paul Williams is that he is sophisticated enough as a composer to write satiric music of a certain form," said De Palma. "I mean he can write Alice Cooper-type music and he can write '50s Beach Boys-type stuff."

De Palma and Williams came up with a contra deal that would benefit both of them. De Palma would cast Williams in the movie, while Williams would provide a score at a cut rate. "As we got to know one another a little bit, [De Palma] said, 'You've got to play Winslow [the Phantom],'" remembers Williams. "That was the original thought, for me to play Winslow. Then we got into rewrites on the script, and I wasn't sure I could act behind a mask, so it seemed like the right idea for me to play the slimy mogul, Swan."

Having raised the $1.1 million dollars to make the film through private investors, shooting began. The title had to be changed to *Phantom of the Paradise* after rock promoter Bill Graham refused to allow the filmmakers to use the Fillmore Theatre as a setting.

De Palma's shooting script tells the story of Winslow Leach (William Finley), a gifted but unknown composer whose magnum opus, a rock cantata based on the *Faust* legend, has been stolen by Swan (Paul Williams), a strange rock impresario. To get Winslow out of the way Swan frames him for a crime, has his teeth removed in a monstrous "hygiene" procedure, and has him thrown in jail. Of course Winslow breaks out of his cell, determined to wreck havoc at Swan's warehouse. They say bad things come in threes, but the torment is not yet over for Winslow, who gets jammed in a record press where he is hideously disfigured and loses his voice.

Not one to let mutilation get him down, Winslow vows revenge on Swan. Donning a leather suit, cape, and a hawk-like metallic mask, he haunts Swan's new extravagant nightspot The Paradise. Swan confronts him and offers a deal. Winslow agrees to stop terrorizing The Paradise in exchange for control over his music. Winslow will agree under one condition: he wants the beautiful Phoenix (Jessica Harper) to sing his cantata. Swan ignores Winslow's request, and turns the beloved cantata over to a heavy metal band fronted by the sexually ambiguous Beef (Gerrit Graham). Winslow goes mad and exacts his revenge in increasingly bloody ways.

It is my long-held belief that most rock music movies suck. It is difficult to translate the excitement of a live performance to the screen, and very few filmmakers are able to pull it off. Despite the occasional cheesy song in *Phantom of the Paradise*, the musical performances are fun, and don't get in the way of the story. The concert scenes have a filmic feel to them that many rock movies miss. Most often concert footage is of the banal *Midnight Special* variety, but De Palma takes full advantage of his celluloid canvas and presents exciting musical numbers. Shot a full two years before *The Rocky Horror Picture Show* — a movie to which it is often compared — *Phantom of the Paradise* may have been the first film to really exploit the carnivalesque aspects of glam rock, using the visually androgynous character of Beef to simultaneously entice and repel the audience.

But it is the story that sets this movie apart. The tale of *The Phantom of the Opera* has been told and retooled hundreds of times, but De Palma manages something that many others have not been able to do: he tells us a story that is familiar, but manages to keep us off balance, unsure of what will come next. What starts off as comedy turns into tragedy. The outrageous nature of his telling of the Phantom's story masks his deeper message about the nature of greed in the entertainment business, a notion that seems more relevant now than when this film was made. He gets his point across subliminally, while keeping the viewer entertained with his great visual flair and wicked sense of humor. There's something for everyone here: comedy, horror, music, and social satire.

The Phantom of the Paradise was not a success when it was released in 1974, but became a cult hit through midnight screenings.

"When the dying starts this little psycho-fuck family
of ours is going to tear itself apart."
– RIDDICK (VIN DIESEL) to JOHNS (COLE HAUSER)

PITCH BLACK (2000)

Pitch Black is a science-fiction film that plays on one of the most human
of all phobias — fear of the dark. Directed by David Twohy, the movie
is run-of-the-mill sci-fi propped up with razzle-dazzle special effects
and an illuminating performance from former bouncer Vin Diesel as
Richard B. Riddick, the convicted murderer with a soft spot.

Pitch Black begins with a bang. Literally. A spacecraft crashes, killing
most of the crew and passengers. Counted among the survivors are the
pilot Fry (Radha Mitchell), a bounty hunter (Cole Hauser), his prisoner
Riddick (Diesel), and a holy man named Inam (Keith David). In the
confusion that follows the bumpy landing, Riddick escapes. Apparently
life on the arid, deserted planet with three suns beaming down 24-7 is
preferable to a life in chains. As the other survivors search the wasteland
for Riddick, they too are being hunted. A species of light-sensitive aliens
are tracking their movements, waiting to strike.

Riddick's stock rises when it is discovered that their new world is
about to be plunged into darkness by an eclipse. Riddick, you see, had
black-market implants shot into his corneas before escaping from an
underground prison, and can see in the dark. The ragtag group must
learn to trust Riddick as he is their best defence against the aliens, who
are lethal and who only reveal themselves under the cloak of darkness.

This isn't the only bad news. They discover the remnants of a scientific research team. A *dead* scientific research team who were brutally
killed by the carnivorous aliens during a similar eclipse 22 years earlier.
It turns out these things live beneath the planet's surface, and get very
hungry waiting for the darkness to come.

The plot of *Pitch Black* is fairly routine. Even casual sci-fi fans will have seen much of this before. As the necessities of survival start to dwindle, the inevitable backstabbing and in-fighting begins, and the characters meet their doom one by one, in increasingly horrible ways. We've seen all this before in everything from *Scream* to *Abbott and Costello Meet the Mummy*.

The main thing that saves *Pitch Black* from "been there, done that" territory is the unexpected relationship twists among the survivors. Screenwriters Twohy and Jim and Ken Wheat manage to insert a gripping human drama amongst the action. "Because we're not all name actors," says Cole Hauser, "you can't assume, 'Okay here's the hero, here's the bad guy, and here's the leading lady that's going to get the good guy and ride off into the sunset.'"

Strong performances help sell this, particularly Vin Diesel's. His Riddick is a muscle-bound killer, a loner whose deep raspy voice is both sexy and scary. He's an action-bound character, but a smart one, who has a winning combination of street smarts and natural intellect. This is the character that keeps the movie afloat, and the one with all the best lines.

"Human blood has a coppery taste," Riddick tells the bounty hunter. "But if you cut it with peppermint schnapps it goes away."

Diesel says he derived much of Riddick's tough guy persona from the nine years he spent as a bouncer in Manhattan nightclubs. "He was like a lot of guys I worked with. I'm drawing heavily from my own experiences. As a bouncer you learn to exude a certain confidence, and you have to learn a lot about people. You have to know what a person is going to do next. You have to read whether they're going to get physical in the next second or whether you can handle a situation with diplomacy and talk something out, or if it is going to erupt into violence.

"You learn about camaraderie because when you are bouncing you have to rely on the other bouncers. You have to rely on the phalanx of soldiers and work together to protect one another against a club filled with 3,000 people."

Think of Riddick as an imposing intergalactic bouncer; instead of

Richard's Favorite Legal Disclaimers

1. "Any references to any religious organization is purely coincidental, and no actual Mormons were used or abused in the filming of this picture." – *Orgazmo* (1997)
2. "No real reapers were hurt during the making of this film." – *Blade II* (2002)
3. "The persons and events in this production are fictitious. No similarity to actual persons or predators, living or dead, is intended or should be inferred." – *Pitch Black* (2000)
4. "No Canadians were harmed in this production." – *Canadian Bacon* (1995)
5. "Any resemblance to persons living, dead, or reincarnated is purely coincidental." – *What Dreams May Come* (1998)
6. "No animals were injured during the making of this film, although some rabbits did have their feelings hurt." – *Happy, Texas* (1999)
7. "All characters portrayed in this film are entirely fictitious and bare no resemblance to anyone living or dead, except for one." – *Jabberwocky* (1977)
8. "The following stunts were performed by professionals, so for your safety and the protection of those around you, Paramount Pictures and MTV Films insist that neither you or your dumb little buddies attempt any of what you're about to see." – *Jackass: The Movie* (2002)
9. "Any similarity with persons living or dead is an accident. Sorry." – *Bad Taste* (1987)
10. "Beavis and Butthead are not real people, in fact they are not even human. They are cartoons. Some of the things they do can cause a person to get hurt, injured, expelled, arrested, and possibly deported. To put it in another way, don't try this at home." – *Beavis and Butthead Do America* (1996)

battling club goers he's taking on aliens. Either way, they only come out at night and turn ugly when they don't get their way.

Twohy has created a spectacular world using a blend of natural locations and digital effects. Shot in the Australian outback, *Pitch Black*'s vision of the futuristic planet is deserted, bleak, and unforgiving. The town of Coober Peety in Queensland turned out to be just the place to create the gritty new world. "It is as barren as it appears," says Twohy. "That is why we went there. I was looking for a blank slate terrain — no telephone poles, no trees — and then by doing some practical applications on the set or in a computer, I can add architecture to the terrain. A lot of stuff was layered in after the fact."

Shooting on location is always difficult, particularly when the site is near an ancient burial ground. "In the days of *Mad Max*, which was shot there before us, you could do whatever you wanted," says Twohy. "It was wide open terrain. You could rip up the landscape. Today it is very ecologically sensitive. The aboriginals tell you where you can and can't shoot. We never got a clear picture since their history is oral, not written. You had to grab an aboriginal and say, 'Is this sacred ground? Is this not sacred ground?' And it would change from week to week. Just another of the vagaries of the filmmaking process. . . ."

Twohy uses his monsters sparingly, never giving the audience the chance to get too comfortable with the sight of them. It's a lesson from old horror movies: what you have to imagine is always more terrifying than what you can clearly see. When we do see the winged predators they seem slightly familiar, like alien bats, or a vicious hybrid of a pterodactyl and the stomach-bursting creature from the first *Alien* movie. "We were likening them to air-sharks," says Twohy, explaining that they are relentless killers with the ability to fly. That we hear them before we see them is a masterful touch that builds suspense and a feeling of dread long before you have even laid eyes on the creatures.

Pitch Black cost $22 million, cheap for an effects-heavy sci-fi film, but did only lukewarm business at the box office. A sequel, *Riddick*, was commissioned largely based on Vin Diesel's popularity after the release of such films as *The Fast and the Furious* and *xxx*. His salary for the sequel was $11 million, half of the entire cost of the first movie.

THE POPE OF GREENWICH VILLAGE (1984)

The story of two down on their luck small-time crooks in New York's Little Italy was adapted from a bestseller by Vincent Patrick. Starring two actors who were poised to become the King and Crown Prince of Hollywood, *The Pope of Greenwich Village* met with indifference at the box office.

The story centers on two Italian cousins, the even-tempered Charlie (Mickey Rourke) and the foolhardy Paulie (Eric Roberts). These two are close, as close as 99 is to 100. "Italians don't outgrow people," Charlie says when explaining why he continues to hang around with his dimwitted cousin. "They outgrow clothes."

Broke and out of work, the pair dream of being rich. The shady Paulie cooks up a scheme to pilfer $15,000 in cash with the help of safe-cracker Barney (Kenneth McMillan). The heist goes bad when a corrupt policeman (Jack Kehoe), who also had his eye on the money, happens across the makeshift gang and is accidentally murdered. Paulie neglected to mention that the money belongs to a local gangster and was supposed to be used to bribe the police. Charlie and Paulie are in *big* trouble with nowhere to turn. They can't go to the police, and as the money they took belongs to Little Italy underboss Bedbug Eddie (Burt Young), they can't seek protection from the mob.

The Pope of Greenwich Village was meant to be a showcase for

Mickey Rourke's intense method acting style, but it is Eric Roberts as the bumbling Paulie who steals the show. Paulie is a loudmouth loser, the kind of guy whose get-rich-quick schemes always backfire, usually with consequences for everyone around him.

You often want to slap Paulie for being so stupid, and he does take his share of lumps, mostly from Charlie, who loves his cousin but doesn't hesitate to hand out some corporal punishment when Paulie messes up. Eric Roberts is so intense he all but breathes fire. His character is stupid, but Roberts plays him as a more dangerous guy, someone who doesn't know how dumb he is. There's an optimism to his foolhardiness that prevents the viewer from hating him, even for all his shortcomings. It's an offbeat, showy performance that eclipses the more experienced technique of the top-billed Mickey Rourke. It's a sensational onscreen accomplishment for Roberts, who in the years since has rarely lived up to his potential. He book-ended *The Pope of Greenwich Village* with strong showings in *Star 80* (1983) and *Runaway Train* (1985), but his subsequent film roles have mostly been forgettable riffs on his earlier, more exciting work. Today he's generally referred to as "Julia's older brother."

Although overshadowed by Roberts, Rourke has some tasty moments of his own. He's a blinkered guy; his whole life revolves around his friends, family, and neighborhood. Life, for Charlie, barely exists north of 14th Street in Manhattan. He is a man-child, someone who got big, but didn't grow up. A total product of his environment — the corrupt neighborhood of Little Italy — Charlie idolized the gangsters and lives by their credo. "Something I learned a long time ago about honest work," he says, "People tell you they got honest work for you. You know what they got? They got a shit job, that's what they got." He's a slacker who craves respect, but doesn't know how to earn it.

Rourke does a nice job with Charlie; you can almost smell his desperation, his longing for a better life. While the characterization occasionally veers toward an ethnic stereotype, he reins it in, turning Charlie into a real person rather than a gold chain-wearing, wildly gesticulating cliché. Rourke has a tendency to play over the top, but I've always seen that as an extension of his real personality, and as such, he has a core of believable humanity.

On the other end of the scale are the performances of Geraldine Page as the dead cop's mother and Kenneth McMillan as the safecracker. They provide a nice counter-point to the ostentatious work of Roberts and Rourke by underplaying their roles. As Page is confronted by two cops investigating her crooked son, her quiet resolve forcefully diffuses the situation without resorting to unnecessarily flamboyant actorly flourishes. She's tough as nails, and by the end of the scene, you know it.

The Pope of Greenwich Village isn't a story-driven film. The run-of-the-mill plot is a poor man's *Mean Streets*, but it's the characters that make this movie worth watching. Anyone who has seen the movie will remember the stickball game, played by suit-wearing, wise-guy wannabes, or Paulie's pained cry after Bedbug's thugs mutilate him. It's an entertaining slice-of-life look at people on the fringes of the underworld.

> "It's a hygiene thing. Ron looks dirty."
> **– PORN PRODUCER**

PORN STAR: THE LEGEND OF RON JEREMY (2002)

Ron Jeremy is the biggest (nudge nudge, wink wink) porn star in the world. With over 1,600 adult films to his credit (including *Blowjob Adventures of Dr. Fellatio*, *Ejacula 2*, and *Dirty Bob's Xcellent Adventures 35*), Jeremy has been working in the adult film business for nearly a quarter of a century.

One would expect a documentary about his life to be salacious, sleazy stuff, and while *Porn Star* does have elements of baseness (how could it not?) it chooses to focus on Ron Jeremy the man, not the movie stud. It could be seen as a porn industry puff piece, as it certainly ignores most of the downsides of working in the sex industry, but that isn't the point of the film. Despite the inclusion of a sequence where he is tested for AIDS during the shooting of *Ally McFeel*, *Porn Star* is not a cautionary tale, like Stacey Valentine's emotionally raw *The Girl Next Door*, it is simply an edgy *E! True Hollywood Story*-style look at an actor who has made his living showing off his nine-and-three-quarter-inch appendage.

Shot over 18 months and edited from 150 hours of film, the film offers up interviews with Jeremy's family who fill in his backstory. We learn that he holds a Master's Degree in special education, and once taught school. We also discover that he doesn't own any luggage, preferring to use garbage bags, even when traveling first class. His friends poke fun at him, talking about his legendary cheapness and suggesting, "He's proof that someone forgot birth control." We also get a glimpse at Jeremy's legendary phone book — actually a ratty binder held together with duct tape and literally crammed with hundreds of thousands of numbers, all written in what appears to be hieroglyphics. In the film the binder is played for laughs, although it might have been interesting if the filmmakers had explored the psychology behind the neurotically compiled address book. It probably reveals some obsessive psychological trait that might have shed more light on Jeremy, and his compulsive need to feel connected.

For his part Jeremy is very open in front of the camera, sometimes almost too much so. He can be a charming guy when he wants to, but there is an air of desperation that bleeds through his well-constructed public persona. "Porn's the purest form of acting. I'd like to see Sir Laurence Olivier perform *Macbeth*, in its entirety, with all that dialogue — *and* a boner. It's not that easy," he says defensively, before adding that he'd rather "have a role in a Steven Spielberg movie" than do more porn.

Director Scott J. Gill doesn't manage to dig as deep as say, Terry Zwigoff's *Crumb*, but he does humanize Jeremy and somehow makes you feel pity for a man who says he has slept with over 4,000 women.

THE PRINCESS AND THE WARRIOR (2000)

German director Tom Tykwer seems to be fascinated by movies that play with time. His best-known movie, *Run Lola Run*, was frenetic, set at a heart-attack pace that turned the clock upside-down and told the same story three times with a trio of different outcomes. That film became an unexpected international hit, prompting Tykwer to reteam with his *Lola* star Franka Potente for his next movie. Once again in *The Princess and the Warrior* he plays with time, but in this one he has shifted gears, slowing the action down to a more restrained and thoughtful pace.

The Princess and the Warrior is the story of two broken people, Sissi and Bodo, and the strange ties that bind them. "I think it is a very descriptive title," says Tykwer, "since the film gives these special strange creatures the same dimension as is usually reserved only for historical heroes. They deserve a description like this, which is not 'The frustrated soldier and the cranky nurse,' although the film could well have been called that. Sissi is a princess in that she is the secret ruler in this psychiatric establishment. In the same way Bodo is a warrior, in a battle against himself and his feelings. Although they are not fanciful characters, they can lay claim to this dimension."

Potente — back to her natural blonde locks after the shocking red hair of Lola — is Sissi, a nurse in a psychiatric institution. She is worshiped by her patients, but her life is monotonous and secluded. While taking care of some banking in the busy city of Wuppertal, she has a chance encounter with a down-on-his-luck ex-soldier named Bodo (Benno Furmann) when he inadvertently causes her to be hit by a truck while crossing the street. As she lies under the vehicle, unable to breath, Bodo slides in next to her to avoid the police who are chasing him. In a very intense scene he saves her life, breathing much needed air into her lungs through a makeshift tracheotomy tube. It's an incredibly well realized moment. Tykwer blocks out all the sound except for Sissi's labored breathing, and there is a stillness that simulates the after-effects of an accident. Anyone who has ever been seriously injured will attest to the peaceful calm that envelops you as your body goes into shock. The scene seems to take forever to play itself out. With her sporadic gasps as a soundtrack, this accident scenario packs more realism into five minutes than any five episodes of *ER*.

Saving Sissi's life is not simply an act of altruism; Bodo uses her to outwit the police, even riding in the ambulance with her while holding her hand. When she wakes, he is gone, and all she has is a button from his coat gripped tightly in her hand. During her long recovery she thinks about Bodo, convincing herself that he is the one great love of her life. Two months after the accident she tracks him down, only to discover that her angel of mercy is a bitter lonely man who wants nothing to do with her.

Sissi makes it her mission to discover whether their paths crossed through simple luck or the complicated mechanisms of fate itself.

"In the cinema people are always being thrown into decisive situations," says Tykwer. "I like the thought of saying over and over, 'What else could have happened to my life? What else could have happened to your life? What could have happened to us?' I think it is wonderful that in the cinema you can set this speculative machine in motion."

Speculation is one of the trademarks of Tykwer's films. His previous two outings — *Winter Sleepers* (1997) and *Run Lola Run* (1998) — examine how fate and coincidence collide to guide the lives of his characters. *The Princess and the Warrior* sees Tykwer push it to a whole new level, weaving a fabric of chance happenings that bring Sissi and Bodo closer. Or *are* they chance? Call it what you will — fate, divine intervention, or coincidence — but the characters become slowly intertwined in ways they could never have imagined. Tykwer wisely doesn't offer any easy answers and leaves much up to individual interpretation, particularly in the final act of the film.

A multi-layered script like this demands believable performances, and in Franka Potente, Tykwer has found just the right actress to portray the iron-willed but unsophisticated Sissi. She is a grown woman with the mannerisms of a child. Potente gives her a strange physicality that at first seems unnatural, almost like a tentative new foal just learning to walk. "I always said, 'She's like a virgin. She doesn't know anything. She's very naïve,'" says Potente. "She's like a child, but very curious, so there is something soft and subtle about her. She is kind of careful, but she's also forward and she's brave. We tried to find something in the body to tell the audience that's what she's like."

"Franka has done an incredible job," said Tykwer. "Sissi seems too inexperienced to walk around like a normal person. It is all Franka's creation, and has nothing to do with the real Franka."

In this film nothing is what it seems on the surface. Take the character of Bodo (Benno Furmann). He is a thief, an ex-soldier, a tough guy who can be reduced to tears at the slightest provocation. He's a conundrum, a deeply damaged man with a violent streak who is capable of acting tenderly, as he does under the truck with Sissi. Furmann brings an unpredictable, dangerous feel to the character; he's like a coiled snake that could strike at any time.

"Benno is somebody who can act wonderfully well with no effort," says Tykwer, "who is very playful but also very physical, for whom a difficult character like this does not seem to be written. In Benno I have found someone who understood in such an intuitive way just how far this character could go. Occasionally one is lucky enough to find that an actor is himself going through a phase in which a certain role speaks to him particularly clearly, in which you suddenly have revelations in which you know that there is nothing more you can do; even if I direct till I'm blue in the face, it simply happens because someone has found out a certain truth for himself. All I can do in a case like that is to create trust."

The Princess and the Warrior got lost in the shuffle. After making a splash at several international film festivals, the movie was sentenced to big screen purgatory when its distributor went bankrupt on the eve of its theatrical release.

RAT PFINK A BOO BOO (1965)

In recent years a number of directors have become known for taking an improvisational approach to their films. British filmmaker Mike Leigh never starts with a locked script, preferring to improvise with his actors until the story fleshes itself out. Ditto Mike Figgis, whose film *Timecode* was made up on the spot. The granddaddy of this technique may well be a man who made 26 no-budget films with a minimum of pre-production. "I like things to just happen," says Ray Dennis Steckler. "I hate to plan things."

Pioneer or crackpot — you be the judge. Steckler (who often multi-tasked, working as director, actor, and cinematographer on his movies) is best known for his 1963 horror musical, *The Incredibly Strange Creatures Who Stopped Living and Became Mixed-Up Zombies*. Not only does it have one of the longest (and wildest) titles in movie history, it also established his modus operandi. Shot in a matter of days with an improvised script and a cast that included friends and family, the film wasn't going to win any Academy Awards, but would make a few bucks at the drive-in. Like all his films, *Incredibly Strange Creatures* may be bad, but it's never boring.

His loopiest movie came two years later. *Rat Pfink A Boo Boo* is a classic example of what happens when a director gets bored midway through a project. Initially called *The Depraved*, it was inspired by a series of obscene phone calls made to Steckler's wife. He imagined a gritty crime drama centering on rock-and-roll duo Cee Bee Beaumont (Carolyn Brandt) and Lonnie Lord (Vin Saxon). Lonnie carries his gui-

Richard's Favorite Alan Smithee Films

Alan Smithee is one of the most prolific directors in Hollywood, and yet has never been nominated for any awards, and has never been seen in public. You see, Mr. Smithee doesn't actually exist. The name was created by the Director's Guild to protect any directors or creative leads who feel their work has been abused. They can apply to have their name removed from the credits, and have Mr. Smithee's name inserted instead. The pseudonym was retired in 1997 after the release and subsequent publicity of Arthur Hiller's comedy (and ironically an Alan Smithee film itself) *Burn Hollywood Burn: An Alan Smithee Film*.

1. *Death of a Gunfighter*: A 1969 western starring Richard Widmark, Lena Horne, and Carroll O'Connor that has the distinction of being the first Alan Smithee film. Robert Totten was originally slated to direct, but clashed with star Widmark and was replaced by Don Siegel.
2. *Stitches*: This 1985 medical school comedy starring Parker Stevenson was actually directed by Rod Holcomb.
3. *Ghost Fever*: A 1987 "comedy" featuring Sherman "George Jefferson" Helmsley and ex-heavyweight boxing champ Joe Frazier. Actually directed by Lee Madden.
4. *Catchfire*: A strong cast headed by real director Dennis Hopper which includes Jody Foster, Dean Stockwell, Vincent Price, and John Turturro flounders in this turgid 1989 thriller.

5. *Shrimp on the Barbie*: This silly 1990 Cheech Marin movie was actually directed by Michael Gottlieb.

6. *Bloodsucking Pharoahs in Pittsburgh*: Not even the special effects of master technician Tom Savini could save this 1991 stinker, actually directed by Dean Tschetter.

7. *National Lampoon's Senior Trip*: Not bad by Smithee standards. This 1995 Matt Frewer comedy is credited to co-directors Kelly Makin and Smithee, when the original director took his name off a segment titled *Forrest Humps*.

8. *Smoke 'N' Lightin'*: Two Miami mechanics steal a luxury car for the night in this Christopher Atkins vehicle from 1995. Written and really directed by Mike Kirton.

9. *Hellraiser: Bloodline*: The horrific fourth part of the successful Hellraiser series was actually directed by Kevin Yagher in 1996.

10. *Wadd: The Life & Times of John C. Holmes*: The excellent theatrical version of this 1998 documentary about porn star Holmes suffered some bad editing choices in the video release, prompting director Cass Paley to call on Mr. Smithee.

tar with him everywhere, because, as the narrator explains, "he never knows when he'll be called upon to sing a song." In a parallel story three thugs are seen vandalizing the city. One night they choose Cee Bee's name at random from the phone book and begin making menacing calls to her. Their reign of terror escalates, and soon they start stalking Cee Bee, banging on her patio door and harassing her.

Steckler breaks the tension here, inserting a song by Lonnie — "You Ain't Nothin' But a Rat Pfink." Back to the action. After another phone call, Cee Bee is abducted, despite the best efforts of her gardener Titus (Titus Moede) to rescue her. While waiting for the bad guys to contact him, Lonnie sings another song — mysteriously backed by an invisible quartet — as Titus nurses his bruised head and ego. The kidnappers demand

$50,000, far more money than Lonnie can raise in a few short hours.

It's at this point that Steckler says he became tired of the story, and really started to improvise. One night after shooting he let his imagination run wild and came up with the most ridiculous idea imaginable. Lonnie and Titus would step into a closet, only to emerge as super-heroes Rat Pfink and Boo Boo. Here the tone changes completely; it's like a whole new film. The grainy black and white of the first half inexplicably gives way to green, yellow, and orange tints as good versus evil. *Rat Pfink A Boo Boo* is a very weird movie, but contains some classic cult dialogue:

Rat Pfink: Remember Boo Boo, we only have one weakness.

Boo Boo: What's that?

Rat Pfink: Mmm . . . bullets.

While this movie betrays every inch of its low-budget origins, it actually contains some pretty good camera work. When not making movies Steckler worked as a director of photography for ABC's *Wide World of Sports* and a variety of Warner Brother's television shows. He knew where to put a camera; too bad he didn't have money for second takes, decent props, or lighting.

Rumor has it that the movie's unusual title was also the result of financial restraint. Not so, says Steckler. "The first story was that the artist made a mistake, printed *Rat Pfink A Boo Boo* instead of *Rat Pfink And Boo Boo* and I just didn't have the money to fix it. The real story is that my little girl, when we were shooting this one fight scene, kept chanting, 'rat pfink a boo boo, rat pfink a boo boo . . .' And that sounded great." Is this a good movie? No, not really, but I guarantee you've never seen anything like it.

SANTA CLAUS CONQUERS THE MARTIANS (1964)

The Monster Times called this one "the worst science-fiction flick ever made, bar none!" I don't agree. I would say that *Santa Claus Conquers the Martians* is one of those films that ping-pongs back and forth from so bad it's good right back to bad again. This may be the biggest Christmas turkey ever . . . either way, it is a lot of fun.

This movie started with the best of intentions. Producer Paul Jacobson wanted to make a movie for kids to see during their Christmas holidays. "Except for the Disneys, there is very little in film houses during the season that the kids can recognize and call their own," he said. Jacobson had a background in kid's entertainment, having served as unit manager on *Howdy Doody*. He set off to make a film that would entertain and delight kids, and perhaps make him a few dollars in the process.

Jacobson outlined the story, a genre-buster he described as a "Yuletide science-fiction fantasy." In his fable, Martian elders, concerned that their offspring are becoming obsessed with Christmas television shows from Earth, hatch a nefarious plot to kidnap Santa Claus. Their plan is to bring him to Mars to make toys for the alien children. A convoy of evil Martian henchmen is sent to Earth, but the dozens of street-corner Santas confuse them. Who is the real Santa? They abduct two spirited human kids, Billy and Betty, who are able to lead them to the North Pole and identify the real St. Nick. Voldar, the grumpy Martian expedition leader, is ordered to bring the hostages back to the red planet, but en route tries, unsuccessfully, to eject them from the spacecraft. This earns the ire of the head Martian Kimar, who exiles Voldar. Santa, meanwhile, having gone where no magical elf has gone before, quickly sets up his intergalactic Toy Shop with the help of the dopey Martian Dropo.

While Santa teaches the gospel of good cheer to the extraterrestrials, Voldar is busy plotting revenge. His planned coup d'état is foiled by Santa and his new Martian friends using "weapons" from the Toy Shop — ping pong balls and soap bubbles. Having battled evil, spread the message of Christmas, and taught the Martians how to build toys, Santa and the kids return to Earth, leaving Dropo in charge as the new outer-space Santa.

Glenville Mareth was hired to refine Jacobson's plot outline and add some "hilarious" dialogue. Here's a taste:

> KIMAR: Dropo, you are the laziest man on Mars. Why are you sleep-ing during working hours?
> DROPO: I wasn't sleeping, chief. It's just that I haven't been able to sleep these last few months. I forgot how. So I was just practicing.
>
> BETTY: What are those funny things sticking out of your head?
> MARTIAN: Those are our antennae.
> BETTY: Are you a television set?

With the script in place, Jacobson set out to raise the $200,000 needed to produce the picture. Private investors anted up most of the money, providing him with the means to rent a converted aircraft hanger at Roosevelt Field on Long Island to act as his studio. There, using an inexperienced, non-union crew, Jacobson and director Nicholas Webster started rolling film.

There is a high-school drama club quality to the production that I find quite charming. Given the quality of the script and the actors, this movie would still be bad even if it had good sets and some level of pro-duction value, but the shoddy nature of the movie actually works to its advantage, lending it an appealingly earnest, "Hey kids, let's put on a show!" feel. The green-skinned aliens look like they were hanged by their heels and dipped in large vats of green goo, their helmets resembling a curious hybrid of a colander, some exhaust tubing, and a scuba mask. Cardboard sets waver and bend and the special effects are mostly out-of-focus shots of miniature models. Continuity and logic seem to have been lost on the filmmakers — a snow-covered man goes inside, but why doesn't the snow on his shoulders melt?

It's easy to poke fun at the performances in *Santa Claus Conquers the Martians*, so let's get on with it. The cast was new to moviemaking, and it shows. As Santa Claus, John Call, a minor-league Broadway actor, certainly looks the part, but in a drunken mall-Santa kind of way. His incessant "Ho, ho, ho" isn't the comforting chuckle of the Jolly Old Man in the Red Suit, but rather a risqué titter from an old lecherous uncle.

An eight-year-old Pia Zadora makes her film debut as one of the Martian girls. *Santa Conquers the Martians* did not give the boost to Zadora's career that she might have hoped; she would have to wait until 1982 to find fame. Zadora's career highlight was also her undoing. She won a Golden Globe for Best New Female Star for her trashy turn in *Butterfly*, but became a laughing stock when it was suggested that her billionaire husband might have bought her the award. She has since appeared in several straight-to-video B-movies.

Both Call and Zadora's characterizations, however, come off like Academy Award winners when compared to Bill McCutcheon's portrayal of Dropo. This goofy character is meant to appeal to the childish side of all of us, but only manages to be annoying instead of endearing.

Some people connected with *Santa Claus Conquers the Martians* went on to have productive careers. Actor Ned Wertimer surfaced on *The Jeffersons*, and Martian-extra Josip Elic appeared in *One Flew Over the Cuckoo's Nest*. The score was composed by Milton DeLugg, who later wrote the theme songs for *The Gong Show* and *The $1.98 Beauty Show*. Just be careful with DeLugg's closing song, "Hooray for Santa Claus." It's one of those tunes that you will find yourself thinking about months after you see the movie, and try as you might, you won't get it out of your head.

No one sets out to make a bad movie, and in Paul Jacobson's case he thought he was making a really good movie. He may have been deluded on that score, but his movie has turned a profit many times over, been released on video, and become something of a camp classic. There has even been some talk of doing a remake, written by *The Tick* creator Ben Edlund, with James Doohan (Scotty from the original *Star Trek*) starring as Santa.

"This picture is an indictment of gang rule in America and of the callous indifference of the government to this constantly increasing menace to our safety and our liberty. Every incident in this picture is the reproduction of an actual occurrence, and the purpose of this picture is to demand of the government: 'What are you going to do about it?' The government is your government. What are YOU going to do about it?"
— **Opening statement from** *SCARFACE: THE SHAME OF THE NATION*

SCARFACE: THE SHAME OF THE NATION (1932)

This movie may seem tame by today's standards, but it was considered so controversial in 1930 when it was shot, that its release was delayed for two years while director Howard Hawkes retooled it to meet the approval of industry censors. The thinly veiled story of Mafioso gang lord Al Capone features 28 onscreen murders (and several more off-screen), the first use of machine guns in a movie, and the troubling notion that crime does pay. The bullet-ridden brutality of *Scarface* certainly made this the most violent film of the 1930s.

The film opens with a protracted moral statement that describes the movie as an "indictment of gang rule in America." From there it takes off like a rocket. In the opening scene we see the shadowy figure of Tony Comonte (Paul Muni), whistling an Italian aria before executing someone with a shot to the head and calmly walking away. Hawkes quickly establishes Comonte as the proto-gangster, a flashily dressed homicidal maniac with a fondness for fast cars and life's fast lane — the kind of wise guy who prefers machine guns because their rapid rat-a-tat-tat is a more time-efficient way to off one's enemies.

His human side is reflected in his affection for his sister (Ann Dvorak). Insanely protective of her, he doesn't seem to just love her, but actually seems to be *in* love with her. Tony's underworld boss is Johnny Lovo (Osgood Perkins), a sophisticated con who reports to Big Louis (Harry Vejar), the Mafia kingpin.

Tony's Napoleonic urge to fight his way up to number one is kicked into overdrive after he is arrested for the murder shown in the first scene. When he is released from jail on a special writ he tries to convince Johnny to kill Louis because of the big boss's reluctance to cash in on Prohibition law and get into bootlegging. When Johnny tells Tony to lay off, all hell breaks loose.

Paul Muni seems born to play the role of the savage Comonte, but he very nearly passed on the role. He had only made two films (but had been nominated for his first screen role in 1929's *The Valiant*) and was a star in Yiddish theater and a hit on Broadway when Hawkes approached him. "I'm not that kind of guy," Muni reportedly told the director when offered the role. He explained that he was a sedentary man, not at all the tightly coiled character in the script. Hawkes wouldn't take no for an answer, and even hired a former middleweight boxing champion to teach Muni to punch and look vicious. It worked. His Tony is an animal, and unlike the mobsters played by Edward G. Robinson and James Cagney, has no redeeming qualities whatsoever. Armed with a bad attitude and a machine gun, he is more than just a caricature; in Muni's hands Tony becomes a layered character with many idiosyncrasies, and it is these foibles that lead to his comeuppance.

A strong supporting cast includes Boris Karloff (*Scarface* was shot before, but released after *Frankenstein*) as the thug Gaffney, and George Raft (who was friends with many real-life mobsters) as Tony's coin-flipping righthand man. Visually the film impresses, with Hawkes taking advantage of dramatic truck-and-dolly shots often left out of early talkies due to technical concerns. Perhaps the most startling image to emerge from the film is the "X" motif Hawkes used to signify imminent death. It takes many forms — gown straps, Raft's apartment number, a facial scar, and even wooden rafters on a ceiling. Perhaps the most inventive use of the "X" symbol is in a bowling alley scene when Boris Karloff is killed. The camera shows his ball hitting the pins, and as the last pin drops, so does he. It's a strike, which, of course, is denoted by an "X" on the score sheet.

Producer Howard Hughes ponied up the reported one million dollars to make the film, and encouraged Hawkes to tone down the violence to make the movie more marketable and less susceptible to the censor's scissors. This resulted in two versions of the film, the original ending where Tony is hanged for his crimes, and an alternate in which Tony dies a cowardly, but dreadful death, gunned down by police as onlookers cheer. The latter was shot without the help of Hawkes or Muni, and has thankfully been shelved. *Scarface: The Shame of the Nation* (the subtitle was added to appease the censors) is as exciting as any gangster film of its time, and impressed director Brian De Palma enough to mount a bloody update of it in 1983 starring Al Pacino.

"The whole world is a circus if you know how to look at it."
— DR. LAO

THE SEVEN FACES OF DR. LAO (1964)

March 1964 was a busy month in show business. The British tabloids reported that George Harrison had met model Patti Boyd on the set of *A Hard Day's Night*. Liz Taylor divorced her fourth husband, Eddie

Fisher. Later that same month Taylor married Richard Burton, telling reporters at the wedding that "it will last forever." Barbra Streisand became a sensation on Broadway, starting a three-year run at the Winter Garden Theatre as the star of *Funny Girl*. Dusty Springfield had a Top 40 hit with "Stay Awhile." On television Honor Blackman's last episode of *The Avengers* aired in the U.K.

There was a fair amount of action in the movie theaters too. The first installment of the Inspector Clouseau series, *The Pink Panther*, was released, becoming a big hit. Disney's *The Misadventures of Merlin Jones* with Tommy Kirk and Annette Funicello opened in U.S. theaters. Sophia Loren could be seen starring in *The Fall of the Roman Empire*. But the most engaging film to hit the screens that month was director George Pal's *The 7 Faces of Dr. Lao*, with Tony Randall and Barbara Eden.

George Pal possessed one of Hollywood's greatest imaginations. As a director he made a string of films, sometimes with very low budgets, that helped define the science-fiction/fantasy genre. In *Destination Moon* he told the story of a group of businessmen who send the first spaceship to the lunar surface. Pal showed us how scientists saved mankind by building a giant ark in *When Worlds Collide*.

Using a combination of live and stop-motion effects, he created worlds and creatures that hadn't been seen before, but his films were more than a series of special effects. He may have destroyed Los Angeles in *The War of the Worlds*, but he managed to weave a thread of humanity through the story. He always infused his fantastic stories with real people in unreal situations. It's a technique that makes his films special. In a George Pal film the viewer can look in wonder at the special effects but still enjoy a good story, populated by real, fully rounded characters. Often the lower budget science-fiction films of the '50s and '60s fell prey to the trap of supplying visual special effects with little or no believability character-wise. Pal never believed, as so many in Hollywood did, that sci-fi films were second-class citizens compared to Westerns or musicals. From the 1940s on George Pal raised the bar for all other fantasy filmmakers.

The source material for *The 7 Faces of Dr. Lao* is an obscure novel by Charles Finney, a marine who wrote the book while stationed in China. Published in 1935 by Viking Press, *The Circus of Dr. Lao* featured illustrations by well-known Russian illustrator Boris Artzybasheff, and told the story of a mysterious Asian magician/ringleader and his menagerie of weird and wonderful creatures. Literally the greatest show on earth (or any other planet) with a supernatural twist.

The book is at times funny and satirical, painting a vivid picture of small town Abalone, Arizona, the site of the traveling circus's latest show. Finney populates his book with a cast of colorful characters. The townspeople are described in succinct, but sparkling detail. In one of my favorite passages Agnes Birdsong is described as someone who "the boys said was damned good company after she learned to smoke and drink."

The star of the book, of course, is Dr. Lao, a mysterious impresario who oversees a sideshow that features such "unbiological creatures" as Apollonius, Satan, a satyr, Medusa, and the Great God Yottle. Finney is sketchy on the details of Dr. Lao's background. We never learn what kind of doctor he is, or the source of his magical powers.

Seasoned wordsmith Charles Beaumont was hired to tailor the novel for the screen. As one of the main writers on the original *Twilight Zone* television series, Beaumont was skilled at fleshing out this type of magic realism story where ordinary people encounter metaphysical forces tinged with moral issues. He took liberties with the book, including subverting the ending.

Beaumont starts the action with a ruthless businessman, Clint Stark (Arthur O'Connell) who secretly learns of a plan to build a railroad near the town of Abalone. Seeing dollar signs, he tries to buy up the town with the hope of turning a handsome profit. The shortsighted townspeople are more than happy to sell, with the exception of Ed Cunningham, a crusading newspaper reporter (John Ericson) who tries to fight Stark's plans. Along the way we meet the greedy inhabitants of Abalone, and a pre-*I Dream of Jeanie* Barbara Eden, who plays Cunningham's love interest. While Cunningham wages a war of words against Stark, a mysterious circusmaster arrives in town and takes out an ad in the newspaper.

Flip-flopping between pidgin English and eloquence, Dr. Lao (Tony Randall) changes his demeanor to suit whatever situation he is in. Using his mysterious powers, he morphs into Merlin the Magician, Pan, Medusa, The Abominable Snowman, Apollonius of Tyana, and a Talking Serpent to teach the townspeople about themselves and how they can solve their problems.

Beaumont's treatment of the story played fast and loose with Finney's original text, particularly in Dr. Lao's interactions with the people of Abalone. In the book he has no appreciable effect on the people who come to see his show. For the film, however, it was decided that he should transform the townsfolk with his magic, teaching them the folly of their ways.

There is a lot to like about *The 7 Faces of Dr. Lao*. In the truest practice of satire Beaumont and Pal hold a mirror to society. The people of Abalone are stock characters who represent various types of human nature and learn about life and morality from the strange displays of Dr. Lao. Beaumont's script is never heavy-handed; he uses humor to examine the human condition. The use of Dr. Lao's sideshow attractions blurs the line between fact and illusion, questioning the very nature of human spirit.

Also featured are some great (for 1964) special effects, designed by Academy Award-winner William J. Tuttle. To modern eyes accustomed to *Jurassic Park*-style CGI, Dr. Lao's Loch Ness Monster and other creatures may look quaint, but are a wonder of stop-motion puppetry.

Tony Randall's portrayal of Dr. Lao and six of his seven alter egos (John Ericson doubled as the horned god Pan in an odd dance sequence) is a marvelous bit of work. Usually I would have trouble with a Caucasian actor playing an Asian character, particularly when that character is central to the story, but Randall treats Dr. Lao with respect. His character believes in the good of his patrons, and is truly perceptive. In addition to using a stereotypical Hollywood Chinese accent, Randall also peppers the film with English, Southern, and French accents, thereby obscuring the doctor's mysterious past, adding intrigue to his portrayal.

It is unusual for a film made at this time to promote racial tolerance, but Pal subtly does so by having the people of small town Abalone ultimately embrace the unusual Dr. Lao.

The 7 Faces of Dr. Lao is appropriate for kids and adults alike.

"Our ability to manufacture fraud now exceeds our ability to detect it."
— **VIKTOR TARANSKI (AL PACINO)**

SIMONE (2002)

■ ■ ■ ■ ■

Simone is a wickedly funny satire on the movie business and the nature of celebrity. Al Pacino is Viktor Taranski, a middling filmmaker who has never had a hit. When his star walks out on him in mid-production on his latest film he must find a replacement or the movie will never be released. A chance meeting with an eccentric computer programmer with terminal cancer leads Viktor to his new leading lady, a synthespian named Simone (a shortened version of Simulation One). The blonde, blue-eyed vision of beauty doesn't actually exist except on a floppy disc, but becomes an overnight sensation after the release of the picture.

Taranski must resort to trickery to keep his secret and her identity under wraps. As she becomes more and more popular — at one point being nominated for two Best Actress Academy awards in the same year, and winning both of them — Taranski realizes that his personal success is completely linked to her existence, and it eats away at him. The movie skewers the Hollywood star system and gently pokes fun at Simone's fans, who completely accept her as a real, breathing superstar.

"We, the audience, worship these celebrities and in this case the ultimate joke is that we are worshiping a celebrity that is thin air," director and screenwriter Andrew Niccol told *Reel to Real* in 2002. "Then you have to ask yourself how real are the so-called *real* celebrities. Even they are artificial to some degree. We have digital newscasters. We have actors acting from the grave. Oliver Reed died during the making of *Gladiator*, and they finished the film with a digital Oliver Reed. Even the so-called real actors have digital work done to them. I've stretched actors to make them look slimmer and I've fixed their complexions. You can now do face replacements. You have a stuntman do a stunt and then you'll insert the actor's face. So it is being done now, and it is most successful when you don't know it's a digital effect."

Pacino shines as Taranski. Gone are the dark days when he simply yelled his way through a role. The histrionics have disappeared and he has started acting again. His Taranski is an interesting character, a man who cares only about art, but finds himself tangled up in the most artificial business in the world. Pacino plays him with humor and restraint. "I thought it was so subversive after it was done to have Al Pacino, one of the world's great actors say, 'Who needs actors?'" says Niccol.

Catherine Keener is here playing an entertainment executive for the third time in the same year — *Death to Smoochy* and *Full Frontal* were the other two — and hands in the kind of solid, funny, sexy performance she is known for. Winona Ryder has a small role as a fiercely difficult actress named Nicola Anders. I remember thinking that after her dreadful performance in *Mr. Deeds* it seemed like Ryder had forgotten how to act. Well, she's back in my good books after seeing her in *Simone*. While she doesn't exactly *steal* the movie, she is very good.

Richard's Favorite
Bits of Movie Wisdom

1. "The length of a film should be directly related to the endurance of the human bladder." – Alfred Hitchcock

2. "In science-fiction films the monster should always be bigger than the leading lady." – Roger Corman

3. "The camera lies all the time – lies 24 times a second." – Brian De Palma

4. "The only thing an actor owes the public is not to bore them." – Marlon Brando

5. "Anyone can direct a picture once they know the fundamentals. Directing is not a mystery. It's not an art. The main thing about directing is . . . photograph the people's eyes." – John Ford

6. "If you get an impulse in a scene, no matter how wrong it seems, follow the impulse. It might be something and if it ain't – take two!" – Jack Nicholson

7. "I cut my finger – that's a tragedy. A man walks into an open sewer – that's comedy." – Mel Brooks

8. "There's a fine line between being a Method actor and being a schizophrenic." – Nicolas Cage

9. "Making a martial arts film in English, is to me, like seeing John Wayne speaking Chinese in a Western." – Ang Lee

10. "Come to work on time, know your lines, and don't bump into the other actors." – Spencer Tracy on acting.

"The calla lilies are in bloom again. Such a strange flower, suitable to any occasion. I carried them on my wedding day and now I place them here in memory of something that has died."
– TERRY RANDALL (KATHERINE HEPBURN)

STAGE DOOR (1937)

Catchphrases can be a blessing and a curse. For instance, Arnold Schwarzenegger's reading of the Terminator's most famous line "I'll be back," struck a chord with audiences, and became a favorite punch line of every hack comedian hoping to get a cheap laugh at Arnold's expense. On the one hand it helped embed the image of the muscleman in popular culture; on the other it forever labeled Arnold as the brunt of jokes.

It's not a new phenomenon. Way back in 1937 Katherine Hepburn uttered a line that would plague her for the rest of her career. In *Stage Door* she plays a wealthy, headstrong amateur actress who delivers the line, "The calla lilies are in bloom again," in a monotone voice as she makes her stage debut. Lines like that make guys like Rich Little rich. It transcended the popularity of the movie, becoming the quote that everyone used when poking fun at Ms Hepburn and her distinctive voice. The movie, of course, has much more to offer than just that one famous line.

Based on a stage play by Edna Ferber and George S. Kaufman, *Stage Door* sees Hepburn and Ginger Rogers (in her first major role sans Fred Astaire) leading a large ensemble cast (including future stars Lucille Ball, Ann Miller, and Eve Arden) as residents of the Footlights Club, a seedy boarding house for wannabe actresses. Terry Randall (Hepburn) is a prim-and-proper rich kid with stars in her eyes. She doesn't fit in with the rest of the women, who respond to her well-bred ways with wisecracks. "How many doors are there to this place?" asks Terry. "Well, there's the trap door, the humidor, and the cuspidor. How many doors would you like?" replies Jean (Rogers).

Eventually the inexperienced Terry is given the chance to act, and during rehearsals delivers the classic interpretation of the calla lilies line. Although she's thrilled to be a working actress, her big break comes with a heavy price. Kaye (Andrea Leeds), another roomer at the hostel, had her heart set on the part that Terry won and kills herself on opening night. With just minutes before the curtain rises Jean tells Terry the tragic news, blaming her for Kaye's death. Distraught, Terry refuses to go on, but is talked into performing as a tribute to Kaye. The tragedy stirs something in her, pushing her acting to new levels.

Stage Door sparkles with good dialogue. Shooting started without a finished script, so director Gregory LaCava relied on improvisation between the actresses for much of the back and forth in the boarding-house. This lends a spur-of-the-moment, natural feeling to the movie and adds to the chemistry among the cast members.

On the strength of these strong performances, *Stage Door* was a breakthrough for two cast members. Ginger Rogers was already an established song-and-dance star with three dozens films to her credit, but this was her first dramatic role. No longer typecast as a hoofer, she used *Stage Door* as a springboard, as she went on to make many dramas, including 1940's critically acclaimed *Kitty Foyle*. Lucille Ball had appeared in 40 movies, although mostly in non-speaking parts with names like "Davy's Girlfriend at Racetrack," or "blonde telephone operator." Her small but effervescent role in *Stage Door* gave her a chance to share her comic gift. It was just the kind of role she needed to graduate from uncredited parts to starring in low-budget comedies.

Although the film was nominated for four Academy Awards, Katherine Hepburn wasn't honored. Her famous line, however, lived on, which may have been a delicious irony for Hepburn. She borrowed the line from her failed 1933 Broadway vehicle *The Lake*, which was met with critical indifference. The quote from the unsuccessful play that she believed in so much had finally achieved immortality.

> "I'd give each one of 'em a stick and, one for each one of 'em, then I'd say, 'You break that.' Course they could real easy. Then I'd say, 'Tie them sticks in a bundle and try to break that.' Course they couldn't. Then I'd say, 'That bundle . . . that's family.'"
> — ALVIN STRAIGHT (RICHARD FARNSWORTH)

THE STRAIGHT STORY (1999)

Edgy, weird, and dangerous are several words commonly used to describe director David Lynch's work. *Eraserhead, Blue Velvet, Wild At Heart,* and *Mulholland Drive* are noted for their dark view of America's soft underbelly, earning Lynch the nickname "Jimmy Stewart from Mars." "Disney," "gentle," and "heart-warming" are some words I never thought I'd hear connected to a David Lynch movie, but that was before I saw *The Straight Story*.

Written by Lynch's live-in companion and long-time editor Mary Sweeney, this is the most linear, and well, straight-ahead story Lynch has ever committed to film. Alvin Straight (Richard Farnsworth) is a true-to-life character who embarks on a long journey to visit his estranged brother Henry (Harry Dean Stanton) who has recently suffered a stroke. It's a road picture with a twist. You see, Alvin is up there in years, walks with a cane, has a host of medical problems, and doesn't have a driver's license. To make the trip he rides a second-hand John Deere lawn tractor 240 miles from his home in Iowa to Wisconsin. "I call it the four-mile-an-hour road picture," says Sissy Spacek, who plays Alvin's daughter Rose. Along the journey, which Lynch wisely takes his time with, we learn much about the plainspoken Alvin. He speaks of the relationship with his wife that produced 14 children, his years as an Army sniper, and his predilection for drink. The dialogue is simple and straightforward, but packs an emotional wallop as we get inside Alvin's skin.

For Farnsworth *The Straight Story* was the role of a lifetime. The Los

Angeles-born Farnsworth was 79 and in ill health when he began shooting the film. He began his career in motion pictures as a teenaged stuntman, driving a chariot for Cecil B. DeMille. For the next 40 years he worked anonymously, doing stunt riding and tricks in 300 films and television shows, even co-founding the Stuntman's Association in 1961, before director Alan J. Pakula cast him in a meaty supporting role as an aging ranch hand in 1978's *Comes a Horseman*. His work on that film garnered him an Academy Award nomination, and led to many other roles, including his much celebrated portrayal of Bill Miner in the Canadian film *The Grey Fox*.

Alvin Straight was Farnsworth's last role, and a fitting capper to his long and interesting career. His graceful performance is deceptively simple, presented with the kind of ease that can only come with years of experience. It's the kind of dignified, natural performance that runs the risk of seeming too real, like he's not acting at all. That's because he is so deep into the character that he seems to transcend the story, almost as if you're watching a documentary. His eyes have seen it all and betray the wisdom of human experience. He wears the wrinkles on his craggy face like a badge of honor, the result of a life well lived. Much like Farnsworth himself. "He's got a quality that's so strong, and he makes every word and glance seem real," says Lynch. "He has innocence, and that's a gift."

The Straight Story is a beautiful piece of work, a movie that takes its time to unfold, but delivers rewards to those willing to wait for the payoff. It is the first film of Lynch's that he did not write, his first G-rating, and the first made in collaboration with Disney. He cites a good working relationship with the studio, but doesn't concern himself with the business of making movies. "Business is so far down the ladder of importance when it comes to the film that it shouldn't even be discussed," he told *The Guardian*. "It's sick how much attention it gets, but then, the world is ass backwards. It would be fantastic to be able to make movies and never put them out. I love getting them to where they're really right for me — that part is beautiful. When it's time to release them, the heartache begins."

> "Fame is the one addiction that you can never overcome. You can kick heroin, but you can never beat the fame high."
> — **ALLISON ANDERS**, director of *SUGAR TOWN*

SUGAR TOWN (1999)

Writer /director Allison Anders has specialized in making deeply personal, quirky films about the music business. Her first film, 1987's *Border Radio*, followed three musicians on the lam after stealing money from a club owner. Ten years later she made *Grace of My Heart*, an underrated little jewel about a songwriter who sets aside her dreams of being a star to write hit songs for other artists. Rounding off her music biz trilogy is 1999's *Sugar Town*, a look at the jaded L.A. scene, written with collaborator Kurt Voss in just eight days.

Anders and Voss weave together a gallery of characters, beginning with a "supergroup" of '80s has-beens poised to make a return to the pop charts. In a clever bit of casting they hired three guys who are each worthy of their own episode of *Behind the Music* — Duran Duran's John Taylor, Spandau Ballet's Martin Kemp, and Michael Des Barres, the former husband of super groupie Pamela Des Barres and singer from Detective — to play the comeback kids Clive, Jonesy, and Nick. Clive is married to Eva (Rosanna Arquette), an actress who has never progressed past performing in B-movie fare like *Bury Your Bones in My Garage*. A monkey wrench is thrown into their relationship when it is discovered Clive has an illegitimate son. Meanwhile Carl (former X bass player John Doe), an aging roadie who has grown sick of the road, grudgingly goes on tour to earn money to care for his family. The final plotline involves a manipulative up-and-coming singer named Gwen (Jade Gordon) who tries to seduce Liz's (Ally Sheedy) boyfriend Burt (Larry Klein). Burt is also the producer who is manufacturing the comeback of the band. See how it all ties together? Like the ambitious

Magnolia or *Short Cuts*, *Sugar Town*'s disparate elements all collide as the plot tendrils intertwine toward the movie's climax.

Anders and Voss manage the sprawling material well, cramming lots of humor and action into a tidy 92 minutes. Weaving the threads of a story through a tapestry this complicated has inherent dangers. The challenge is to find an emotional balance without swerving into melodrama or irony. For the most part they succeed, although the film's final third has some plot resolution problems and a rather unsatisfying *de rigeur* ending. A cast that seems to be having a ball, however, pumps up the movie's energy level. Musicians Taylor, Kemp, Des Barres, and Doe all give very natural performances, breathing life into stereotypes that might have fallen flat if not played with so much élan. Rosanna Arquette also deserves mention for her portrayal of Eva. Having survived the ups and downs of Hollywood stardom herself, Arquette delivers a smart, funny performance informed by insider knowledge of what the downside of fame feels like. *Sugar Town* aims to uncover a little-seen facet of show business — mid-level stars trying to live their lives, while clamoring for another shot at the brass ring. Ultimately, it's a glib story of desperation where the serious and satiric collide.

"Bad luck isn't brought by broken mirrors, but by broken minds."
— DR. FRANK MANDEL (UDO KIER)

SUSPIRIA (1977)

Based on the Thomas De Quincey essay "Levana and Our Ladies of Sorrow" from the book *Confessions of an Opium Eater*, *Suspiria* is veteran Italian horror director Dario Argento's masterpiece. Shot with technologically outdated Kodak Technicolor film stock, the movie is painted in lurid tones of red, blue, and yellow, as Argento unfolds the story of American ballerina Suzy Banion (Jessica Harper) and a coven of witches.

"It was always meant to be an acid trip," says Argento. "I went to Germany to shoot it, to accent all the expressionistic fairy-tale aspects." To add to the film's surreal fairy-tale feel, cinematographer Luciano Tovoli studied Walt Disney cartoons to create the vibrant psychedelic quality Argento wanted.

Suspiria drips with atmosphere from the opening minutes. Before the first drop of blood is spilled Argento earns his nickname "the Italian Hitchcock" as he establishes a feeling of anticipation and uncertainty with a series of fluid camera moves and a nerve-jangling score by Goblin. Like other Argento films the plotting is sloppy, but the lack of a clear narrative lends *Suspiria* much of its nightmarish quality.

In a nutshell, here's what happens: There is a ferocious storm brewing as Banion arrives at her new school, a dance academy located in the Black Forest. She is turned away at the door, and as she is leaving to find a hotel she sees a young woman running from the school. When the woman turns up dead, Banion begins her own investigation into the death. Her search for the culprit leads her into the hands of ancient and unspeakable horror.

Fans of gore will not be disappointed — one of Argento's specialties is coming up with new and creative ways to murder people — but the real terror here comes from his use of prolonged suspense. He's not afraid to draw out a scene until it reaches its breaking point, white-knuckling it until the suspense is almost unbearable. *Suspiria* is a genre classic that may not appeal to all viewers, but will certainly leave an impression on anyone who sees it.

13 CONVERSATIONS ABOUT ONE THING (2002)

This is a difficult, wordy little picture that asks a single question: "How do we achieve happiness?" Of course there is no answer, but director Jill Sprecher and her sister, co-screenwriter Karen, present four scenarios that offer up interesting variations on the fragile nature of happiness.

"I really love the short story form," says Jill Sprecher. "*13 Conversations* was envisioned as an anthology of a theme. For me, there's nothing really better than reading a good short story. I love Mark Twain, O. Henry — I fall back on the American classics a great deal." Matthew McConaughey is Troy, a swaggering lawyer who is slowly torn apart by guilt after committing a hit-and-run. Walker (John Turturro) and Patricia's (Amy Irving) marriage is collapsing under the weight of his infidelity. Beatrice (Clea DuVall), a good-natured young woman who cleans rich people's houses, has her life and outlook altered forever after a near-fatal accident. The final and best storyline involves Gene (Alan Arkin), an insurance claims adjuster who fires Wade, his happiest employee, simply because he can't stand to see him smile day after day. "There is something Chekhovian in the depth and absurdity of Gene's obsession with Wade," says Arkin, "even after trying to right this incredible wrong, he's still reluctant to let it in, to look at himself too closely." This is an odd film — one that takes some warming to — but it does get under your skin, particularly Alan Arkin's scenes, which he executes with the skill, insight, and timing of a master.

TADPOLE (2002)

－ ━ ━ ━ ━ ━ ━

A quirky little film shot in two weeks on a shoestring budget, *Tadpole* was one of the finds at the 2002 Sundance Festival, where it took home a Best Director award and a five-million-dollar distribution deal from Miramax films. Oscar Grubman (Aaron Stanford) is an intelligent 15-year-old with a problem. He is hopelessly in love with his stepmother Eve (Sigourney Weaver), a scientist who married his father (John Ritter) after his marriage to Oscar's mom dissolved. Things become complicated when Oscar sleeps with Eve's best friend Diane (Bebe Neuwirth), intoxicated by the fragrance of the scarf Diane happened to borrow from Eve. It's a wickedly funny scene, and one that displays how blinded by love he is. It's *The Graduate* by way of *Oedipus Rex*.

Despite its unusual subject, *Tadpole* works on many levels. First-time actor Aaron Stanford is terrific as the lovesick Oscar. "Gary initially was, I think, dead set on a 15-year-old to do it," Stanford told *Ensiders.com*. "But they ended up not looking at anybody who was under 20, because of who the character is, because he's not a real 15-year-old. One of the lines in the script is, 'he's a 40-year-old trapped in a 15-year-old's body.' They needed someone who was able to physically pull off 15 while at the same time having a sort of wisdom behind the eyes, an older soul."

As good as Stanford is, it is Broadway veteran Bebe Neuwirth who steals the show. As the 40-something temptress Diane, she wrings every bit of impish humor from the character. Sigourney Weaver provides the emotional core of the film. As Eve, a woman married to her work as much as to her husband, her reaction to Oscar's advances provides real feeling, a sensitive turn that deepens the story.

Tadpole is a funny, insightful coming-of-age story with great performances.

TARGETS (1968)

■ ■ ■ ■ ■ ■ ■

Few directorial debuts have been so startling, so self-assured as Peter Bogdanovich's 1968 film *Targets*. Working with a microbudget, Bogdanovich skillfully knitted together two seemingly unrelated stories and gave horror legend Boris Karloff his last good role.

Like so many filmmakers, Bogdanovich got his big break courtesy of Roger Corman. The legendary director/producer offered Bogdanovich some outtakes from *The Terror*, a low-budget Corman shocker, and the services of Boris Karloff, who contractually owed Corman two days on set. Bogdanovich's task was to find a way to turn those elements into a movie, quickly and cheaply.

Working with his then-wife Polly Platt, Bogdanovich pounded out a script (allegedly with some unaccredited help from Orson Welles and Samuel Fuller) partially inspired by the 1966 shooting spree of University of Texas clocktower-sniper Charles Whitman. To that, Bogdanovich added a parallel story involving Karloff as Byron Orlock, a monster movie legend nearing the end of a long and distinguished career.

Orlock wants to retire from films. His presence in Hollywood has been reduced to pumping out bad drive-in horror movies, and he wants out. He feels that his films are inconsequential in light of the real-life horrors of Vietnam and inner-city violence. A money-hungry director,

Sammy Michaels (played by Bogdanovich), tries to convince Orlock to take one more kick at the can and make one last film.

At the same time in this fractured timeline of a story, a Vietnam vet named Bobby Thompson (Tim O'Kelly) is nearing his breaking point. From the outside he looks like a normal all-American kid, but he has come back from the war deeply psychologically scarred and with an unhealthy (for those around him, at least) fascination with guns. He seems in control until one beautiful cloudless California morning when he overloads, shoots his mother, his wife, and even an unlucky delivery boy. In a confession note left with the bodies he writes chillingly that he expects to be caught, but will kill many more before that time.

Here Bogdanovich begins to meld the two unrelated stories, building tension until their inevitable confrontation in the climax of the film. Orlock is seen grudgingly preparing to make a personal appearance at a drive-in to promote his last film, *The Terror*. Bobby lies in wait on an oil storage tank, steadily picking off motorists on the freeway, while calmly eating a sandwich with a Pepsi chaser. After narrowly escaping the police, Bobby flees to the drive-in to hide under the cloak of darkness. Orlock arrives by limo, preparing to meet and greet with his fans. At dusk Bobby makes his way behind the huge movie screen and begins shooting. As panic ensues everyone tries to escape, except for Orlock.

Bogdanovich never lets go of the tension in *Targets*. It builds and builds until the very closing seconds of the film, and more astoundingly he does it without resorting to gimmicks. There are no fancy camera moves à la Brian De Palma, no suspenseful music to manipulate the viewer, just superb editing and pacing. The scene in which Bobby randomly guns down motorists on the freeway while eating his lunch is particularly unnerving. Shot from his point of view, high atop an oil storage tank, we don't see close-ups of the dead or any blood; they are anonymous victims of a lunatic, seen through the scope of a gun and shot between bites of his sandwich. The absence of music in the sequence makes it terrifying, almost as though we're seeing news footage or a scene from a documentary on serial thrill killers. Bogdanovich has rarely ventured into the thriller realm, and it's a shame, because he has a master's touch with suspense.

I had to wonder while watching *Targets* if Bogdanovich was taking a metaphorical shot at his boss, B-movie king Roger Corman, by staging a sniper scene at a drive-in, the very place Corman made his money. Or was he showing contempt for the unsophisticated middle-American audiences who flocked to the open-air theaters on the weekends?

Tim O'Kelly is effective as Bobby, his outward calm just a shell to hide the rage and pain that lives within, but the film really belongs to his octogenarian co-star. Boris Karloff once said, "As long as they want me, I'll work till the end." And he did; in a career that spanned almost 200 films, Karloff stayed in front of the cameras until just a few months before his death in 1969 at age 81. *Targets* would have been a great capper to his long career, but unfortunately he continued to say "yes" to virtually any producer who would hire him, and in the last year of his life made several Mexploitation horror films with titles like *Alien Terror* and *Isle of the Snake People*. See *Targets* instead, and appreciate how good an actor Karloff was. He portrays Orlock as a kind yet cynical, world-weary fellow. "I'm an anachronism," he says, feeling left behind by the changing pace of life in a world that he helped create but has no place in.

To see Karloff at his best check out the "Appointment in Samarra" scene. He tells a haunting fable about the consequences of trying to escape our fate in one long 95-second take as the camera slowly glides into his face. His deep, slightly lisping voice (familiar to all as the narrator of *The Grinch Who Stole Christmas*) dances over the macabre lines, weaving a spooky story about the Angel of Death that cleverly foreshadows the conflict yet to come in the movie. Karloff himself considered Orlock to be his greatest performance.

Targets was not a success when first released in 1968. A sniper story, even one that could be considered anti-gun, was too timely in the wake of the Kennedy and King assassinations. As a result the film was poorly marketed and only played in limited release.

THE TERROR OF TINY TOWN (1938)

Producer Jed Buell could be called many things, but politically correct isn't on the roll call. He elevated bad taste to an art form, producing novelty Western movies with unusual casts. In 1939 he unleashed *Harlem on the Prairie*, specifically geared toward the 800 or so African-American theaters in the United States. But his "finest" moment came a year earlier with the release of *The Terror of Tiny Town*, the world's first (and to date, only) all-midget musical motion picture.

Buell stumbled across the idea for the movie following an offhand remark by his assistant. "If this economy drive keeps on," he said, "we'll be using midgets for actors." Buell assembled his cast through talent agencies, radio broadcasts, and newspaper ads promising "Big Salaries for Little People." He even recruited a troupe of 14 circus performers from Hawaii. In all he cast almost 60 actors with an average height of 3'8", ranging from teenagers to pensioners.

The storyline (by Fred Myton and Clarence Marks) involves a feud between the Preston and Lawson ranches. Tension between the two families has reached an all-time high, as each believes the other is responsible for a series of mysterious cow disappearances. What they don't know is that evil gunslinger Bat Haines ("Little Billy" Rhodes) is actually behind all the trouble in Tiny Town, working in cahoots with the corrupt sheriff. Our hero (you know he's the good guy because he's wearing all white) Buck Lawson (Billy Curtis) suspects that someone other than the Prestons might be the source of the town's woes, but is preoccupied with wooing the lovely Nancy Preston (Yvonne Moray). Haines realizes that Buck is onto him, and tries to frame him for the murder of Tex Preston (Billy Platt). Proclaiming his innocence, Buck avoids a lynch mob, and at the end there is the inevitable showdown between good and evil in a cabin wired with dynamite.

This sounds like a typical Saturday matinee bottom-of-the-bill serial Western, but add in actors of small stature, a duck that walks backward, and cowboys who chase one another around on Shetland ponies, and you've got big-time entertainment.

The Terror of Tiny Town is the height of exploitation filmmaking. The diminutive actors are never treated with any dignity, and jokes are made constantly at their expense. In the film's prologue Buck proclaims that once this movie is seen, "I'm going to be the BIGGEST star in Hollywood." "No way," counters Bat Haines, "*I'm* going to be the BIGGEST star in Hollywood." In fact, the script is a goldmine of cheesy "big" and "small" jokes. "That's a BIG order for me," says one character. "You'll get SMALLpox from him!" warns another.

Modern exploitation films never get this bizarre. Despite the run-of-the-mill story and action, the very idea of the novelty casting of little people makes *The Terror of Tiny Town* a fascinating time capsule of a different era in Hollywood's history. Tinsel Town has never been a dignified place, but this film is astonishingly politically incorrect, and that is what makes it a must-rent. It displays the lengths producers will go to put bums in seats. Like it or hate it, you have to admit that you've never seen anything quite like it, which in the cookie-cutter world of modern cinema, is quite a feat.

The Terror of Tiny Town was a box office success, easily earning back its $100,000 production cost. It was such a hit that Buell developed sequel fever, planning a series of little people movies. The first was a retelling of the Paul Bunyan yarn announced in *Variety* on July 20, 1938. Fortunately for the Lilliputian actors and audiences alike, that film was never made.

While most of *Tiny Town*'s cast returned to their day jobs after the shoot, several of the actors had long careers in Hollywood. At 2'6" Yvonne Moray became known as a smaller version of Greta Garbo, and went on to appear in several films. But it was Billy Curtis who had the most productive career, and was responsible for one oft-told Hollywood legend. He appeared in 40 movies and television shows until his death in 1986.

The most famous entry on his filmography is 1939's *The Wizard of Oz*. His uncredited performance as City Father pales by comparison to his behavior on the set. Charles Schram, a makeup man at MGM recalls, "Billy Curtis was the handsomest and had the most style [of the 124 little people hired for the movie]. He was quite arrogant. He looked down on the others because he had had a degree of success in vaudeville." He apparently swaggered around the set, and made several passes at Judy Garland, who rebuffed him saying, "Mother wouldn't approve." Curtis also claims credit for saving Margaret Hamilton from an on-set fire, and helping Judy Garland sneak off the lot to meet her boyfriend. Both stories have been denied.

But it was one comment from Judy Garland that immortalized Curtis and his Munchkin brethren forever. "They were drunks," she said, allegedly referring to Curtis. "They got smashed every night, and the police had to pick them up in butterfly nets."

> "If we never looked at things and thought of what might be, why we'd all still be out there in the tall grass with the apes."
> — DR. JUSTIN PLAYFAIR (GEORGE C. SCOTT)

THEY MIGHT BE GIANTS (1971)

The title *They Might Be Giants* is an allusion to Don Quixote and his fight with a series of windmills he mistook for giants, an offbeat premise that fuels this film. George C. Scott plays wealthy, retired New York City judge Justin Playfair, who, downhearted over the loss of his wife, becomes convinced he is Sherlock Holmes. He sees injustice everywhere, and figures it must be the work of the world's most evil man — Sir Arthur Conan Doyle's Dr. Moriarty. Dressed in a deerstalker hat, he searches New York for his nemesis with the aid of a female psychiatrist conveniently named Mildred Watson (Joanne Woodward). Watson is a dedicated career-driven woman who has never allowed herself much of a personal life — until now. She falls for the retired judge, at first drawn to him in a professional sense, and later to his keen deductive powers as a detective. Their love story is poignant and humorous, as two damaged people come together, each providing the other with a crucial slice of humanity that was otherwise missing in their lives.

A subplot involving a conniving brother who is trying to have Playfair committed to an insane asylum so he can take control of his fortune spices up the action, but it is the performances of Scott and Woodward that keep the film fresh and enjoyable. Scott plays the judge as a sensitive and loveable character, a far cry from the gruff roles he usually undertook. In an endearingly deluded way he really believes he is the legendary sleuth, and because of his conviction, the audience begins to believe it too. Once the game is afoot, funny scenes abound. Woodward's ill-fated attempt to cook dinner displays her comic timing, while a food throwing riot in a supermarket is flat-out slapstick.

The central theme of this lighthearted story is reflected in the title. In the back of a taxi cab Playfair says, "They might be giants," and at once the movie's premise gels. There just *might* be windmills, just as Playfair just *might* be Sherlock Holmes. Imagination can be a powerful thing, and *They Might Be Giants* bristles with flights of fancy.

When asked how he made Playfair so convincing, Scott said, "I didn't play the character as if I were portraying Sherlock Holmes. I played him as a delusional man who *fantasized* that he was Sherlock Holmes." In a broader pop culture sense, the film inspired two art rockers from Brooklyn, New York, supplying the name for their band. They Might Be

Giants won an Emmy for their theme song from the sitcom *Malcolm in the Middle*, and have their own offbeat take on the film. "It's about how insanity is groovy. It was the insanity-chic period of cinema," says John Linnell. "It's one of those 'Who's crazy?' movies."

"'Who belongs in the asylum? The crazy people or the people who aren't crazy?'" adds John Flansburgh.

> Maria: If I get a cold, you cough. If I go on a diet, you
> lose the weight and if we should ever have a baby,
> I'm not so sure I would be the mother!!!
> Joseph: I would be happy just to be the father.
> **– Dialogue from *TO BE OR NOT TO BE***

TO BE OR NOT TO BE (1942)

By age 33 Carole Lombard was one of the leading stars in Hollywood. Nicknamed the Profane Angel because of her bawdy sense of humor and beautiful visage, she commanded a fee of $35,000 per movie, making her one of the highest paid female stars of the time. She and her movie star husband Clark Gable embodied the glamour of Tinsel Town. It was a seemingly charmed life. Lombard's fairy tale came to a tragic end on January 16, 1942, just months before her last film, *To Be or Not To Be* premiered.

To Be or Not To Be is one of the most biting satires to ever hit the silver screen. Conceived and written by German ex-patriot director Ernst Lubitsch, the film is set just before the 1939 Nazi invasion of Poland. Jack Benny and Carole Lombard play Joseph and Maria Tura, stars of a Polish troupe of actors. Their lives, professional and personal, are thrown into turmoil because of the German occupation of WWII. The actors are pressed into service to protect the Polish underground. Impersonating Nazi officials, they become involved in a variety of schemes to undermine the German campaign. The troupe is successful, uncovering a treacherous double agent before safely fleeing the country in Hitler's plane.

The tale of Polish actors thwarting the Nazis was a change of pace for director Lubitsch. After leaving Germany in the late 1920s he helmed a series of movies such as *Ninotchka* and *Trouble in Paradise* that gave birth to a common Hollywood phrase — "the Lubitsch Touch" — that referred to witty, sophisticated films. Possessing a firm but loving hand with actors, he was able to wheedle great performances from his casts, often displaying what he envisioned for a role by acting out the scenes for them. *To Be or Not To Be* was darker, more biting than anything Lubitsch had done before, or would do after.

Lubitsch may have had a personal reason for attacking the fascist regime. As a well-known actor in Germany, a cruel caricature of his profile was circulated on a Nazi propaganda poster as an example of the typical Jewish face.

The idea of framing a comedy around the exploits of the Nazis wasn't exactly a new idea. Charlie Chaplin had stirred up controversy in 1940 with *The Great Dictator*, an anti-fascist spoof set in the fictional land of Tomania, but *To Be or Not To Be* is a different sort of bird. More derisive than Chaplin's offering, Lubitsch paints the Nazis as buffoons, and his movie rides a thin line between comedy and outright propaganda. While there is nothing remotely funny about the Nazis or their deeds, surefire objects for ridicule are authority and arrogance, and in this case the flawed logic of the fascists is a perfect target. Many critics in 1942, however, thought the Nazis were no laughing matter, with one, Bosley Crowther of *The New York Times* saying that he is "unable even remotely to comprehend the humor." It's worth noting that the sentiment of the times was playing against this movie, much as today's audiences may have reacted strongly to a farce about the events of 9-11 released shortly after that tragic day.

As "that great, great actor Joseph Tura," Jack Benny hands in his best big screen performance. Although blessed with unerring comic timing and a deadpan glance that could send audiences into spasms of laughter without saying a word, movies weren't his forte; he was best suited to the more intimate medium of television. Having said that, he is a delight in *To Be or Not To Be*. His dialogue shines, particularly the one-liners. "I'm going to have to do the impossible," he says, "I'm going to have to surpass myself." His Joseph is so conceited, so self-centered he is a riot to watch.

In one unforgettable scene Joseph is in the midst of the *Hamlet* soliloquy from which the movie takes its name, as Sobinski (a very young Robert Stack) rises to leave the theater. Benny's reactions to the snub are worth the price of admission, as he silently watches the patron leave during the performance, too stunned to even speak. It's the deadpan leer Benny was famous for, but it was rarely ever used to better effect.

Benny may have the showier role, but the picture really belongs to Lombard, whose last role was tailor-made for her. As Maria Tura, the manipulative ingénue of a small Polish acting troupe, she is a wonder to behold. The years spent churning out one- and two-reelers for Mack Sennett gave her a master's touch in the comedic scenes; her work at Paramount honed her dramatic skills and her great beauty gave her charisma to burn. Combined, these elements add up to a tour de force performance that she rightly considered to be her best ever. She died in a plane crash while on a war bond tour just three weeks after shooting on the film wrapped.

Although *To Be or Not To Be* was a flop at the time of release, it has belatedly earned praise from film historians who praised Lubitsch's handling of the risky material and his skillful weaving of comedy, propaganda, and drama. The style of the film stands alone in the Lubitsch canon; it isn't as fluffy and sophisticated as his other movies, but given the subject matter coupled with his own personal feelings, perhaps a little heavy-handedness is to be expected.

To Be or Not To Be was remade in 1983 as a vehicle for Mel Brooks and Anne Bancroft. The stories are not identical, and while Brooks earned good notices as the hammy actor, it is the Lubitsch version that is required viewing.

THE TOXIC AVENGER (1984)

Director Lloyd Kaufman describes his work as "a Cuisinart of genres," which is Lloyd-speak for his brand of extreme cinema that combines ultra-violence, slapstick, and horror with the sensibilities of *Mad* magazine. In 1984 Kaufman directed *The Toxic Avenger*, a film that would define his vision of exploitation movies. The film was so over-the-top it took almost one year after completion to find a movie theater in the United States that would screen it. Despite the outrageous X-rated content of the film, it spawned a cottage industry, and put Kaufman's company, the fiercely independent Troma Films, on the map.

The Toxic Avenger stands alone in the history of cinema as the only movie where a kid's head is crushed beneath the wheel of an automobile to be made into a children's environmentally correct Saturday morning cartoon show. "That's pretty cool," says Kaufman.

In the early 1980s Kaufman and former Yale classmate Michael Hertz had reached a crossroads. Their film production company Troma had made a name and decent box-office returns, pumping out a string of low-budget sex comedies geared toward the B-movie market. In mid-1983 though, the Troma mantra of "guaranteed bottoms would give you guaranteed bottom line," hadn't held true.

Their fearless commitment to the public's desire to watch scantily clad women in unpredictable (and unlikely) situations had insured that there would be a small but loyal audience for their films. So entrenched was their reputation for making jiggle movies that one pundit suggested that their name actually stood for "Tits R Our Main Asset."

"Troma tries to give people something they haven't seen before," says Kaufman of his company's manifesto. "They will be challenged. Troma tries to provoke people. We're trying to get people's juices flowing with the hope that [they will see past] this baby food mentality of $100 million movies, which have to be all things to all people. We're trying to get rid of that. You can live on baby food, but it is boring. We're the jalapeno peppers on the cultural pizza."

The two-man production team made their name with the 1979 sex-romp *Squeeze Play*. "We came up with the title referring to the squeezing of women's breasts," says Kaufman. "I was very surprised when I found out that, co-incidentally, this was also a strategy in softball." The story of the Beaverettes — an amorous all-girl softball team — established Troma's recipe of outrageous humor mixed with social comment, all served with a healthy dose of T&A. Setting the film apart from the run-of-the-mill sex romps were Kaufman's hot topic references to the then-burgeoning women's lib movement. But it was the movie's combination of sports and sex appeal that seduced audiences, turning *Squeeze Play* into the neophyte company's first financial success. More importantly, it taught the duo about what plays on the silver screen.

Three more teen sex flicks followed — *Waitress, Stuck On You, The First Turn On* — making the Troma brand synonymous with rollicking, playful films.

"Disney has a brand," says Kaufman, "and according to the *New York Times* Troma is the only other studio where people go for the brand name." Indie film legend Roger Corman calls Kaufman's vision the point "where the anarchic meets the ridiculous." Typical of the humor is a scene in *Stuck On You* where chickens are shown pornography so they will lay more eggs. It's a scene that was shocking at the time, but would now fit perfectly in the mainstream films of the Farrelly Brothers or Trey Parker and Matt Stone.

Troma gained a reputation for no-holds-barred, anything goes, gonzo filmmaking. Was there anything they wouldn't do? "I wouldn't do something that suggests Adolph Hitler or Hillary Clinton are good people," says Lloyd. "I wouldn't do that. I don't believe I would do a movie with Barbra Streisand or Julia Roberts either."

With notoriously low budgets, Troma turned a profit (sometimes just barely) by identifying their customers and pandering to them. Small, sexy comedies, released one theater at a time with imaginative promotional gimmicks, became a hallmark of the Troma team.

Then the big boys caught on.

By and large Troma had operated under the radar of the majors, but as their success grew, they couldn't stay underground for long. Soon, larger budget, broadly released sex farces were eating away at the Troma niche. Troma product was squeezed out of the theaters, which were booked solid with studio teen comedies. Faced with diminishing returns, Kaufman and Hertz needed to find a new direction.

The direction came to Kaufman while reading *Variety*. A voracious reader, he was always scanning the newspapers and trades for inspiration. What he read would change the face of Troma films, and pop culture, despite being news that would have sent anyone else running in the opposite direction. In large block letters the headline screamed, "The Horror Film Is Dead." A regular film producer would have looked at the news, and decided to make comedies, dramas, or gangster movies — anything *but* horror films. But Lloyd saw an opportunity to open a Pandora's Box of sex, violence, humor, and the world's first superhero from New Jersey.

"We knew from film history that since the beginning the horror film was very viable, and wasn't going to go away," Lloyd told the Australian webzine *Tabula Rasa* in 1994. "We figured, well, if people weren't going to make horror movies temporarily, maybe there's an open window we could jump into and make a film in that genre, so when the vogue comes back, we'll be at the forefront."

Ignoring the proclamations of "the machine's trade paper," Kaufman set out to write *Health Club Horror*, featuring a disgusting-looking creature. An article in *I.F. Stone's Weekly* about South American children who played with "pixie dust" found at a local dump stuck in Kaufman's head. The dust was actually irradiated waste from X-ray machines.

"The children had fun frolicking in the beautiful, shiny sparkles, and it ended up killing them," writes Kaufman in his 1998 book *All I Need To Know About Filmmaking I Learned From The Toxic Avenger*. "To this day I find this chilling."

The resulting film, now called *The Toxic Avenger*, was set in the "Toxic Waste Dumping Capital of America," Tromaville, New Jersey. While working at a health club, 90-pound weakling health club janitor Melvin Furd (Mark Torgl) is constantly bullied by Bozo (Gary Schneider) and his gang. When a prank misfires, Melvin lands in a barrel of toxic waste and mutates into the lumpy-headed Toxic Avenger (Mitchell Cohen). "Toxie," as he is affectionately known, soon wins the respect of the people of Tromaville as he wages a war against crime, armed only with a mop. He is a hero to the underdog, but hated by the town's corrupt mayor and police chief, who call in the National Guard to battle Toxie.

One unforgettable scene is the famous head-crushing sequence. Removed from the R-rated version of the film years ago, it was restored for the director's cut DVD. Like so many of Kaufman's inspirations, this one came from a real life incident when he accidentally ran over his four-year-old kid sister Susan. (She's fine.) Recently Kaufman unveiled the secret behind the gory effect. "It was just a melon in a wig!" he says. Although Troma reports that the scene where a dog is shot garnered the most complaints, the head-crushing sequence (repeated several times) remains one of the film's highlights.

Like all Troma films, *The Toxic Avenger* is an acquired taste. Gallons of fake blood are spilled, hands are plunged into deep fryers; in fact, all of Toxie's charitable acts of crime fighting are far more gruesome than anything the bad guys ever do. Oh, yeah, there's a sex scene between Toxie and Sara — a blind patron of a Mexican restaurant — that is not for the faint of heart. Ultimately though, the film is a good underdog tale, with some surprising performances. Andree Maranda is effective as Sara, while Dick Martinsen as Officer O'Clancy, the most Irish cop ever, is more comedic than stereotypical.

By far, *The Toxic Avenger* is the most successful (in a cult way) of the Troma catalog. Toxie became a Saturday morning cartoon character, had his own line of Marvel Comics, and has spawned three Troma-produced sequels. Two were produced in 1989 at the height of Toxie-mania — *The Toxic Avenger Part II* and *The Toxic Avenger III: The Last Temptation of Toxie*. A full 10 years passed before Kaufman once again turned his eye toward the superhero.

"We only do things we believe in, and frankly for 10 years I was not interested [in The Toxic Avenger]. He was getting fat. He was using a cellphone. He had an agent and then suddenly he came out of retirement. He's like John Travolta," said Kaufman on the release of *Citizen Toxie* in 2000. "It's a shot-for-shot remake of the Orson Welles classic, with all the gore, lesbian, and dismemberment scenes added that the evil Howard Hughes forced Welles to take out in the first place."

"People like me win . . ."
– MURRAY (DAVID HEWLETT) in *TREED MURRAY*

TREED MURRAY (2001)

At the heart of *Treed Murray* is a very simple idea: An upper-class advertising executive is literally forced up a tree by a gang of disenfranchised youth. He bargains with them, plays head games with them, and in

Richard's Favorite Credits

1. "The director would like to thank: Jenny – who gave me strength and major booty." – Kevin Smith's *Dogma* (1999)

2. "Manure courtesy of Seattle Slough."
   – *Harper Valley PTA* (1978)

3. "This line available . . . your name here." – *The Adventures of Priscilla, Queen of the Desert*

4. "Thanks to John Woo for use of his kitchen knife."
   – *Psycho* (1998)

5. "Ms Streisand's clothes from . . . her closet."
   – *A Star is Born* (1976)

6. "Dedication: To every politician who has ever jeopardized a baby's health with unsanitary kisses, who has ever delivered a three-hour Fourth of July oration about himself and George Washington, who has ever promised peace, prosperity, and triple movie features in exchange for a vote, this picture is not too humbly dedicated." – *The Senator Was Indiscreet* (1947)

7. "The Monster – ?" (Boris Karloff is not listed in the credits) – *Frankenstein* (1931)

8. "Interesting fact: Actor Richard Crenna invented tartar sauce."
   – *Hot Shots: Part Deux* (1993)

9. "Filmed entirely on location on Earth."
   – *Better Than Chocolate* (1999)

10. "The film is over – You can go now."
    – *One Crazy Summer* (1986)

return they give as good as they get. Imagine *Twelve Angry Men* taking a bough, or an out-on-a-limb *Lifeboat*. "I pitched this movie to people as *Die Hard* in a tree," laughs director William Phillips.

Murray (David Hewlett) is an upwardly mobile young ad executive taking a shortcut through a large city park on his way home from work. His path is blocked by a 14-year-old gangbanger named Carter (Kevin Duhaney), who demands money. The suit doesn't take the kid seriously, which only exacerbates the situation. When Carter becomes threatening Murray reacts by knocking him to the ground with his briefcase, dismissing him with a flick of his hand. Murray realizes the state of affairs has gotten out of control when the rest of Carter's gang, led by the charismatic Shark (Cle Bennett), emerges from the woods. It's everybody's worst urban nightmare — to be surrounded by a hostile gang bent on causing you pain and anguish — so he does what anyone would do. He runs like hell.

Lost, exhausted, and feeling trapped with the gang hot on his heels, Murray finds sanctuary in a beech tree. Unfortunately his briefcase at the base of the tree gives him away, and the kids discover his hiding spot. He tries to buy his way out of the dangerous circumstances by offering his wallet and watch, but the kids don't just want money, they want respect. They want the dignity that Murray took from Carter by pushing him to the ground. Shark demands an apology, but will only accept it face to face. Murray has to come down from the tree.

This is the point at which the movie becomes truly interesting. Screenwriter and director Phillips adds a massive dose of verbal pyrotechnics between Murray and Shark. Murray refuses to come down from the tree, afraid of the consequences, and tries to talk his way out of trouble. The sky is beginning to darken as Murray tries to negotiate with his captors using every trick he has every learned at work — acquiescence, bargaining, manipulation. Nothing works. In Shark he has met his match, an equally clever salesman. Throughout the night their banter becomes a psychological war of words, revealing the true murky nature of the characters. As the night lifts and daylight begins to fill the sky it's clear that first impressions can be deceiving. Murray isn't necessarily the good guy; Shark and company aren't completely bad.

Treed Murray should be a template for first-time, low-budget feature filmmaking. It's the kind of film that could be taught in film school to show how to make a riveting, ambitious movie that makes the most of its modest resources. Phillips takes a one-location scenario and relies on the script and carefully chosen actors to imbue the movie with life and vitality. Despite careful planning, however, there were problems during shooting.

"When you are trying to get your first feature off the ground one thing you have to do is get yourself a project with limited cast and limited locations and keep things really cheap," says Phillips. "I thought that would be the case here. Of course, it's not easy. Putting a man up a tree turned out to be quite difficult."

The tree was a 25-foot-tall American Beech tree in the heart of the Boyd Conservation area in Toronto. "It's a beautiful tree that went up and up and up, so high we couldn't even get the actors up that high without vertigo setting in or the insurance going through the roof," says Phillips. "It was a huge tree. When the temperature and the moisture changed, a type of moss or algae would start to form, so the tree would go from flat matte grey to brilliant green. That was a problem because there was this artificial limb we put on it. We needed something strategically placed so David Hewlett had something to hold on to and work with. We put this limb on, and you can't damage the tree, so you couldn't hammer it in. So we had to create these straps, and the straps were covered with exactly the color of the bark. But we found that when the bark changed color the straps wouldn't. We constantly had to paint the straps.

"In the middle of the shoot the tree went to seed. The beechnuts became ripe on this tree and they started raining down. So we'd be doing these scenes, and beechnuts would be bouncing off the brims of the gang member's hats. Then the birds would come to eat the beechnuts. You'd have thousands of birds flying into the tree."

"It sounds so bloody easy," adds Hewlett who was positioned on a branch almost 20 feet above the ground for 16 of the 19 days of the shoot. "The ideal thing to do in the Canadian summer is to put sugar blood all over somebody's head and put them in a tree. Every wasp and stinging beastie landed in my hair. I spent the entire time waving off wasps.

"Also, you are so far from the Kraft service that by the time the coffee got up to me it was half spilled and cold," he laughs. "It was hell."

Location problems aside, Phillips makes the best of a limited scenario, keeping the dialogue crisp and the camera work fluid. Even though the action never strays from the one location, the film is at once simple, yet ideologically complex and exciting. Without judgment or manipulation, the well-written script shifts sympathy from character to character, forcing the viewer to change allegiances several times throughout the course of its 89 minutes. There is no black and white, right or wrong, just damaged people coming to grips with the idea that the great gap between them isn't so great after all.

The performances are believable, particularly those of David Hewlett and Cle Bennett as Shark. Hewlett is superb, running the gamut of emotions that Murray is forced to deal with when stuck in the tree, whilst Bennett is menacing but smart.

While the issues raised in *Treed Murray* are universal, there is one thing that makes it a story that could only have happened in Canada, where guns and gangs are not synonymous. When a revolver appears in the latter half of the film, everyone, including the gang members are unsure how to deal with it because guns aren't that commonplace. In the U.S. the entire story might well never have happened; Murray would likely have been shot long before he had the chance to hide in the tree.

Ancient philosopher and playwright Aristotle boiled down the perfect structure for a dramatic presentation to three acts — Act One: Put someone in a tree; Act Two: Throw rocks at them; Act Three: Get them out of the tree. William Phillips has entertainingly updated Aristotle's idea to fit cinema culture.

"You don't go to work every day. You go to a bar every day."
— MARIE (ESZTER BALINT)

TREES LOUNGE (1996)
- - - - - - - - -

Early in his career Steve Buscemi twice played frustrated film directors. In 1992's *In the Soup* the former New York City fireman turned "King of the Indies" tries to finance a boring 500-page script, and inadvertently becomes the pawn in a crime spree. As Nick Reve in 1995's comedy *Living In Oblivion* he was at the helm of an independent film with a bungling crew. Perhaps as a result of impersonating one onscreen, in 1996 he decided to play the part in real life, and direct his own movie.

For his directorial debut he chose a script he had been working on since 1990. Centered on a seedy bar remembered from his youth, *Trees Lounge* is the story of Tommy Basilio (Buscemi), a 31-year-old loser who spends too much time at the bar. According to the screenplay Tommy is "pale, thin, unemployed but possesses a fair amount of humor and charm." It's a character close to Buscemi's heart; he wrote it as an exercise in imagining how he might have turned out had he not left Valley Stream (a small town near Kennedy Airport and home of the real Trees Lounge) after high school. It's not a pretty portrait.

Tommy is an unemployed auto mechanic, fired for "borrowing" money from the till, whose pregnant girlfriend (Elizabeth Bracco) has just left him for his former boss (Anthony LaPaglia). He passes the time at Trees Lounge, a dive bar populated by hollow-eyed winos, drinking until he passes out or gets kicked out. His drinking is so out of control that when he pops in and announces he's only staying for one drink, the bartender bets him 10 bucks that he can't have just one. Tommy's fortunes seem to change following the death of his ice cream vendor uncle, when he is offered the opportunity to take over the neighborhood Good Humor route. The downward spiral, however, continues when a 17-

year-old customer, Debbie (Chloe Sevigny) develops a crush. Never one to deny himself a drink or a woman, Tommy succumbs to her charms. Despite Tommy's assertion that nothing happened, that "we just made out like teenagers," Debbie's father goes ballistic and destroys the ice cream truck with a baseball bat.

The role of Tommy is crucial to the success of *Trees Lounge*, as the movie is character-driven rather than plot-driven. Audiences must feel a certain empathy for Tommy or the whole thing would be a wasted exercise. Buscemi does a great job of defining Tommy's character. He's a beer-and-a-shot guy who sees salvation at the other end of the bar, if only he could stop drinking. "This character is the closest to myself that I've ever played," Buscemi said at the time. "I guess it's my realistic dark side." He's simultaneously pathetic and likeable, but Buscemi makes the character endearing enough that the viewer becomes frustrated with him as he throws his life away.

Unlike many other movies in the barfly canon, *Trees Lounge* isn't without hope. There is a sense that Tommy is at a crossroads in his life, and if he makes the right decisions he won't end up like Bill, a lounge regular who is an echo of what Tommy may become if he doesn't straighten up.

In 1997, after the release of the film, Buscemi rescued the neon sign from the real Trees Lounge from the scrapyard as realtors were converting the tavern into a sports bar. He paid $200 for it, storing it in his father's backyard in Valley Steam until the woman who ran the bar for 40 years asked if he would give it to her. He handed over the sign, and closed that chapter in his life.

> "If I couldn't do the Twist everyday, I'd die."
> — **JANET HUFFSMITH, waitress/dancer**

THE TWIST (1992)

■ — ■ — ■ — ■ — ■ — ■

The idea of dancing with the Prime Minister of Canada was not particularly appealing to me. While Pierre Trudeau, Joe Clark, and Brian Mulroney may have been able to cut a rug, they were hardly my dream dance partners. That all changed one Thursday night in 1992 when I went to a party celebrating the release of Ron Mann's documentary *Twist: An Instructional Dance Film*. The guest of honor was Canadian Conservative Prime Minister Kim Campbell. Ms Campbell, Canada's short-lived first female PM, was set to twist on the dance floor for a crowd of media types gathered for a photo op.

I knew she was scheduled to arrive shortly before nine, and I was determined to twist with the Prime Minister. What a great story to tell my grandchildren! I could envision sitting by my fireplace, toddlers crowded around me.

"Tell us about the time you danced with the Prime Minister," they would coo.

"Well . . . it was really nothing," I would say for the thousandth time, "we danced on a sultry summer night, and she looked longingly into my eyes. . . ."

Back to reality. It didn't happen. I stood on the sidelines with everyone else while Campbell and director Ron Mann shook their hips to Chubby Checker. Afterward I asked Mann how the PM was as a dance partner. "She dances conservatively," he said.

Dancing with the head of state is just one of Mann's many accomplishments. As Canada's leading pop cultural documentarian, his subjects have included jazz musicians (1981's *Imagine the Sound*), performance poets (1982's *Poetry In Motion*), comic books (1988's *Comic*

Book Confidential), and marijuana (1999's *Grass*). "I'm interested in popularizing unpopular culture," he says, "and making it accessible."

At first glance the dance craze might seem like a thin idea for a feature-length documentary. Actually, the twist was one of the major turning points in our recent cultural history. The simple, even silly-looking dance was the catalyst that blew apart the conservative, uptight moral code of the 1950s, bridging the generation gap by introducing teenage culture to the establishment. Our parents did the twist. Even the first lady of Camelot Jacqueline Kennedy twisted at a nightclub in Palm Springs.

"What is interesting about the twist is that it became a metaphor for everything of that period," says Mann. "It was a metaphor for society at the time. It became a metaphor for the appropriation of African-American culture. It became a worldwide phenomenon of people going nuts. It was liberating. It reflected the tone of the times."

Reflected the tone, and perhaps created the tone of the times. Many pop culture historians have suggested that the twist was the beginning of the sexual revolution. "It was a dance that led to free style dancing, which sociologically led to the late '60s," says Mann. "In terms of pop culture, it was a time when adults and kids were dancing together for that brief time. It symbolized the change out of the '50s and into the '60s. What I like to call squareness awareness."

Mann cuts and pastes rare film clips to create *The Twist*, the result of three years of scouring film libraries and searching for vintage clips that weren't always easy to find. "People think that there is a warehouse somewhere where all these images are kept," says Mann. "That simply isn't true. There are only six hours of pre-1962 *American Bandstand* in existence. Most of the material, certainly from the early '60s, that was on television was on two-inch tape. They had executives with PhDs in economics who wiped out the tapes because they were $300 each. Much of the film that is still around from that period is deteriorating. People think it still exists, but it just fades away. As a cultural historian I am interested in recovering these images that are not represented in mainstream television and motion pictures."

There are some real gems among the footage that Mann collected for this film. Any student of popular culture will be amused to see Marshall McLuhan discussing the twist on television. He admits that he has done the twist, but declares it unsexy, likening it to a "conversation without words." Mann has also unearthed some great performance footage of Louis Prima doing "The Saints Go Twisting In." The deft editing job was the result of studying reams of rare material. "We went through 350 hours of rock and roll footage of social popular dance. I have curated an archive to the point where even Michael Jackson's company calls us up to look at African-American dance."

As a complement to the old clips, Mann has assembled new footage of interviews with a host of the creators and main practitioners of the twist. Mann shot three days' worth of original interviews at Lulu's Roadhouse in Kitchener, Ontario, with musicians Hank Ballard, Chubby Checker, Joey Dee, the first go-go dancer Janet Huffsmith, and ex-*American Bandstand* dancers Carole Spada and Joe Fusco. Mann also tracked down Betty (Romantini) Begg who was on the dance show the day Checker performed his hit song for the first time. "It was the first time we could move our hips on TV," she says.

"It was a big twist love-in," says Mann, "because some of these people hadn't seen one another in 30 years."

I particularly found the interview with Hank Ballard fascinating. Ballard wrote and recorded "The Twist" as an R&B tune, but found little success with it. White radio stations wouldn't play the song because Ballard was well known for writing R&B songs with suggestive lyrics. Enter Chubby Checker. His voice was virtually indistinguishable from Ballard's, but he was a clean-cut kid who says in the film that he has "the talent to make anything seem clean."

We know the rest. Chubby covers the song and becomes a pop culture phenomenon, while Ballard remains a relatively obscure figure. It surprised me that Ballard seems to harbor no ill will for Checker. In one of the more revealing interview clips, Ballard seems genuinely pleased by Checker's success. One would expect bitterness, but there doesn't appear to be any.

A film about the twist would not be complete without music. The doc's soundtrack includes dozens of twist songs culled from the huge catalog of dance music recorded in the early '60s. Everyone jumped on the twist bandwagon, and hundreds of twist songs were released in a very short time. Mann had a dream list of songs he wanted, but wasn't able to lay his hands on all of them. "As an independent filmmaker there is an economic censorship that exists," says Mann. "You can't afford certain songs. 'Twistin' the Night Away' by Sam Cooke is one of the top three twist songs. I couldn't use it because it wasn't available, or it was too expensive."

He was able to secure the rights to many songs, although his favorite twist song got away from him — "Twistin' Off a Cliff" by Duane Eddy. It's only 40 seconds long, with a twangy guitar riff followed by the blood-curdling scream of someone falling off a cliff. "It even charted," he says.

The Twist garnered good reviews, even from the Prime Minister of Canada. She told me she thought it was a marvelous film. I told her I was disappointed that I didn't get the chance to dance with her. She promised me a twist the next time she goes out dancing. That was nine years ago. Never trust a politician.

> "It remains an undisputed fact that every man has one moment of total selflessness in his life."
> — The NARRATOR

TWO FAMILY HOUSE (2000)

-- -- -- -- -- -- -- -- -- --

Write about what you know. That's one of the golden rules of letters, and a tenet that screenwriter Raymond DeFelitta followed when scripting *Two Family House*. "It's a story I'd heard over the years from both my uncle and my father that involved the purchase of a two-family house, where my uncle planned to open a bar on the ground floor and use the second floor apartment as his home," he says. "But once he purchased his two-family house my uncle faced a moment of truth. How he reacted to what followed is what makes his story exceptional and worth telling today."

It's Staten Island in 1956. Buddy Visalo (Michael Rispoli) is a lovable loser who dreams of being a crooner. His lone shot at the big time failed to bear fruit after his pessimistic wife Estelle (Katherine Narducci) wouldn't let him go to an audition for the Arthur Godfrey show. Godfrey hired Julius LeRosa, another American-Italian singer, for the job instead, and Buddy is eaten up inside that maybe, just maybe, that job could have been his. Since then he has been reduced to partaking in an endless stream of get-rich-quick schemes that never pan out. He has one last plan that he is sure could be a winner — buy a two-family house, live upstairs, and convert the bottom into a bar where he could perform and cater to his customers.

Buddy's friends are lukewarm to the idea, particularly when they see the building. It's a run-down tenement with unwanted lodgers in the upper apartment — the lovely and very pregnant Mary O'Neary (Kelly Macdonald) and her boozy husband Jim (Kevin Conway). Despite Buddy's best efforts to evict them they simply won't go. When Buddy's plan to intimidate the O'Nearys into leaving backfires, Mary becomes so distraught that she goes into labor. Following the birth the loutish Jim disappears, more interested in booze than in babies. Mary and the newborn are left alone to fend for themselves. Buddy evicts her, but feels so guilty he sets her up in a small apartment in the neighborhood.

In time Buddy realizes that Mary is the only person who truly believes in him and that he has fallen hopelessly in love with her. He juggles his married life, his old friends, his mistress, and the new bar until his life seems ready to fall apart. Then he finds the strength to turn his back on the things that make him unhappy and follow his dream to be Buddy Visalo, singer and bar owner.

Two Family House is a simple, old-fashioned movie. Director DeFellita has created a sweet, understated romance whose story rings with grace and honesty. He has looked back to the great filmmakers of the 1940s and '50s, men like George Stevens and David Lean, who created emotional moments that were earned, not taken.

"I'm not a hardcore independent filmmaker," says DeFilitta. "My tastes are older and perhaps a bit quaint. But what I appreciate is not out of vogue — it's just out of practice. Very often the simpler a movie appears to be, the richer it becomes for me."

At the core of *Two Family House* is Michael Rispoli as Buddy, a warm teddy bear of a man. Rispoli may be best known as Jackie Aprile on the first season of HBO's *The Sopranos*, but if there were any justice he would have been noticed for his work in this film. His Buddy may look like Fred Flintstone, but he has more wit, imagination, and intelligence than his pals at the local bar and refuses to accept his lot in life. He's a dreamer with stars in his eyes, and it is his journey that propels the whole film; if you didn't believe in him the movie's spell would be broken. Buddy has been bloodied by circumstance but is unbowed and it is that theme of achievement through doggedness that makes him and this movie so appealing.

"Michael has the toughness of that type of neighborhood guy so ingrained that he doesn't have to show it," says DeFilitta. "He *is* that rare, odd combination of hard-nosed pragmatist and softer, more artistic dreamer."

Another of the film's revelations is Kelly Macdonald as Mary. There is great chemistry between her and Rispoli, but it is her strength and independence that shine through. Since her debut in 1996's *Trainspotting* through to her roles in *My Life So Far* and *Gosford Park*, Macdonald has been searching for the breakout performance that she so richly deserves. She takes a chance with Mary, playing her as plain-spoken and blunt, and winning over the audience with her audacity rather than charm. It's a spunky performance, one that brims with excitement and life.

DeFilitta has nothing but praise for Macdonald. "I had seen Kelly in *Trainspotting* and every time I watched her in a film I always suspected that she had smaller parts that got bigger because she was so good."

The other female lead, Katherine Narducci, another refugee from *The Sopranos*, was cast partially because she resembled DeFilitta's real-life aunt. "Photographs of Estelle from the late 1940s and early 1950s could be pictures of Katherine today," he says, "the two women look so much alike." Narducci brings more to the role than her looks. In what may be the toughest part in the film, she plays the soul-destroying wife, but makes us feel sympathy rather than hatred for her. She is basically a good person, and while she would rather condemn Buddy to a life of drudgery than see him try and take a chance, we get the feeling it is because she is afraid to break from social convention, not that she is deliberately trying to ruin his life. She may be spoiled and difficult, but she isn't evil, and Narducci subtly conveys this in a well-mannered and funny performance.

Two Family House is an uplifting look at human nature and how dreams sometimes come true.

THE VIRGIN SUICIDES (2000)

The Virgin Suicides is one of those rare occasions when a film surpasses the book it is based on. Writer and first-time director Sophia Coppola manages to render the complex novel down to its core, without losing the heart and suburban spirit of the book. She sensitively handles the story of the Lisbon sisters and the neighborhood boys who love them.

"I read the book and loved the story and the characters," said director Sophia Coppola. "and the way he [author Jeffrey Eugenides] was talking about this teenage world without being condescending. How everything is so epic when you are experiencing it for the first time — your first love, obsession — you have all these heavy things on your mind, like the mystery between girls and boys."

Set in the upscale suburb of Grosse Pointe, Michigan, in the early 1970s, the film introduces us to the Lisbon sisters. They are five blonde and sweet girls ranging in age from 13 to 17, who have captivated the neighborhood boys with their angelic beauty. The group of guys, led by Tim Weiner (Jonathan Tucker), worship the sisters from afar, using binoculars to secretly watch them.

The girls are unattainable, not because they don't like the boys, but because their strict parents (James Woods and Kathleen Turner) barely let them out of the house. In a misguided effort to protect their kids from the big bad world, the elder Lisbons are overprotective and smother the girls with rules and regulations. The attempted suicide of the family's youngest daughter Cecilia (Hannah R. Hall) leads them to a psychologist (Danny DeVito) who tries to reason with her, saying that she isn't old enough to know how hard life can get.

"Obviously, doctor," she replies, "you've never been a 13-year-old girl."

The doctor suggests the parents give the girls more freedom, unlock the gates of the suburban prison. The Lisbons take his advice, open up their home, and throw a party. "The first and only party of their short lives," the narrator explains. At the party Cecilia makes a second, more successful attempt at ending her life.

For the sisters left behind, life goes on after the death of their youngest sibling. In the fall they return to school, where Lux (Kirsten Dunst) falls for a boy with one of the greatest names ever, Trip Fontaine (Josh Hartnett). When we first meet him he is walking down a school hallway with the strains of Heart's *Magic Man* playing on the soundtrack. His strut combined with the music tell us all we need to know about his character. Trip is a good-looking smooth operator with feathered hair.

Lux breaks her curfew, and the girls are grounded . . . forever. The resourceful kids figure out ways to stay in touch, and in one of the best scenes in the film they communicate by playing records over the phone. Like ancient peoples who would commune through smoke signals, the boys and girls "speak" to one another through music. The phone rings. One of the girls picks it up as Todd Rundgren's *Hello, It's Me* seeps out of the receiver. They volley songs back and forth. Gilbert O'Sullivan's sad sack version of *Alone Again (Naturally)* is answered with *Run to Me* by the Bee Gees. It's a lovely sequence that displays the emotional power the music has in the mind of a 14-year-old.

In the end, as the title suggests, the sisters kill themselves, leaving the boys with only their memories and a handful of souvenirs from the girl's lives — a diary, lipstick, and some rosary beads.

Coppola has taken a beautifully but densely written book and boiled it down to its essentials. Eugenide's novel is obsessed with details, so much so that the book threatens to collapse under the weight of its own minutiae. On film, Coppola follows the golden rule of directing, "show us, don't tell us," and avoids the downfall of the book. The wonderfully choreographed Lisbon party scene, for example, quickly conveys the whole awkwardness of the social gathering, from the well-meaning interruptions of the parents to the harmless flirting of the girls.

Seventies vintage pop songs play a large role in the film, perfectly evoking the era and setting the movie's tone. At the school dance ELO's *Strange Magic* reflects the mysterious sexual awakening the Lisbon girls experience as one by one they join their dates on the dance floor. The music works as a mood enhancer for the film, and doesn't detract from what is on the screen, but rather adds to it. A luscious contemporary score is provided by Air, a Parisian prog-rock electronica band.

"I wanted Air to do the score because I was listening to them while I wrote the script," Coppola says. "I know to the author of the book *The Virgin Suicides* it's very much about memory and *how* you remember things, and the idea of piecing these girls together through fragments of memory. I thought that by having music that sort of separated you from the time and was contemporary but related to 1970s soundtrack music I could achieve that kind of feel. Also Air have a dreamy quality to them that separates you from reality, and they are so good at making the perfect melancholy feeling."

A cast of seasoned pros heads the production. James Woods is father Lisbon, a dorky high school math teacher who is up to his ears in estrogen and uncertain how to deal with it. "He loved the script," Coppola says of Woods, who is best known for playing tough, smart-ass guys. "I think it is always interesting to see actors in parts that are different for them. It was fun to see his other side. In real life he's very charming and lovable, and went to MIT and has this Mensa-sized brain. I saw that he had that side, a sensitive side. You wouldn't believe it. James Woods has a sensitive side!"

As the mother Kathleen Turner is a harridan who is so freaked out by her daughters' blooming sexuality that she smothers them, and eventually loses the thing she held most dear, her family. "I hadn't seen Kathleen Turner since I was 14," says Coppola, "I think it was strange for her to have a meeting about a script with me, because the last time she saw me I was a gawky little kid. As soon as we started working together she took me very seriously as her boss, so I have to give her credit for being so cool like that."

As the most luminous of all the sisters Kirsten Dunst shines as Lux. On her face you can see the struggle of a young woman trying to find out who she is but never quite succeeding. Even when she is smiling there is a sadness that comes through, as though "the imprisonment of being a girl" is too much for her to bear. And in the end, I guess it was.

The Virgin Suicides is Sophia Coppola's directorial debut, and it is a strong, self-assured piece of work. She balances the dark humor of the piece with real emotion and treats the young characters with respect, not as some strange mutations who are trying to learn the ways of the adult world. She realizes that the boys who loved these girls couldn't give them the one thing they needed most: understanding.

"Under their calm façade, I think most people would love to get back to the jungle . . ."
— TOM (FAB FILIPO)

waydowntown (2000)

Calgary-born director Gary Burns co-wrote the script for *waydown-town* with his hometown in mind. He came up with the idea for the movie based on a pet gripe of his, the "plus 15" walkway system in Calgary, Alberta's downtown core. Built 15 feet above the city's streets, these walkways connect many of the downtown's office buildings. "The unfortunate result of this ever-expanding system is that these walkways have sucked the life out of the downtown core," says Burns. "I imagined a film where the main characters inhabit this architectural anomaly; a metaphor for modernism gone wrong."

Burns, working with co-writer James Martin, fleshed out a story about a group of co-workers who bet a month's salary to see who can stay indoors the longest. Since their offices are all connected by the walkways it isn't much of a stretch to imagine that they could stay inside until they retire. "The film really questions why we're working where we are working," says Burns. "Is this where you want to spend the rest of your life?"

We meet the contestants in this crazy game almost a month into their wager. No one thought the match would last this long, and the players are nearing the end of their tethers. The challenge was the brainchild of twentysomething Tom (Fabrizio Filippo) and office drone Randy (Tobias Godson), two cubicle dwellers at the firm of Mather, Mather, and Mather. Their colleague Sandra (Marya Delver) signed up to show she was one of the guys, and Curt (Gordon Curry) is a girl-crazy desk jockey who is convinced he will win the bet. Tom's cubicle-mate Brad (Don McKellar), a lifer with almost 20 years at the company, doesn't join in on the bet, but seems to be pondering a final wager with himself.

The effects of braving the great indoors for 24-hour days are beginning to show. As we near lunchtime, Tom unwittingly gets involved in a dysfunctional tryst in the parking garage, experiences the fantasy of flying, and spots saluting superheroes out of the corner of his eye. Sandra is obsessed with the recycled air being filtered through the building's vents and has become addicted to the perfume inserts from fancy magazines. Randy is irritable and seems to be losing his short-term memory. Curt, convinced that having sex will prolong his chances of winning, hits on a vulnerable co-worker. We also learn that Curt has a leg up over the others. In university he won a similar bet by not going outdoors for a full year.

By the time lunch is over, so is the bet.

Like many films before it, *waydowntown* unmasks the soulless nature of corporate life. What makes it stand apart from its predecessors like *The Man in the Gray Flannel Suit*, *The Apartment*, and *Clockwatchers* is its thoroughly modern approach to the subject of office burnout. These people aren't just bored; the climate-controlled cocoon they live and work in has dehumanized them to the point where they are office somnambulists, the zombies of the corporate caste system. Brad, the quiet guy, is the ultimate example. He's a man so broken that he spends his days playing video games at his desk and stapling motivational slogans like "Don't compromise — prioritise!" to his chest. When he sends Tom a nasty note suggesting that he is destined for the same fate, Tom realizes for the first time that he is completely desensitized, and that his job largely consists of "saying hello and making small talk." It's interesting that in the film's 87-minute running time we never actually learn what any of them do to earn their paychecks. Burns is making the point that all corporate businesses are the same — vast, anonymous, and oppressive. In *waydowntown*'s world the lines between work, leisure, and trade have been erased.

Initially Burns wanted to shoot the entire film in one long continuous shot that would have necessitated the use of digital video, which allows for 92 minutes of non-stop taping. That idea was tossed out, but the plan to use digital video stuck.

"There were a couple of reasons for staying with the video format," said Burns. "I figured the only way the film was going to fly is if we had unlimited access to the malls and walkways. I think a small crew that looks like a television crew has a better chance of having the run of downtown."

Burns also liked the realistic look digital video provided. Under the fluorescent lighting of the office areas and the mall he found that video lent an "edgier look" and a heightened sense of realism. "I think if you do go with video, you're not shooting video to look like film. That would be a big mistake," he says. "If you're going to shoot video, embrace the video and say, 'This is what we want, we love the look of this.'"

The young ensemble cast is uniformly good, although Fab Filippo as Tom is the leading light. His sardonic narration tries to make sense of the unusual situation, but it is his character's realization that the artificial world he lives in is turning him into a nasty, self-centered person that elevates the film. In a darkly comedic morality tale like this we need some redemption, and in Filippo's character we get it. By lunchtime on the 24th day of the bet he is on the road to salvation.

Also notable is Canadian auteur Don McKellar in the role of Brad. His character best sums up the mood of the film by incessantly replaying a computer program of Neil Armstrong's first steps on the moon. With a click of his mouse he topples over Armstrong every time, causing him to do a face-plant on the lunar surface. The constant sabotage of Armstrong on the computer screen is a metaphor for emotional stumbles that Brad and his office mates suffer in their 9 to 5 existence. McKellar subtly underplays Brad, barely concealing a bubbling volcano of rage beneath his spiteful stare. It is a great comedic performance.

waydowntown is set in Calgary, but the dark urban satire is universal. Many viewers will relate to the themes of alienation and despair, but hopefully will also find catharsis in the story.

> "It is unfortunate that you are no longer able to speak – I should be interested to hear you describe your symptoms!"
> **– MURDER LEGENDRE (BELA LUGOSI)**

WHITE ZOMBIE (1932)

Bela Lugosi is best remembered for bringing Bram Stoker's literary creature Dracula to blood-curdling life on the screen. It was his first North American role, and it branded him for life as a movie creature of the night. At his best he was spine-tingling, at his worst (unfortunately there are too many examples to mention them all) he became a caricature of himself, grimacing into the camera like a madman with a day pass.

Most people under the age of 25 only know about him via Martin

Landau's Academy Award-winning portrayal of him in Tim Burton's bio-pic *Ed Wood*. It is a shame because, while Landau gives an impressive performance, the real Lugosi was nothing like the foul-mouthed, pathetic drug addict seen in the movie. "I particularly found it appalling because he was a real European gentleman," Lugosi friend, and editor of the legendary *Famous Monsters of Filmland* Forrest J. Ackerman told me in 1995. "I never heard him say so much as a 'damn' or a 'hell,' and they had him saying absolutely scatological things about Boris Karloff that he never would have uttered in real life." The depiction of Lugosi in the film is bittersweet and very effective, despite bordering on parody and not giving him his due. He was a classically trained actor, who, like Boris Karloff and Vincent Price, found a niche in horror. *Dracula* is his towering achievement, but he made several other chillers that deserve to be remembered before his debilitating morphine habit dulled his on-screen presence. Chief among them was a low-budget thriller shot after the filming of *Dracula*.

In *White Zombie* (yes, rocker Rob Zombie cribbed the name) Lugosi played the charismatic Murder Legendre, the leader of a legion of zombies on a Haitian sugar plantation. He makes a zombifying potion for Monsieur Beaumont (Robert Frazer), a neighboring plantation owner who has coaxed a young couple to be married on his property. Beaumont lures the couple to his spread because he is secretly in love with Madeline (Madge Bellamy), the soon-to-be wife of the young couple. He slips the bride the evil brew, and after drinking it she appears to die, and the wedding is called off. Actually she has simply been transformed into a soulless zombie spouse for Beaumont!

As an emotionless zombie, she's no barrel of laughs, and Beaumont soon tires of her, asking Legendre to change her back. He refuses, and instead adds Beaumont to his zombie army. When Madeline's "widowed" almost-husband is tipped by a local priest that his beloved might not be dead, but rather *undead*, he seeks her out.

By today's standards *White Zombie* moves v-e-r-y slowly, but the movie just drips with atmosphere, and for a low-budget quickie, looks great. To save money, sets from *Dracula*, *Frankenstein*, and *King Kong* were recycled to create the creepy Haitian landscape where zombies rule and people foolishly trust a guy named "Murder." The scene in which Beaumont is led through an old mill surrounded by blank-faced zombies cranking a huge wooden wheel particularly resonates, makes great use of the sets, and is as effective as any image from *Dracula* or *Frankenstein*.

Snail-like pacing aside, *White Zombie* holds up because of the terrific performance from Lugosi (with amazing makeup from Jack Pierce, who created the looks for Frankenstein, the Mummy, and the Wolfman). His spellbinding Legendre is a hypnotic presence — noble and threatening — who commands attention when he is on screen. On a historical note, *White Zombie* was the first zombie movie, and set the template for virtually all that followed.

> "I want the two-car kids and the one-bedroom kids, the mother-lovers and the ones who can't stand the sight of the old lady! I want all of you! Let's see if those tigers can stop the future!"
> — Thus ends the speech of MAX FROST,
> 24-year-old president of the United States

WILD IN THE STREETS (1968)

Wild in the Streets is a quirky, low-budget film based on the 1960s ethic of never trusting anyone over 30. Darker than the usual teen fare, this satire poked holes in the peace and love ideals of the hippie generation.

This is one of those movies that was released at just the right time to cash in on the Zeitgeist of a generation. Released in the hot summer of 1968, when more than half of the population of the United States was under 25 years of age, the movie exposed the collective power of the young.

James Dean lookalike Christopher Jones plays the charismatic Max Frost. Jones was a rising star in Hollywood, having already played the lead in the television series *The Legend of Jesse James* for 20th Century Fox. Studio publicists reported at the time that his smoldering good looks attracted more fan mail than any actor since Tyrone Power.

In the film, following a hell-raising youth, Frost becomes a multi-millionaire rock star. Convinced that he will not live to see age 30, Max hatches a plan to take over the government. Asked by Senate hopeful Jerry Fergus (Hal Holbrook) to sing at a political rally, Frost uses the opportunity to preach youth empowerment in a song called "14 or Fight." Demanding that the voting age be lowered to 14, he calls for a demonstration on Sunset Strip.

A colorful cast of characters supports Frost in his crusade. His entourage included Sally LeRoy (Diane Varsi), described as "former child star and acidhead"; drummer, anthropologist, and author of *The Aborigine Cookbook* Stanley X (Richard Pryor in his first film role); Fuji Elly (May Ishihara), "Japanese typewriter heiress and beach bum"; a one-handed horn player, The Hook (Larry Bishop); and Billy Cage, a 15-year-old Harvard Business School graduate. Together they form an alliance to act on Frost's mad scheme.

Frost solidifies his relationship with Fergus after thousands of kids show up for the Sunset Strip demonstration. To end the riot the California legislature agrees to lower the voting age to 15, and with the newfound teen support Fergus wins his seat in the Senate. Soon an emergency election must be held to replace a dead 84-year-old senator. It is decided that Sally LeRoy will run for the coveted seat, but unfortunately senators must be at least 25 years old. Sally turns 25 the day before the election, and is eligible to run. Max becomes her campaign manager, penning a song with the memorable couplet, "Sally LeRoy / She's old enough for Congress, boy."

Of course, she wins; there'd be no movie otherwise. Her first order of business is to get the age limit for all elected offices lowered to 14. To insure the passage of the law, the entourage lace Washington D.C.'s water supply with LSD. High and hallucinating, D.C.'s powerbrokers pass the law, smoothing the way for Frost to run for president.

Frost wins the Oval Office, and immediately imprisons everyone over 30 in concentration camps where they wear dark robes and are perpetually stoned on LSD. Max is victorious, but all is not well. The next generation has a new slogan, "We're gonna put everybody over 10 out of business."

Wild in the Streets was American International Pictures biggest budget picture to date. Normally specializing in fast and dirty exploitation and horror flicks, AIP upped the ante with this one, achieving the mainstream success that usually eluded them. The theme song, "The Shape of Things to Come" (credited to Max Frost and The Troopers) became a Top 30 hit, and the film even earned an Academy Award nomination for Best Editing (it lost to *Bullitt*).

The thing that impresses me about *Wild in the Streets* is how skillfully the director Barry Shear and screenwriter Robert Thom pegged the anarchic feel and excitement of the baby boomers' youth movement. If you weren't around in the '60s (or can't remember them), this film is a fascinating time capsule of the decade's mores, clothes, and music. There is a sense that anything could happen, and in this film, it does. To modern eyes *Wild in the Streets* seems campy, in particular a scene in which a hospital gown-clad Shelley Winters, as Frost's overbearing mother, is high on LSD, scaling a chain link fence, screaming, "Feathers! I must have feathers!" Certainly not the most dignified moment in Ms Winters' career, but it does display the drug paranoia that was rampant in the late '60s. With Timothy Leary's mantra of "Tune In, Turn On, and Drop Out," burned into the public's consciousness, *Wild in the Streets* was seen as an update of *Reefer Madness*, with groovy camera angles and cutting edge graphics.

Even though the film is played as a satire, its message was taken seriously by some in the "establishment." During the 1968 Presidential Convention the Mayor of Chicago hired security to protect the water supplies of the city from being laced with LSD. Crazy man, crazy.

Richard's Favorite
Corporate Logos

1. In the opening credits of *The Fearless Vampire Killers* the MGM lion transforms into a vampire.

2. The Universal logo is run backwards in the original 1982 cut of *ET: The Extra-Terrestrial.*

3. *The Great Muppet Caper* begins with Animal roaring like the MGM lion and then eating the surrounding title card.

4. In *Josie & the Pussycats* the MGM lion morphs into a screaming fan.

5. A UFO at the beginning of *Lilo & Stitch* abducts the Walt Disney logo.

6. Opening credits of the 1978 period piece *Paradise Alley* use the 1940's version of the Universal logo.

7. In Gus Van Zant's 1998 remake of *Psycho* the Imagine, Inc. logo drips with blood instead of water.

8. In the original theatrical release of *Strange Brew* the MGM lion appears to be drunk and belches.

9. In *The Bad News Bears Go to Japan* The Paramount Mountain changes into Mount Fuji before the opening credits begin.

10. In the end credits for 1996's *Joe's Apartment* a group of cockroaches bands together to form the MTV logo before crawling off screen.

ZARDOZ (1974)

John Boorman is an ambitious filmmaker. He spikes his films with high-minded ideas, examining the issues that lie at the very core of human existence. His films create new worlds, where outside forces — sometimes natural, sometimes supernatural — collide with the lives of ordinary folk. When he is good, as in *Deliverance*, he hits all the right notes, pitting people of different cultures against one another with unpredictable and entertaining results. But when he is bad, he is very, very bad.

Well intentioned though they may be, movies like *The Exorcist II: The Heretic* and *Excalibur* were noble failures. Filled with interesting mythology, these films, like many in the Boorman canon, collapse under their own weight. Pretentious and just a bit loopy, they are unintentionally funny, although not nearly as bizarre as his 1974 space opera *Zardoz*.

As writer and director of *Zardoz* (WIZARD of OZ, get it?) Boorman has to shoulder the blame for the overblown philosophy behind the film. He set the movie in the year 2293, on an Earth where most of mankind has devolved into "Brutals." They live in the Outlands and worship a giant floating stone head named Zardoz, who spouts a message of hatred toward humans and vomits weapons from his large gaping mouth to arm his mindless followers. "The gun is good," he says. "The penis is evil." During one of the visits a Brutal named Zed (Sean Connery) climbs aboard the huge head only to discover a man (Arthur Frayn) in a robe. Zardoz isn't an omnipotent being, but simply a man pretending to be a god. Confused, frustrated, and looking ridiculous in his racy red loincloth, Zed kills the head's aviator.

He rides the head to the Vortex, an area Zed believes to be Heaven.

He soon learns that the Vortex is not Heaven, but a land inhabited by the Eternals who are protected from the Brutals by an invisible shield. The Eternals are a race of genetically superior, but sexually impotent people who live forever within the boundaries of the shield. They are hard-hearted and bored of life, so filled with ennui that many of them have become Apathetics, who reject all life activities. Zed is taken prisoner by the Eternals, one of whom, May (Sara Kestleman), wants to breed him with the women of the Vortex, to bring much-needed new life to their barren existence. Another woman, the beautiful Consuella (Charlotte Rampling), is both attracted and repulsed by Zed, and wants him destroyed.

The pace picks up at this point, with Zed making love to May, being blinded by Consuella, wowing the Eternals with an erection, wearing a bridal gown, and finally bringing the Apathetics to action while goading the Eternals into seeking death.

I think Boorman meant *Zardoz* to be a comment on the social ills plaguing America in the years following the Second World War. Instead he packs the movie with broad, unfinished ideas without filling in the fine print. Is he suggesting that we are drifting away from the traditional morality of religion and worshiping false gods? Perhaps he's concerned about a nation that is turning more violent, literally becoming "Brutals." Or could it be that we have become apathetic layabouts? Are the elderly Apathetics, shipped off to an out-of-the-way structure and ignored, an allegory for the aged in our society? There is something to be said for all these themes, but Boorman doesn't take a point of view, he simply layers one hypothesis on top of another until they become a jumbled mess. In the hands of a better storyteller some of this might have worked, but Boorman goes for substance over coherence.

Now for the fun part. Viewed through today's eyes *Zardoz* seems hopelessly dated, like a particularly cheesy episode of *Battlestar Galactica*. Connery is a sight with his perfect 1970s porn-star hair and red diaper-cum-hot pants. With his large moustache and an ammo belt crisscrossed around his bare chest he looks like a gay mercenary, or maybe the sixth member of the Village People. The women fare a little better, particularly Consuella. In her see-through top she looks fit for a night on the dance floor at Studio 54.

If the costumes (or in most cases the lack of costumes) are unintentionally hilarious, the dialogue is downright side-splitting. Of course the famous line, "The gun is good. The penis is evil," is ripe for ridicule, but there are many howlers, always delivered with great significance, that invite laughter. "An old man calls me," says Zed. "The voice of the turtle is heard in the land." Woody Allen would have a hard time topping the comedic lines in *Zardoz*. In fact, 20th Century Fox was so concerned that people wouldn't know what to make of the movie's unintentional humor they forced Boorman to add a prologue suggesting that *Zardoz* is a spoof.

Zardoz would have destroyed the career of a lesser actor, but Sean Connery good-naturedly romps through this material, and to this day counts it as one of his favorite movies. It seems like a strange role for the former "Bond, *James* Bond" to take on, but Boorman remembers that "Sean was so desperate for film work at the time that he actually agreed to do this movie." It is a testament to Connery's charisma that his career survived *Zardoz*, but his mugging and overacting provide several truly entertaining moments.

If you want to see great serious '70s science fiction, rent *Slaughterhouse Five*, *Silent Running*, or *The Andromeda Strain*, but if you're in the mood for an overblown, hilarious mock-serious space drama, you can't do any better than *Zardoz*.

THE END . . . FADE TO BLACK

Bibliography

Unless otherwise noted all interviews contained in this book are with the author, spanning from 1992 to 2002. Copyright Richard Crouse, 2002.

Other Sources

Baker, Chris. "Spooky Kooky: Ray Dennis Steckler chews the fat about low-low-low budget filmmaking." *Oakland's Urbanview*. February 6–12, 2002.

Bergan, Ronald. "Paul Bartel: Film director whose black humour lampooned America's dark side." *Guardian Unlimited*. May 19, 2000.

Big Bad Love. Director's Notes.

Bockris, Victor. *The Life and Death of Andy Warhol*. 1989.

Chaw, Walter. "One Conversation with Jill Sprecher." *Film Freak Central*. May 2002.

Chaw, Walter. "Speak of the Devil's Backbone: Film Freak Central Interviews Guillermo del Toro." *Film Freak Central*.

Coates, John. "The Making of Phantom of the Paradise." *Filmmaker's Newsletter*. February 1975.

Corman, Roger and Jerome Jim. *How I Made a Hundred Movies in Hollywood and Never Lost a Dime*. DaCapo Press, 1990.

The Dish. Director's Notes.

Dreyfuss, Randy and Harry Medved. *The 50 Worst Films of All Time*. Warner Books, 1978.

Eisner, Ken. "From Fear to Film: Mile Zero Grew Out of a Period of Anxiety in the Life of Its First-Time Director." *The Georgia Straight*. November 22–29, 2001.

The Experiment. Director's Notes.

Fowler, Thom. "Roman Coppola Talks About His Hip and Cool Debut GQ." *Hollywood Bitchslap.*

Frailty. Press Kit.

Gangster Number One. Press Kit.

Guthmann, Edward. "Peeping Tom a Peek at Greatness Panned in 1960, Michael Powell's horror film is now a classic." *San Francisco Chronicle.* Friday, February 26, 1999.

Hedwig and the Angry Inch. Press Kit.

"Holy Shit! What is all this green stuff?" *Tabula Rasa #1*, 1994.

Hopkins, Jerry. *Bowie.* MacMillan Publishing Co., 1985.

"Jackson on Jackson." *SFX Magazine.*

Jepsen, Cara. "The Curse of Incubus." *Salon.com.* May 3, 2000.

Kaufman, Lloyd and James Gunn. *All I Need to Know About Filmmaking I Learned From the Toxic Avenger.* Boulevard, 1998.

The Kid Stays in the Picture. Press Kit.

Leiby, Richard. "The Life He Left Behind; Actor Steve Buscemi and his altered ego." *The Washington Post.* October 25, 1996.

Lybarger, Dan. "Digital Souls: An Interview With Maurice Prather on Carnival of Souls." *Lybarger Links.* February 3, 2000.

Mason, Phil. "Peter Weller: Robocop." *Total DVD.* February 2002.

McKenna, Kristine. "Straight Shooter: After a painful return to TV, America's oddest auteur gives the real story." *Premiere.* November 1999.

On The Street, Sydney. March 27, 1989.

"The Minus Man: About the Production." *The Owen Wilson Fansite.*

Puig, Claudia. "Lynch tries direction other than dark." *USA Today.* October 1999.

Riordan, Paul. "The Films of George C. Scott." *Images Journal.* 1997.

Riordan, Paul. "He Is Legend: Richard Matheson." *scifistation*.

Sigler, Jeremy. "Perry Henzell." *Indexmagazine.com*. 2001.

13 Conversations About One Thing. Press Kit.

"Suspiria." *Terrortrap*.

Warhol, Andy. *The Philosophy of Andy Warhol (From A To B & Back Again)*. 1975.

Wise, Damon. "That's for Bambi. Wham! Right in the head." *Mojo*. June 2002.

Wyant, Jean Flynn. "Tadpole Grows into Something Bigger Than a Frog: An interview with Aaron Stanford and Gary Winick." *Entertainment Insiders*. June 16, 2002.